DAY HIKING

Yosemite
National Park

DAY HIKING

Yosemite
National Park

Scott Turner

MOUNTAINEERS
BOOKS

MOUNTAINEERS BOOKS is dedicated to the exploration, preservation, and enjoyment of outdoor and wilderness areas.

1001 SW Klickitat Way, Suite 201, Seattle, WA 98134
800-553-4453, www.mountaineersbooks.org

First edition, 2021

Copyeditor: Ginger Oppenheimer
Cover and book design: Mountaineers Books
Layout: Melissa McFeeters
Cartographer: Pease Press Cartography
All photographs by the author unless credited otherwise
Cover photograph: *A fall morning along the Merced River near Cathedral Beach*
Frontispiece: *Yosemite Falls and the Merced River from the Housekeeping Camp footbridge*

The background maps for this book were produced using the online map viewer CalTopo. For more information, visit caltopo.com.

Library of Congress Cataloging-in-Publication data is on file for this title at
https://lccn.loc.gov/2021008630

Mountaineers Books titles may be purchased for corporate, educational, or other promotional sales, and our authors are available for a wide range of events. For information on special discounts or booking an author, contact our customer service at 800-553-4453 or mbooks@mountaineersbooks.org.

Printed on FSC-certified materials

ISBN (paperback): 978-1-68051-276-2
ISBN (ebook): 978-1-68051-277-9

An independent nonprofit publisher since 1960

Table of Contents

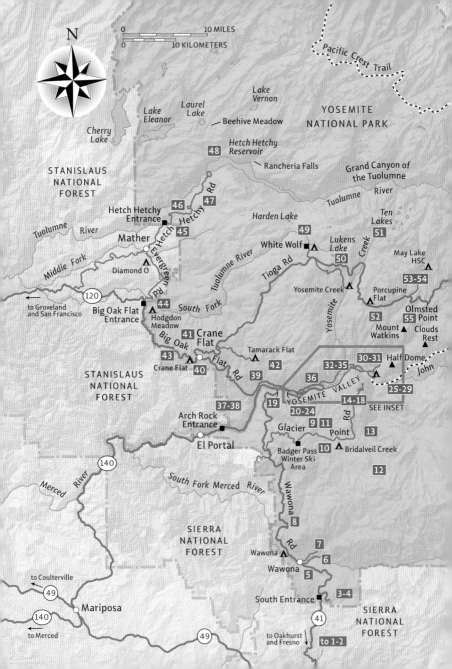

N

0   10 MILES
0   10 KILOMETERS

Cherry Lake

Lake Eleanor

Laurel Lake

Beehive Meadow

Lake Vernon

Pacific Crest Trail

YOSEMITE NATIONAL PARK

STANISLAUS NATIONAL FOREST

Hetch Hetchy Reservoir

48

Rancheria Falls

Grand Canyon of the Tuolumne

Tuolumne River

Tuolumne River

Middle Fork

46 47

Hetch Hetchy Rd

Hetch Hetchy Entrance

Mather

45

Evergreen Rd

Diamond O

Harden Lake

49

White Wolf

Lukens Lake

50

Ten Lakes

51

May Lake HSC

53-54

Tuolumne River

Tioga Rd

Yosemite Creek

Porcupine Flat

Olmsted Point

55

to Groveland and San Francisco

120

Big Oak Flat Entrance

44

South Fork

Hodgdon Meadow

Big Oak Flat Rd

41

Crane Flat

43

Crane Flat

40

Tamarack Flat

42

39

52

Mount Watkins

Clouds Rest

30-31

Half Dome

32-35

36

25-29

John

STANISLAUS NATIONAL FOREST

37-38

19

YOSEMITE VALLEY

14-18

SEE INSET

20-24

9   11

Glacier Point Rd

13

Arch Rock Entrance

El Portal

Glacier Point

10

Badger Pass Winter Ski Area

Bridalveil Creek

12

Merced River

140

South Fork Merced River

SIERRA NATIONAL FOREST

Wawona Rd

8

7

6

to Coulterville

49

Mariposa

Wawona

Wawona

5

3-4

140

to Merced

49

49

South Entrance

41

SIERRA NATIONAL FOREST

to Oakhurst and Fresno

to 1-2

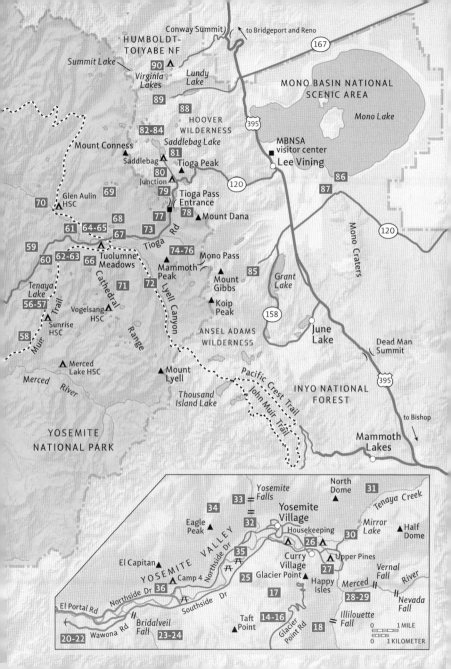

Conway Summit

→ to Bridgeport and Reno

HUMBOLDT-
TOIYABE NF

Summit Lake

90 ▲

Virginia
Lakes

Lundy Lake

167

MONO BASIN NATIONAL
SCENIC AREA

89

88

HOOVER
WILDERNESS

82-84

Saddlebag Lake

Mono Lake

395

MBNSA
visitor center

Lee Vining

Mount Conness

81

Saddlebag

Tioga Peak

80

Junction

79

86

Glen Aulin
HSC

69

87

70

Tioga Pass
Entrance

77

78

120

▲ Mount Dana

61

64-65

68

73

67

120

59

Tuolumne
Meadows

74-76

Mono Pass

60

62-63

66

Mammoth
Peak

85

Grant
Lake

71

72

▲ Mount
Gibbs

Tenaya
Lake

Cathedral

▲ Koip
Peak

Mono Craters

56-57

Vogelsang
HSC

158

58

Sunrise
HSC

Range

Muir Trail

Lyell Canyon

ANSEL ADAMS
WILDERNESS

June
Lake

▲ Merced
Lake HSC

Merced
River

▲ Mount
Lyell

Pacific Crest Trail

Dead Man
Summit

INYO NATIONAL
FOREST

395

Thousand
Island Lake

John Muir Trail

YOSEMITE
NATIONAL PARK

to Bishop →

Mammoth
Lakes

North
Dome

31

Yosemite
Falls

33

Yosemite
Village

Tenaya Creek

34

Eagle
Peak

32

Housekeeping

Mirror
Lake

30

▲ Half
Dome

VALLEY

Northside Dr

35

26

Curry
Village

27

Upper Pines

El Capitan ▲

YOSEMITE

Camp 4

36

25

Glacier Point ▲

17

Happy
Isles

Vernal
Fall

28-29

Merced

River

Northside Dr

Southside Dr

El Portal Rd

Bridalveil
Fall

23-24

Nevada
Fall

20-22

Wawona Rd

Taft
Point

14-16

Glacier Point Rd

18

Illilouette
Fall

1 MILE

1 KILOMETER

Hikes at a Glance

HIKE	DISTANCE IN MILES (ROUNDTRIP)	DIFFICULTY	YEAR-ROUND	KID-FRIENDLY
WAWONA AND MARIPOSA GROVE				
1. Corlieu Falls	2.4	1	•	•
2. Red Rock Falls	1	1	•	•
3. Grizzly Giant Loop	2.1	2		•
4. Mariposa Grove Trail to Wawona Point	7.2	3		
5. Wawona Meadow	3.5	2	•	•
6. Wawona Swinging Bridge	0.8	1	•	•
7. Chilnualna Falls	7.2	3	•	
8. Alder Creek Falls	7.2	3		
GLACIER POINT ROAD				
9. Dewey Point Winter Route	7.5	3		
10. Westfall Meadow	2.8	1		•
11. Dewey Point via McGurk Meadow	7.6	3		
12. Ostrander Lake	12	4		
13. Mono Meadow	3.7	2		•
14. Taft Point	2.4	2		•
15. Sentinel Dome	2.2	2		•
16. Taft-Sentinel Circuit	7.2	3		
17. Pohono Trail	12.8 (one-way)	4		
18. Panorama Trail	8.8 (one-way)	3		
YOSEMITE VALLEY				
19. Turtleback Dome	1.2	1	•	•
20. Inspiration Point	2.3	3	•	
21. Artist Point	1.8	2	•	
22. Old Inspiration Point and Stanford Point	7	4		
23. Bridalveil Fall and West Valley Loop	6.5	3	•	
24. Four Mile Trail	9.4	4		
25. Cooks and Sentinel Meadows	2.6	1	•	•
26. East Valley Loop	6.4	3	•	•
27. Happy Isles	1.6	1	•	•
28. Mist Trail to Nevada Fall	6	3	•	
29. Half Dome	14.6	5		
30. Mirror Lake and Tenaya Canyon	4.6	2	•	•

DOG-FRIENDLY	BACK-PACKING	WATER-FALLS	HISTORICAL	GEOLOGY	VIEWS	LAKES	GIANT SEQUOIAS	FALL COLOR	WINTER ROUTE
•		•						•	
•		•						•	
			•				•		
			•		•		•		•
•			•					•	•
			•						
		•						•	
	•	•	•						
	•			•	•				•
	•			•	•				
	•					•			•
			•	•	•				
				•	•				
				•	•				
	•				•				
		•			•				
					•				•
			•		•				
		•	•		•				
			•		•				
		•						•	
					•				
		•	•		•			•	
		•	•					•	
			•						
		•	•	•	•			•	•
	•	•		•	•				
			•		•	•		•	

HIKE	DISTANCE IN MILES (ROUNDTRIP)	DIFFICULTY	YEAR-ROUND	KID-FRIENDLY
YOSEMITE VALLEY (CONTINUED)				
31. Snow Creek Trail	9	4	•	
32. Lower Yosemite Fall	1.2	1	•	•
33. Upper Yosemite Fall and Yosemite Point	7.6	4	•	
34. Eagle Peak	10.8	5		
35. Middle Valley Loop	6	3	•	•
36. Old Big Oak Flat Road	2.4	2	•	
BIG OAK FLAT ROAD				
37. Foresta Falls	2.3	2	•	•
38. Little Nellie Falls	5.4	2	•	
39. Cascade Creek	8.2	3	•	
40. Clark Range View	3	1		•
41. Tuolumne Grove	3	2	•	•
42. El Capitan	16.6	4		
43. Merced Grove	3.3	2	•	•
HETCH HETCHY				
44. Carlon Falls	2.8	1	•	•
45. Lookout Point	2.7	2	•	•
46. Poopenaut Valley	2.4	3		
47. Smith Meadow Trail	3	3		
48. Wapama Falls	5.3	3	•	
WHITE WOLF TO TENAYA LAKE				
49. Harden Lake	5.8	2		
50. Lukens Lake	2.6	1		•
51. Ten Lakes	12.6	4		
52. North Dome	9.5	4		
53. May Lake	3.5	2		•
54. Mount Hoffmann	6	4		
55. Mount Watkins	9.2	3		
56. Tenaya Lake	3.3	2		•
57. Sunrise Lakes	6.5	3		
58. Clouds Rest	11.6	4		
59. Polly Dome Lakes	5.8	2		
60. Medlicott Dome	4.4	3		

DOG-FRIENDLY	BACK-PACKING	WATER-FALLS	HISTORICAL	GEOLOGY	VIEWS	LAKES	GIANT SEQUOIAS	FALL COLOR	WINTER ROUTE
	•		•	•	•	•		•	
		•	•						•
	•	•			•				
	•	•			•				
		•	•					•	
			•		•				
		•							•
		•	•						•
	•	•	•						
			•				•		•
	•			•	•		•		•
			•				•		•
		•	•						
					•				
•								•	•
					•			•	
		•	•	•	•	•			
						•			
						•			
	•				•	•			
	•			•	•				
	•		•		•	•			
	•				•	•			
				•	•				
						•			
	•					•			
	•			•	•	•			
	•			•		•			
				•	•	•			

HIKE	DISTANCE IN MILES (ROUNDTRIP)	DIFFICULTY	YEAR-ROUND	KID-FRIENDLY
TUOLUMNE MEADOWS				
61. Pothole Dome	1.2	2		•
62. Cathedral Lakes	9.4	3		
63. Budd Lake	5	3		
64. Soda Springs and Parsons Memorial Lodge	1.3	1		•
65. Tuolumne Meadows Loop	6.3	3		
66. Elizabeth Lake	4.6	3		•
67. Lembert Dome	3.8	2		•
68. Dog Lake	2.5	2		•
69. Young Lakes	14.4	4		
70. Glen Aulin and Waterwheel Falls	17.4	4		
71. Vogelsang High Sierra Camp	14.4	4		
72. Lyell Canyon	9.2	3		
TIOGA PASS				
73. Lower Gaylor Lake	4.4	3		•
74. Spillway Lake	8.5	3		
75. Mono Pass	9.1	3		
76. Parker Pass and Mount Lewis	13	4		
77. Upper Gaylor Lakes	5.8	3		
78. Mount Dana	5.2	4		
LEE VINING CANYON AND MONO BASIN				
79. Nunatak Nature Trail	0.5	1		•
80. Bennettville and Fantail Lake	3.4	2		•
81. Gardisky Lake	2.4	3		
82. Greenstone Lake	4.1	2		•
83. Twenty Lakes Basin	8.4	3		
84. Conness Lakes	6.2	3		
85. Parker Lake	3.6	2		•
86. South Tufa	0.9	1	•	•
87. Panum Crater	2.4	2	•	•
88. Lundy Mine and Oneida Lake	7.2	3		
89. Lundy Canyon	3.8	2		•
90. Virginia Lakes	3	2		•

DOG-FRIENDLY	BACK-PACKING	WATER-FALLS	HISTORICAL	GEOLOGY	VIEWS	LAKES	GIANT SEQUOIAS	FALL COLOR	WINTER ROUTE
				•	•				
	•					•			
					•	•			
			•	•					
			•	•					
						•			
				•	•				
						•			
	•				•	•			
	•	•	•	•				•	
	•				•	•			
	•				•				
						•			
						•			
	•		•		•	•			
	•				•	•			
			•		•	•		•	
				•	•				
•				•		•			
•			•			•			
•	•				•	•			
•						•		•	
•	•				•	•		•	
•						•			
•	•					•		•	
			•	•		•			
•				•	•	•			
•	•		•			•		•	
•	•	•				•		•	
•	•					•		•	

Introduction

A wild summer thunderstorm had swept Yosemite Valley the night before. Hail crashed down around my tent while the intervals between lightning and thunder had been a handful of milliseconds. A cool west wind swept in behind the storm system the next morning as I found myself following the Pohono Trail along the spine of Yosemite Valley's southern rim. Early morning light filtered through the boughs of red firs and sugar pines as a chorus of birds sent delicate tendrils of sound reverberating through the cavernous forest. Yosemite Falls, briefly swollen by the deluge, burst forth into space above Cooks Meadow, and the dull roar added a bass note to the avian symphonies above.

I moved forward, tenth of a mile after tenth of a mile, with the reliable *crunch crunch crunch crunch* of boots on decomposing granite keeping a metronomic tempo. A rivulet of recent snowmelt flowed through a green ribbon of corn lilies and ferns to my right as my breathing deepened, keeping in time with my footfalls. After many hours, or perhaps only minutes, I lost track of any semblance of the outside world—politics, pandemics, personal problems, parenting. Somehow, without even knowing I crossed a threshold, I had passed into the timelessness of the Yosemite Wilderness.

Here in the heart of the Sierra Nevada Mountains lies the crown jewel of America's National Park Service: Yosemite National Park. With an all-star roster of names rivaling the 1927 Yankees—Half Dome, Yosemite Falls, El Capitan, Glacier Point, Nevada Fall, Tuolumne Meadows, and the Mariposa Grove of giant sequoias—Yosemite hiking reigns supreme as the quintessential American nature experience. With trails ranging from intimate, family-friendly excursions through peaceful meadows and sequoia groves to heart-stopping ascents up the side of massive granite domes, Yosemite promises superlative experiences and lifelong memories for everyone.

Yosemite's most famous advocate, John Muir, once described Yosemite as "the grandest of all the special temples of Nature I was ever permitted to enter." This guide presents the best day hikes exploring the 747,956 acres of this temple of nature as well as several noteworthy hikes on the park's margins within adjacent national forests. Each hike showcases the qualities that make Yosemite exceptional: soaring alpine summits, glaciated wonderlands, sparkling lakes, precipitous cliffs, fall color, winter hiking, a constellation of flora and fauna, and history spanning thousands of years of human habitation.

THE WRECK OF MATTER AND THE CRUSH OF WORLDS

The story of Yosemite begins with the rocks underfoot and the monoliths towering overhead. The astonishing array of geological features in the park attests to the combined powers of water, ice, time, and fire. Each

Opposite: *Lower Chilnualna Falls is one of Yosemite's many waterfalls (Hike 7).*

World-famous views of Half Dome from Glacier Point

of those elemental forces has imposed its artistic will on the rock of Yosemite, carving out one of the most iconic landscapes on the planet.

Although the Sierra Nevada's signature granite rocks developed relatively recently in the range's geologic story, these igneous, meaning "of fire," rocks dominate the landscape throughout the heart of the range. Between 85 and 115 million years ago, a massive pocket of magma cooled slowly into an enormous block some 400 miles long, from north to south. This block, known as a batholith, cooled and solidified, remaining underneath layers of much older metamorphic rocks for nearly 100 million years. About 10 million years ago, tectonic pressure

forced the batholith upward, with a pronounced upward tilt on the eastern end and a downward tilt on the western end.

The newly uplifted eastern edge of the batholith formed a serrated crest, known today as the Sierra Crest, standing 10,000 feet high at pass level and rising as high as 13,120 feet at Mount Lyell. From that crest, rivers and glaciers flowed down the now ramp-like range, carving out valleys and canyons to the east and the west along natural faults while washing away much of the older metamorphic rock that originally lay atop the range. When the climate cooled about 2.5 million years ago, massive glaciers formed, which carved out some of the park's notable valleys while scouring out lakes and

U-SHAPED VALLEYS, ERRATICS, AND POLISH

One of Yosemite's earliest champions, John Muir, proposed the first viable theory of Yosemite Valley's origins. Muir hypothesized that massive glaciers originating from the Tuolumne and Merced Rivers' headwaters must have flowed downhill along the modern courses of the Tuolumne River, Tenaya Creek, and the Merced River, gouging out a tremendous amount of rock as they went. The glaciers melted as the last ice ages receded, revealing the valley's sculpted cliffs and smaller hanging valleys that produce the park's waterfalls. Water then filled the valley, creating a lake impounded by a terminal moraine, a mass of rock deposited by the glaciers at their farthest extreme. Sediment carried by the creeks eventually filled parts of the lake, creating the current landscape of a flat valley graced with sprawling meadows and a meandering river.

Muir's theory of glaciation came remarkably close to the modern scientific explanation of Yosemite Valley's origins. Modern geology accepts the glacial theory, which accounts for the characteristic U-shape of Yosemite and many of the Sierra's other notable canyons, including Kings Canyon, Tehipite Valley, and Hetch Hetchy Valley. Glacial scouring of the range's bedrock also created many of the region's lakes, some of which eventually filled with sediment to become meadows. Glaciation also polished domes and canyons in the high country while littering boulders, known as erratics, throughout basins and valleys. Hikers can enjoy the evidence of glaciation in and around Tuolumne Meadows, Tenaya Lake, and Olmsted Point.

polishing dome-like outcrops in the high country. Periods of glaciation continued until as recently as 10,000 years ago, when the last of the ice age glaciers began retreating to the high elevations of the park.

Omnipresent though the granite may seem, it's only part of the story. The oldest rocks in the Sierra Nevada date back to the Paleozoic Era (540 to 250 million years ago). They originated as sedimentary rocks before heat and pressure metamorphosed them into hornfels, marbles, slates, and schists over millions of years. These rocks covered the range prior to the rise of the granite, and eons of erosion washed much of it into the San Joaquin Valley. Remnants of these ancient rocks cap the Sierra Crest surrounding Tioga Pass down to the floor of Mono

Basin, where dramatically different rocks become more prevalent.

Additional rock building occurred 20 million years ago when a period of volcanism, which is still active in and around the Mammoth Caldera, introduced a large volume of basaltic rock on the eastern edge of the range. Evidence of this volcanism is apparent around Mono Lake at the Mono Craters as well as farther south around Mammoth Lakes.

FLORA AND FAUNA

The park's wide elevation range (2127 feet at El Portal to 13,120 feet at Mount Lyell) supports five major vegetation schemes that contain a myriad of habitats. Visitors can experience chaparral and oak woodland, lower montane forest, upper montane forest, subalpine zone, and alpine zone within a few hours of driving. Occasionally, hikers can experience several biomes within the span of a single hike.

Chaparral and oak woodlands dominate the lowest elevations of the park, and those communities occasionally extend up to 6000 feet on south-facing slopes. Mixed-coniferous forests dominate Yosemite's habitats between 4000 feet and 10,000 feet. The lower elevation forests—commonly known as the lower montane forest, within Yosemite Valley to about 7000 feet—feature a mixture of deciduous and evergreen trees and chaparral species, including black oaks, bigleaf maples, dogwoods, canyon live oaks, ponderosa pine, incense cedar, Douglas fir, California bay laurels, and manzanita. Between 5000 and 8000 feet, Jeffrey pines, white firs, sugar pines, and—in three separate groves—giant sequoias replace hardwoods and the lower elevation conifers. Another change occurs above 7500 feet as the lower montane forest transitions into upper montane forest. This forest includes lodgepole pine, mountain hemlock, red fir, and Western white pines as the dominant species.

The subalpine zone includes increasingly stunted and hardy conifers, primarily lodgepole and whitebark pines that thrive above 9000 feet. Around 11,000 feet, trees devolve into wind-blasted shrubs known as

The Fallen Monarch provides perspective on the immensity of giant sequoias (Hike 3).

CLIMATE CHANGE

Yosemite's biodiversity has faced numerous threats before as a result of hunting, grazing, and resource exploitation. However, none of those threats match the ongoing impacts of climate change. Climate change in California can be summed up in two words: "hotter" and "drier." The combination of heat and drought has sparked massive wildfires, including the 2013 Rim Fire (257,000 acres) and the 2018 Ferguson Fire (97,000 acres). Millions of conifers have died as reduced rainfall and an ever-rising snow line has left the lower and middle elevation forests vulnerable to bark beetle infestations. Many of the larger and older tree specimens, including even the giant sequoia, have shown signs of weakening and of mortality. And as the forests suffer, numerous threats may lead to many of Yosemite's most vulnerable arboreal, floral, and fauna species becoming further imperiled.

krummholz. Above 11,000 feet, plant life struggles to survive in a harsh alpine environment that spends much of the year buried beneath snow. Some parts of this alpine environment still contain the vanishing remnants of the glaciers that once covered the upper elevations of the park, including the Lyell Icefield on the north slopes of Mount Lyell.

One of the most remarkable features of the park's floral scheme is the giant sequoia. Yosemite National Park harbors three groves (Mariposa, Tuolumne, and Merced), with one small grove (Nelder) just outside the park boundaries. These massive trees can reach heights exceeding 300 feet and ages exceeding 3000 years. If considered in terms of overall volume, the sequoia is the largest single-stemmed tree on the planet. Each of the groves is rich in history, particularly Mariposa Grove. It was in the shadow of the Grizzly Giant Tree that John Muir and President Theodore Roosevelt spoke, which helped pave the way for Yosemite's establishment as a national park.

The park also harbors a wide range of fauna, including 90 species of mammals, 262 species of birds, 11 species of amphibians,

44 species of reptiles, and countless insects. The park contains several endangered and threatened species, including peregrine falcons, bald eagles, the Yosemite toad, Sierra Nevada red fox, Sierra Nevada bighorn sheep, and California wolverines. Several common species present safety concerns, including black bears, rattlesnakes, mountain lions, mosquitos, and ticks. Those species are covered in more detail in the safety and regulations sections.

Mule deer are known for their large ears.

HISTORY

For several thousands of years, the only folks wandering the meadows and forests of what we now call Yosemite Valley were the Miwok people. The Miwok of Yosemite referred to the valley as "Ahwahnee," which roughly translates to "gaping mouth"—a reference to the valley's appearance. The indigenous residents of Ahwahnee referred to themselves as the Ahwahneechee, or "the people of the mouth." The Miwok ranged throughout the Sierra Nevada, forming close trading and even familial partnerships with the Mono people on the eastern side of the range.

Hundreds of years of indigenous inhabitation came to a sudden and screeching disruption in 1851 when the Ahwahneechee clashed with Gold Rush pioneers along the Merced River. A band of Miwoks raided Savage's Trading Post near today's Hite Cove Trailhead, killing several pioneers. Local miners, led by James D. Savage, formed the Mariposa Battalion, which pursued the Miwoks into a vast valley laced with waterfalls and dominated by towering granite formations. Lafayette H. Bunnell, a member of the battalion, applied the word "Yosemite," which to Bunnell sounded more "American" than the word "Ahwahnee." Bunnell mistakenly believed that "Yosemite" was the Miwok word for "grizzly bear." In a twist of irony, the word "Yosemite" was closer to the Miwok word for "killers," a misunderstanding that continues to reflect this bloody period of the valley's history.

European-American explorers and pioneers trickled into the Yosemite region in the decade that followed. Entrepreneur James Hutchings and artist Thomas Ayres began promoting the valley to entice tourism. Meanwhile, Galen Clark, who later became the Yosemite Grant's first guardian, was the first European-American to encounter the big trees at Mariposa Grove. Advocacy from individuals such as Clark and US Senator John Conness, from California, led to Abraham Lincoln signing legislation to formalize the Yosemite Grant in 1864, leading to the country's first instance of establishing government protection and preservation for public land.

After the establishment of the Grant, the federal government ceded Yosemite Valley and Mariposa Grove to California as a state park. For the next decade, a series of court battles established authority and powers for the park's new commissioners board, all while more tourists streamed in on newly established roads. Among those new arrivals was a Scotsman by the name of John Muir who sought employment with Hutchings as a carpenter and timber harvester. After setting up his workshop/living quarters along the base of Yosemite Falls, Muir set to exploring the valley and surrounding wildernesses. After falling in love with Yosemite Valley and its surrounding high country, Muir applied his trademark eloquence in voluminous writings, becoming one of the most well-known outdoorsmen and outdoor advocates in American history.

Although the areas surrounding Yosemite Valley and Mariposa Grove had become a national park in 1890, Yosemite Valley itself and Mariposa Grove remained in the custody of the California government. Citing the state's mismanagement, John Muir spent several days in 1903 pitching President Theodore Roosevelt on the necessity

Opposite: *One of the elms John Hutchings planted in the 1800s blanketed in snow (Hike 26)*

of returning the valley to federal custody as part of Yosemite National Park. Roosevelt succumbed to Muir's persuasion, helping to pave the way for legislation including Yosemite Valley and Mariposa Grove into the national park three years later. With the establishment of the National Park Service a decade later in 1916, the ever-more-popular Yosemite Valley commenced a decade of development, conservation efforts, growing pains, and an evolution in management wisdom. An additional 677,000 acres of wilderness in the surrounding high country enlarged Yosemite to nearly its current size during the 1940s, incorporating the high country of the Tuolumne River and Merced River watersheds.

Today, Yosemite receives over four million visitors per year, with most visiting between the spring thaw and mid-September. Although congestion remains an issue, the efforts of the park rangers have resulted in a park that is remarkably well organized, managed, and maintained, regardless of how bad that traffic may seem on a summer afternoon. The park even continues to grow, with a new acquisition in 2016 of 400 acres encompassing Ackerson Meadow.

FEES, PERMITS, AND REGULATIONS

The park collects **entrance fees** at each vehicle entrance station (**South Entrance**, **Arch Rock**, **Big Oak Flat**, **Hetch Hetchy**, and **Tioga Pass**). You can also pay entrance fees or purchase a variety of parks passes, including the America the Beautiful Pass, which covers entrance fees across the National Park System, online and at park entrances. This pass is a fine investment for park users who plan multiple trips to America's national parks and monuments within a twelve-month period.

The park waives fees on four Free Entrance Days: the third Monday in January (Martin Luther King Day), the first day of National Parks Week in late April, National Public Lands Day in late September, and November 11 (Veterans Day). The National Park Services Interagency Annual Military Pass waives entrance fees year-round for active-duty servicemembers, veterans, and Gold Star Families.

Yosemite does not require **day hiking permits** for any hike in the park, with one exception: **Half Dome**. The park allows a maximum of 300 hikers to climb Half Dome each day, and it regulates those permits through a complex reservation system. The majority of those permits, 225, are available via a preseason permit lottery conducted through recreation.gov (the Half Dome cables reservation is www.recreation.gov/permits/234652), and the website guides you through the reservation process. The remainder of the permits are made available via a second lottery during the hiking season based on cancellations, and you can apply for those permits two days in advance of the day you plan to hike. The park notifies you by email whether you won a permit. Prior to starting your hike, you will need to pick up the paper permit from the Valley Visitor Center.

Hikers looking to backpack in the Yosemite Wilderness must obtain a **Wilderness Permit** prior to their hike. The park places a quota on permits issued for each backcountry trailhead, and given the park's popularity, you will have a much better chance of getting a permit if you reserve in advance during the park's peak season (May through October). Yosemite Conservancy, the park's nonprofit partner, processes permit reservations 24 weeks (168 days) in advance of the date of a hike. You can submit your reservation via Yosemite Conservancy's online application form, and the Conservancy notifies you of the results of your application within 48 hours. After the Conservancy confirms your permit reservation, you must pick up the actual permit on the day of or the day before your hike. A limited number of permits may be available on a first-come, first-served basis at the ranger station or visitor center closest to the trailhead of your choice.

Because of the high volume of visitors Yosemite experiences every year, and also because of the park's directive to preserve its habitats, cultural resources, and wildlife for perpetuity, park visitors must abide by the following **regulations:**

- **Food storage.** Yosemite is home to hundreds of American black bears, an omnivorous, opportunistic predator with a voracious appetite, spectacular olfactory prowess, and a prodigious capacity for thievery. Obstacles such as a locked car door are trivial to a determined bear. Fed bears often become a dangerous liability that often must be exterminated by the very park rangers who are tasked with protecting them. Yosemite hammers home the necessity of storing any item with a scent—not just food—in a food storage locker. The park provides these lockers at most trailheads, every campsite, and many other locations where you may have to park a car.

- **Fires.** The park places strict regulations on where you can have campfires. You may commonly have a campfire within a designated picnic area or campsite with fire grates. In wilderness areas, you may usually have a campfire in an already established campfire ring, but you may not have a campfire above 9600 feet ele-

vation. You always must fully extinguish campfires to eliminate the danger of sparking a wildfire. The park frequently institutes fire restrictions that further limit the above rules, so be sure to check the current level of restriction through the park website before your visit.

- **Pets.** Pets are allowed on paved roads, paved bike trails, campgrounds (not including Camp 4), and in other developed areas such as Curry Village. You cannot bring your pet on unpaved trails, except Wawona Meadow. Pets must also be kept on leash, pet food must be stored like any other food, and pet owners must clean up after their pets. Pets are allowed on all national forest trails described in this guide.

- **Motorized and mechanized equipment.** These umbrella terms refer to boats, motor vehicles, bicycles, mountain bikes, hang gliders, wagons, carts, aircraft, and scooters. Motorized and mechanized devices are prohibited within wilderness areas and on many of the trails outside of wilderness areas. The exceptions are the 12-mile paved bike path that encircles Yosemite Valley and the Wawona Meadow Loop.

- **Firearms.** Thanks to a 2010 law that established the legality of carrying a gun in a national park, you may bring a gun with you on a hike. However, you may not fire that weapon under any circumstances within the national park, which reduces the firearm to mere deadweight. Numerous facilities prohibit firearms, and those facilities are clearly marked.

- **Other weapons.** You cannot use a bow and arrow, slingshot, howitzer, or nuclear weapon (no matter how much the mosquitos bother you) within the park.

Morning magic at Valley View

The following are prohibited in the park:

- **Destroying or disturbing natural, cultural, or archaeological features.** Yosemite National Park contains a wealth of cultural features and natural features. The preceding sentence only remains true if park visitors refrain from doing any damage, deliberate or otherwise, to park resources. The park may close some areas to protect sensitive features or facilitate habitat restoration.

- **Disturbing, hunting, or feeding wildlife.** Maintain a distance of at least 30 feet from any park wildlife, to the best of your ability. Otherwise, you face the possibility of an injury as well as necessitating that park rangers must euthanize a newly aggressive animal. You may not hunt on national park land.

- **Switchbacking or cutting trails.** This practice causes damage to trails and habitat while hastening erosion over newly exposed earth. The park must then fix the damage, which costs precious dollars and manpower.

- **Polluting or contaminating water sources.** This includes food waste, soap of any kind, and human waste. It doesn't matter if you brought a special organic, chemical-free soap; any foreign contaminant is prohibited within park watercourses.

- **Disposing of human waste within 100 feet of water or within sight of a trail.** Catholes must be 6 to 8 inches deep, and you must pack out your toilet paper. In the Tuolumne River drainage, the park asks you to dig catholes at least 300 feet away from the water since the Tuolumne drains into Hetch Hetchy Reservoir, which also doubles as San Francisco's water supply.

- **Camping within 200 feet of water.** Set up camp on durable surfaces at least 200 feet away from water except within designated campsites.
- **Leaving trash in toilets or elsewhere.** Many of the toilets in the park are vault toilets, wherein human waste collects in a huge underground vault. While using a vault toilet, put yourself in a park employee's shoes for a moment. Imagine your boss telling you to fish trash out of the toilet because a tourist didn't check the rules first. Next, experience a vault toilet. This regulation quickly becomes self-explanatory.
- **Drones.** The use of any unmanned drone in the park is forbidden.
- **Backcountry camping without a permit.** All backcountry campers must possess a valid permit while also adhering to the approved itinerary and the approved group size. Note that permits govern the day of the planned hike as well as the planned starting trailhead. Wilderness permits do not govern which trailhead you use for your exit.
- **Boondocking.** This practice, wherein visitors camp out in their cars or motorhomes outside of designated areas, is strictly forbidden within the park, especially within Yosemite Valley. If you attempt it, expect the rangers to send you packing.

WHEN TO VISIT

There's never a bad time to visit Yosemite National Park, but road, weather, and fire conditions can affect where you can go as well as what you'll see when you get there.

Seasons

Yosemite experiences all four seasons in their full, unadulterated glory. This is particularly true in the middle elevations (3000 feet to 6500 feet) where displays of golden foliage, heavy frostings of snow, rivers swollen with spring snowmelt, and blazing sunshine are the hallmarks of each season.

In the lower elevations (1500 feet to 3000 feet), dormant vegetation springs to life in an emerald spectacle following a few storm cycles in late fall and early winter. The spring wildflower season, spectacular during wet years, begins in late February, but by the time mid-May arrives, most of the grasses and flowers succumb to interior California's blazing summer heat, which reigns from late May through October.

In contrast, the high country (6500 feet to 13,500 feet) lies under a heavy snowpack from November and possibly well into summer. Snowpacks can reach depths of over 20 feet in areas like Tuolumne Meadows and Tioga Pass, creating a truncated summer that lasts from July to September. Cool temperatures and shorter days follow swiftly from mid-September into mid-November before the long, harsh winter settles in again. Spring begins in April as the higher sun angle and warm temperatures begin melting the snowpack, causing prodigious snowmelt to course through Yosemite's rivers, creeks, and streams.

Roads

Several roads provide access to Yosemite National Park from the San Joaquin Valley, and one road provides access to the park from the Mono Basin east of Tioga Pass.

From Fresno, State Route 41 leads north through Oakhurst to the park's South Entrance, where it continues north as Wawona Road to Glacier Point Road and beyond to Southside Drive in Yosemite Valley. State Route 140 leads northeast from

Merced through the Merced River Gorge to El Portal and the park's Arch Rock Entrance before continuing east to a junction with Big Oak Flat Road and the Southside Drive/Northside Drive split. State Route 120 leads east from Manteca to the park's Big Oak Flat Entrance, at which point it joins Big Oak Flat Road, and then beyond to Crane Flat. At Crane Flat, SR 120 splits from Big Oak Flat Road, becoming Tioga Road as it traverses the Yosemite high country to exit the park at the Tioga Pass Entrance. Big Oak Flat Road connects SR 120 to SR 140, providing access from the Big Oak Flat Entrance to Yosemite Valley.

Within Yosemite Valley, the one-way Southside Drive provides access to trailheads and facilities on the south end of the valley, while the one-way Northside Drive provides access to trailheads and facilities on the north end of the valley. El Capitan Drive connects the two roads east of El Capitan Meadow, and Sentinel Drive also connects the roads south of Yosemite Village. The Happy Isles Loop Road, which is partially closed to automobile traffic, provides access to parking areas serving the John Muir Trail.

From a junction just west of Big Oak Flat, Evergreen Road leads north to the village of Mather, from which point you can continue north on the gated Hetch Hetchy Road to reach Hetch Hetchy Valley. Note that the gate is generally open from sunrise to sunset, although the hours vary according to season.

Also note that, depending on the extent of the snowpack, three roads close from mid-November into late May: Tioga Road from Crane Flat to Tioga Pass, Glacier Point Road from Badger Pass to Glacier Point, and the access road to Mariposa Grove.

On the east side of the Sierra, the main artery is US Highway 395, which runs north from Victorville north of Los Angeles to the Lake Tahoe Region. SR 120/Tioga Road ascends through Lee Vining Canyon from US 395 at Lee Vining to Tioga Pass and Tuolumne Meadows. Several other roads leading to June Lake, Virginia Lakes, and South Tufa area provide access to trailheads within the Inyo and Humboldt-Toiyabe National Forests.

Roads within Yosemite National Park can close at any time for a variety of reasons, including snow, rockfalls, downed trees, and wildfires. During the winter, Glacier Point Road and SR 120/Tioga Road between Crane Flat and Lee Vining lie beneath the snowpack, prompting closures from late fall to late spring and occasionally early summer. Snow can also close any road in the park's lower elevations, particularly when plowing efforts cannot keep up with snowfall. All vehicles entering Yosemite National Park during winter conditions are required by federal law to carry snow chains, even if your vehicle has four-wheel drive or snow tires. The park's website provides regular updates on road conditions and closures.

Trail Conditions

Trail conditions vary from route to route and from season to season within the park. During the winter, snow can bury almost any route in this guide to the point where it is difficult or even dangerous to hike. Certain routes in the Valley, such as the Four Mile Trail or the Mist Trail, close during the winter, and snow buries every route in the high

Opposite: *Golden bigleaf maples frame the wispy flow of Bridalveil Fall (Hike 23).*

country from late fall to potentially early summer. The more popular routes are always kept well maintained, but some of the more obscure routes receiving less traffic are subject to obstacles such as downed trees, rockfalls, and erosion—especially where those trails pass through recent burn zones. Many trails have unimproved creek crossings that can be dangerous during peak runoff. Trail descriptions in this guide refer to specific conditions or features that may impact travel on any given route.

Weather

From El Portal to Yosemite's high point at Mount Lyell, temperatures can range from triple-digit heat at the lowest elevations to subfreezing temperatures at the highest elevations. Thanks to California's climate scheme of warm, dry summers and cool, wet winters, the park may also experience multiple months of drought during the summer followed by five months of frequent precipitation producing snowpacks that linger for two-thirds of the year from mid-fall to early summer.

Within Yosemite Valley, the average winter high temperature ranges between 30 and 45 degrees (all temperatures listed in Fahrenheit). Spring high temperatures range between 60 and 75 degrees. Summer temperatures range between 80 and 90 degrees. Fall temperatures range between 55 and 75 degrees. You can generally expect temperatures in El Portal (1900 feet) to be 10 to 20 degrees warmer than the Valley, while temperatures at Tuolumne Meadows (8500 feet) may be 15 to 25 degrees cooler.

One notable exception to summertime drought occurs during California's monsoon season, which runs from early July into early September. During this period, thunderstorms may appear seemingly out of nowhere, usually during the afternoon, and they can produce bursts of intense precipitation coupled with lightning and thunder. During these times, lightning strikes become a significant hazard, especially for hikers at higher elevations in exposed areas.

VISITOR SERVICES

Yosemite National Park and the surrounding national forests provide a wealth of visitor services, ranging from visitor centers and wilderness offices to museums and art galleries showcasing the park's rich history.

YOSEMITE IN WINTER

Although many of Yosemite's trails either close or become inaccessible because of road closures (Tioga Road and Glacier Point Road, specifically), the park offers numerous winter activities, including downhill skiing, cross-country skiing, snowshoeing, and backpacking. Hiking in the valley can be a delight during winter, especially on a quiet morning following a snowstorm. Yosemite Hospitality operates an expansive snow play and ski area at Badger Pass, which is also the hub of numerous snowshoe and cross-country ski routes. A smaller snow play area that provides access to routes around Crane Flat lies at Crane Flat Campground. Be prepared to carry chains at any time between November and May as chains become mandatory when snowy conditions prevail.

Within Yosemite, you will find three visitor centers. The **Wawona Visitor Center** lies within the village of **Wawona**, and it also houses the wilderness permit office for the southwest Yosemite region as well as the **Pioneer Yosemite History Center**.

Yosemite Valley contains a small city's worth of services scattered throughout the valley's east end. Visitor services dedicated to information and education include the **Yosemite Valley Visitor Center** and **Wilderness Center**, the **Ansel Adams Gallery**, and the **Yosemite Museum**. The east valley area also contains Yosemite Valley's lodging, markets, souvenirs, outfitting shops, restaurants, laundromats, and a host of other services providing more convenience than you will find at virtually any other national park.

The **Big Oak Flat** and **Hetch Hetchy** areas offer limited visitor services confined primarily to their respective entrance stations and information stations. Wilderness permits for Hetch Hetchy trails can be obtained at the **Hetch Hetchy Information Station**.

The hub of visitor services for Yosemite's northern high country is found at the **Tuolumne Meadows Visitor Center**, accessible via **Tioga Road**. The nearby Tuolumne Meadows Wilderness Center processes wilderness permits for the **Tuolumne Meadows Trailheads**. A market and restaurant can be found adjacent to the Tuolumne Meadows Lodge. **Tioga Pass** does not feature any visitor services aside from the Tioga Pass Entrance Station at the park's eastern boundary.

East of the park's boundary along the Sierra Crest lies a separate national forest jurisdiction, **Inyo National Forest**. Inyo National Forest encompasses hikes within

Upper Lee Vining Canyon and at many spots within **Mono Basin**. The **Ansel Adams Wilderness** and **Hoover Wilderness** sit within Inyo National Forest boundaries. The **Mono Basin Scenic Area Visitor Center** provides information on the region's trails and history, and rangers at the center also issue wilderness permits. Note that the South Tufa Trail lies within a California State Natural Reserve with its own set of distinct rules. Numerous restaurants, hotels, markets, gas stations, and other conveniences can be found along US Highway 395 in Mammoth Lakes, June Lake, Lee Vining, and Bridgeport.

LODGING

Lodging opportunities within and outside Yosemite are varied and multitudinous, ranging from the humblest of remote campsites to elegant, historic lodges. Most of the noncamping options (hotels, tent cabins, and High Sierra Camps) in the park are operated by Yosemite Hospitality, and reservations can be made for these options 366 days in advance of your planned visit through the http://travelyosemite.com website.

Hotels

Within Yosemite National Park, you will find three full-service lodges: the Yosemite Lodge in Yosemite Village, the majestic Ahwahnee east of Yosemite Village, and the Wawona Lodge. All three lodges operate via a concessionaire, and you can book rooms in advance through the Travel Yosemite website (see Appendix II).

Additional lodging lies outside the park in the El Portal, Oakhurst, Fish Camp, Midpines, Mariposa, June Lake, Lee Vining, Twin Lakes, and Bridgeport areas. Those options are more numerous and varied and are best reviewed through a travel search engine for pricing, quality, and availability.

Tent Cabins

Yosemite's unique collection of tent cabin facilities offers a middle path between the luxury of the Ahwahnee and the no-frills accommodations of the park's campgrounds. Two of the tent cabin facilities, Curry Camp and Housekeeping Camp, lie within Yosemite Valley. Curry Village features additional cabins and traditional hotel rooms, along with a host of amenities, including a market, restaurant, coffee shop, flush toilets, and showers. Housekeeping Camp also has its own general store.

The other two tent cabin lodges, White Wolf and Tuolumne Meadows, lie outside the valley along Tioga Road. Both lodges also have a small restaurant and general store as well as showers and flush toilets.

Camping

Yosemite National Park contains thirteen campgrounds. Of those thirteen campgrounds, seven offer reservations (Wawona, Upper Pines, North Pines, Lower Pines, Hodgdon Meadow, Crane Flat, and Tuolumne Meadows). Month-long reservation windows open for each campground five months in advance on the 15th of each month. So, for instance, if you wish to book a campsite in July, reservations would become available on the morning of February 15.

Yosemite Valley contains four campgrounds (Upper Pines, North Pines, Lower Pines, and the walk-in Camp 4), and competition for campsites during the spring and summer is ferocious. Of the four, only **Upper Pines** (238 sites) and **Camp 4** (35 sites) are open all year. **Lower Pines** (60 sites) and **North Pines** (81 sites) open

from mid-spring to mid-fall, serving as an overflow for sprawling Upper Pines. All four campgrounds have running water, and all four campgrounds, excluding Camp 4, permit dogs.

South of Yosemite Valley, you will find one campground in Wawona, **Wawona Campground** (93 sites), and one on Glacier Point Road, **Bridalveil Creek Campground** (110 sites). Wawona Campground is open year-round, and it takes reservations from early spring to early fall. Bridalveil Campground opens in early July and remains open into late September on a first-come, first-served basis.

North of Yosemite Valley, you will find two campgrounds along Big Oak Flat Road, **Crane Flat** (166 sites) and **Hodgdon Meadow** (105 sites). Hodgdon Meadow is open year-round, provided Big Oak Flat Road is open, and it accepts reservations from early spring to early fall. Crane Flat is open from late June through early October, weather permitting, and it accepts reservations during that time frame.

The remainder of the park's campgrounds lie along Tioga Road between Crane Flat and Tioga Pass. **Tamarack Flat** (52 sites), **White Wolf** (74 sites), **Yosemite Creek** (75 sites), and **Porcupine Flat** (52 sites) all open during early summer and close early in the fall, with dates fluctuating depending on the extent of the snowpack. All four of those campgrounds operate on a first-come, first-served basis. Only **Tuolumne Meadows Campground**, the park's largest with 304 campsites, permits reservations at 50 percent of its sites during its opening dates through the summer, snowpack permitting.

Numerous federal campsites lie outside the park in the Sierra, Stanislaus, Inyo,

COPING WITH CONGESTION

Yosemite's popularity, combined with limited parking and road infrastructure, creates a significant problem during the Valley's high season (late April through October and Christmas break): congestion. You can avoid at least some of the worst of the congestion by using public transportation wherever possible. YARTS and the Yosemite Valley Shuttle make it possible to leave your car outside the Valley, which eliminates parking hassles. If you absolutely must drive a car into the park, consider arriving early—as in, really early. Finding a parking spot before 7 AM is a much more realistic scenario than finding one at 10 AM. Early birds really do get the worm when it comes to Yosemite's limited parking.

and Humboldt-Toiyabe National Forests. A smaller number of nearby private campsites also lie outside the park. Reservation and seasonal availability varies according to region, with eastern Sierra campgrounds having a narrower operating season and western Sierra campgrounds having a broader operating season.

High Sierra Camps

No survey of the lodging options in Yosemite would be complete without mention of the fabled High Sierra Camps. This quintet of backcountry tent cabin sites—Glen Aulin, May Lake, Sunrise, Merced Lake, and Vogelsang—offers convenient stopping points along the High Sierra Route, a 49-mile backcountry excursion that begins and ends at Tuolumne Meadows. A lottery system determines who gets to visit the camps, each of which offers an array of luxuries, including hot meals, pit toilets, and pre-pitched tents. Visit the Travel Yosemite website (see Appendix II) for more information.

TRANSPORTATION

Yosemite National Park features a sophisticated and effective public transit system that makes it possible to visit many

hiking destinations without having to use a car. **The Yosemite Area Regional Transit System**—more commonly known as YARTS—provides shuttle service into the Valley from several gateway communities, including Merced/SR 140 (blue line), Fresno/SR 41 (yellow line), Mammoth Lakes/SR 120 and US 395 (green line), and Sonora/SR 120 (pink line). The YARTS shuttles run seasonally, with the Merced, Fresno, and Sonora lines starting service in mid-May and ending service in mid-September, and the Mammoth Lakes line starting service in early June and ending in late September, depending on when Tioga Pass opens.

Visitors exploring Yosemite Valley can use the year-round **Yosemite Valley Shuttle** to travel to and from twenty-one separate stops between Yosemite Village and Happy Isles. The seasonal **El Capitan Shuttle** extends shuttle service from Yosemite Village west toward El Capitan, Cathedral Beach, and the Four Mile Trailhead.

A handful of shuttle options convey visitors to other popular destinations outside of Yosemite Valley. The **Mariposa Grove Shuttle** accesses Mariposa Grove from mid-March to the end of November. Given the limited parking at Mariposa Grove, the shuttle is the park's preferred method for reaching the grove's trailheads. The park also operates the **Tuolumne Meadows Shuttle** (fee required), which carries passengers between the Tuolumne Meadows Lodge and Olmsted Point. A separate branch of the shuttle travels between Tuolumne Meadows Lodge and Tioga Pass with a stop at the Mono Pass Trailhead.

Yosemite Hospitality, the park's concessionaire, offers additional shuttles that depart from the valley to popular destinations along Glacier Point Road and Tioga Road. The **Glacier Point Tour Bus** (fee required) travels between Yosemite Lodge and Glacier Point, which enables one-way, downhill hikes on the Panorama and Four Mile Trails. During winter, a separate shuttle travels between Yosemite Lodge and the Badger Pass Ski Area. Finally, Yosemite Hospitality offers the **Yosemite Valley to Tuolumne Meadows Hikers Bus** (fee required), which travels from Yosemite Lodge to Tuolumne Meadows with stops at Crane Flat, White Wolf, Yosemite Creek, May Lake Junction, Tenaya Lake, and Tuolumne Meadows. This latter bus enables point-to-point hikes from the Tioga Road and Tuolumne Meadows trailheads that lead to Yosemite Valley.

TRAIL ETIQUETTE

Established by the Center for Outdoor Ethics, the seven Leave No Trace Principles are a set of ethics guidelines that will inform your decision making on the trail. Because of Yosemite's popularity, it is imperative that hikers do their part in minimizing their impact, and these principles are the established protocol for accomplishing this goal.

1. **Plan ahead and prepare.** You can avoid a lot of common errors by knowing the regulations and concerns of the park and the surrounding national forests, monitoring weather conditions, traveling outside of the times of highest use, visiting in small groups when possible, and using a map and compass to ensure you don't have to mark your way with additions like cairns or ribbons.

2. **Travel and camp on durable surfaces.** Avoid camping on vegetation, especially meadows, and make sure you camp at least 200 yards away from water. There are a few off-trail routes in this guide, but those routes stick to durable surfaces. If there is a trail, stay on it to the best of your ability.

3. **Dispose of waste properly.** Put all trash and other refuse into the appropriate receptacle. You are responsible for carrying out everything you bring with you. The one exception here is poop, which you must bury in a 6-to-8-inch-deep cathole. Pack out your toilet paper in a plastic bag because it takes a long time for paper products to biodegrade and animals may dig it up.

4. **Leave what you find.** Yosemite National Park contains an astonishing wealth of natural, historical, and cultural artifacts. This remains true only if visitors refrain from taking, disturbing, or damaging those artifacts. Please do your part by leaving everything the way you found it.

5. **Minimize campfire impacts.** Given how dry the environments can become in Yosemite, you can have a fire only in an approved container. Keep your fire small so that sparks don't drift off into dry brush. Make sure your fire is dead out before you turn in for the night and scatter the ashes around to allow them to cool thoroughly.

White Cascade spills into an expansive pool by Glen Aulin (Hike 70).

6. **Respect wildlife.** Respecting wildlife is a formal law at Yosemite. You are not supposed to handle or bother wildlife in any way, and you should attempt to keep at least 30 feet between you and any wildlife you encounter. Feeding wildlife alters their behaviors and can make them aggressive. It can lead to injuries, and in some cases, it can force the park to euthanize the aggressive animal.

7. **Be considerate of other visitors.** A good rule of thumb here is to remember that every person you cross paths with on the trail spent a lot of precious time, money, and effort to get here. They are all trying to enjoy their trip, and therefore you should offer whatever courtesy is within your power to ensure that you don't hamper someone else's experience. Specifically, this principle asks that you yield to others on the trail to reduce conflict and let the sounds of nature—and not those killer tunes blasting from your Bluetooth speakers—prevail.

WATER SAFETY

Yosemite's abundance of running water is one of its most celebrated virtues. At the same time, that icy water, often rushing at speed and in prodigious volumes, is also one of its greatest threats.

Waterfalls

Waterfalls exert a powerful pull on hikers, and, sadly, on occasion that pull proves to be lethal when people get too close to the edge.

Maintain a safe distance from the edges of waterfalls, especially during the spring and early summer when runoff swells waterfalls and makes them much more dangerous.

Creek Crossings

As with waterfalls, Yosemite's watercourses can become raging torrents during the spring and summer thaw. During those times, even the most innocent-looking creek crossings can become treacherous, possibly fatal. Always consult the rangers in advance of any exploration into the backcountry to get the latest information on creek crossing hazards, especially during spring and early summer.

Giardiasis

Giardia, a nasty little microorganism that causes severe intestinal issues, is present in nearly all of Yosemite's water sources. Even if it appears to possess crystal purity, always treat the water using your preferred purification method (pump filters, UV radiation, iodine, chlorine, or, most effectively, boiling) before you drink water from a stream, lake, or river.

TERRAIN SAFETY

In a land full of sheer, vertical cliffs and towering precipices, gravity combined with granite can become a considerable danger. Stay alert and keep the following factors in mind at all times:

Rockfall

While rare, rockfalls do occur and can present a considerable danger. The most common location for rockfalls is along the walls of Yosemite Valley. If a rockfall risk is present, the park may close the relevant trail. In the event of a rockfall, do your best to retreat away from the valley walls toward the center of the valley.

Living on the Edge

On an almost yearly basis, hikers fall to their deaths after getting too close to the edge of thousand-foot cliffs. It may seem obvious that your best bet for avoiding such a fate is to stay well back from the edge of a cliff. However, you may face other trail conditions where steep drop-offs or ice create gravity-related perils. Consider using trekking poles as a means of improving your balance, and if the trails are icy, be sure to carry microspikes or crampons, depending on the conditions as reported by park rangers.

Slips and Falls

Some of the trails in this guide are rocky and dusty, creating the potential for slips and falls. Some of the same trails, such as the Mist Trail leading to Vernal Falls, can be perpetually wet: wet, rocky trails paired with gravity can produce the potential for injury. Trekking poles can provide stabilizing balance, while sturdy hiking boots or shoes with good tread can minimize the likelihood of slipping.

WILDLIFE

Wildlife encounters are a memorable part of the Yosemite hiking experience. Follow these guidelines to ensure that those memories are good as opposed to traumatic ones.

Fed Bear = Dead Bear

Bears have a powerful sense of smell, and they live in a perpetual state of hunger. For this reason, it is imperative that you store every food item and every scented item according to the park's directions. The park provides food storage lockers at every campsite and most trailheads. If you're backpacking, use an approved food storage cannister. If a bear does get to your food, it may become aggressive, which may result in rangers having to euthanize the bear.

Mountain Lions

These beautiful apex predators are a miracle of evolution thanks to their grace, speed, stealth, and prodigious hunting ability. So, naturally, they are a subject of abject terror for many hikers. Mountain lion attacks are an extremely remote possibility, and most hikers will never see a mountain lion. However, in the extraordinarily unlikely chance that you meet one, face it down and make a ton of noise. Appear as large as possible and do not run. Fleeing may trigger a predatory response that convinces the cat that you're a meal. If attacked, fight. Report any sightings or incidents with mountain lions to the rangers immediately.

Bloodsucking Fiends

Ticks in the lower elevations and mosquitos in the higher elevations are the bane of hikers everywhere. Both parasitic vampire bugs will seek out warm-blooded humans and suck blood for sustenance. Ticks lie in wait along the tips of branches and grasses, and they latch onto human hosts, burying their head in the skin and sucking blood until engorged. Some ticks, specifically the black-legged tick, may carry Lyme disease, a debilitating bacterial disease that can cause severe physical symptoms. When hiking in overgrown areas, perform frequent tick checks and wear light-colored clothing so you can spot them on your body.

Mosquitos tend to thrive in the high country wherever water accumulates, which in Yosemite means pretty much everywhere. Although most mosquitos don't carry diseases, their bites leave itchy, maddening bumps that will plague you for days. Bug nets over your head, clothes treated with permethrin, and topical insecticides containing DEET are the most effective deterrents. Other organic deterrents produce a limited effect without the drawback of applying a toxic chemical on your skin.

Rattlesnakes

Rattlesnakes, also occasionally known as "danger noodles" and "nope ropes," reside within the park in the lower and middle elevations. They are seldom seen in the high country. Rattlesnakes are venomous, and their rattles serve as an early warning system to alert hikers that they have gotten too close. Despite their fearsome reputation, rattlesnakes are only aggressive when cornered or surprised. Give them a wide berth,

A tagged California black bear browsing for nosh in a meadow

and all you'll get from the encounter is a jolt of adrenaline and a picture to terrify your nonhiking friends with.

TRAIL SAFETY

Combined with the wisdom that comes from knowing the local wildlife, terrain, and water issues, the following will help ensure your safety from other things that can get you.

Share Your Itinerary

The best practice is to leave an itinerary with a trusted loved one, as well as with a park ranger, especially if you're heading deep into the backcountry. Be sure to stick to that itinerary as faithfully as you can.

Hide Your Valuables

Yosemite is a big place that receives a wide variety of visitors from every walk of life. While crime is rare, it does exist here. For that reason, don't leave valuables in a place where they might entice a criminal.

Navigation

The most reliable method for navigating remains the traditional **map and compass**, although electronic methods (GPS, navigation apps) have become more prevalent over the last decade. Each trip description in this guide refers to a USGS 7.5-minute topographic map quadrant covering a given area as well as a secondary map, usually produced by Tom Harrison Maps. Navigation apps may be useful, but be aware that geographic obstacles such as canyon walls or dense forest cover may cause your **GPS unit** to malfunction. GPS units may also fail for a variety of other reasons and are best used in conjunction with solid, traditional navigation skills. Finally, many of the apps that provide GPS tracks for hikers to follow

are unreliable for a host of reasons; compare those tracks to official sources before relying on them.

Altitude

As elevation increases, many people begin to experience uncomfortable physiological symptoms associated with decreased oxygen, a condition known as **altitude sickness**. The best precaution against altitude sickness is acclimation, a process wherein hikers slowly gain elevation over a period of several days before attempting to recreate at higher elevations. If you do begin experiencing symptoms associated with altitude sickness, including headaches, dizziness, elevated heart rate or palpitations, vomiting, fatigue, or dizziness, immediately head to a lower elevation. Once altitude sickness sets in, leaving higher elevations is the only way to mitigate symptoms.

Dealing with Heat

During periods of extreme heat (85 degrees Fahrenheit and above), hikers become prone to **heat-related injuries**, including dehydration, heat cramps, heat exhaustion, and heat stroke. The best way to avoid heat-related injuries is to avoid hiking in the heat. If the forecast calls for high temperatures, hike early in the morning or late in the afternoon when temperatures are more moderate. Be sure to carry abundant water; consider carrying a liter for every hour you plan to spend on the trail during high temperatures. Also consider carrying water purification systems since Yosemite has enough running water that a water source is usually close by, but it will need to be treated. Carry and consume electrolyte supplements to replace the salts and minerals that your body leaches out while sweating.

Dealing with Cold

Hypothermia, a condition where your body loses internal heat faster than it can produce it, can be a significant hazard even when it's not all that cold. Be sure to carry extra clothing, preferably in the form of layers that you can add or subtract as the temperature fluctuates. Use extreme caution at water crossings, as the icy waters generated by snowmelt can induce rapid-onset hypothermia.

APPAREL AND GEAR

The difference between a happy day in Yosemite and a miserable experience often boils down to how prepared you are. This short review of clothing and hiking gear is a good starting point for achieving this preparation.

What to Wear

Temperatures can vary wildly in Yosemite National Park from moment to moment. Experienced Sierra hikers plan for these vacillations by dressing in layers that they can add and subtract as the weather dictates.

When buying or packing hiking clothes, **avoid cotton**. Synthetic fabrics wick away moisture and dry quickly, making them safer materials to wear while hiking. Cotton absorbs moisture and stays wet, creating the potential for hypothermia during cold conditions. Choose **synthetic and wool fabrics** for every clothing item you wear, including your undies, socks, shirts, pants, and base layers. A good rule of thumb is to layer according to the three Ws: wicking, warmth, and weather. The wicking layer is a good synthetic or wool layer that won't

No shortage of spots to relax on the slopes above Budd Lake (Hike 63)

absorb too much moisture and inadvertently chill your bones. The warmth layer can consist of one to several different layers that you can add and subtract according to temperature fluctuations. Finally, the weather layer consists of a weatherproof jacket or poncho that can shield you from rain or snow.

Although **footwear** comfort and preferences vary from person to person, good traction and a durable sole are important requirements for any shoe you wear. Your best bet is to experiment with different shoes on local hikes while consulting with the footwear department at your favorite outdoor retailer. Once you've chosen the shoe that works for you, be sure to break it in before your trip to avoid getting blisters.

Blisters occur thanks to a combination of moisture, friction, and heat. Your feet get hot, then they sweat. Repeated friction caused by walking results in painful hot spots that then evolve into blisters, especially when shoes fit improperly. Moleskin, a sort of sticky fabric, can stop a blister if you apply it to a hot spot in time. Sock liners can cut down on friction, as can wearing properly sized shoes. If a blister occurs, blister gels can protect the blister and prevent it from bleeding due to continued friction.

What Else to Bring

Congratulations! You are no longer naked. However, not being naked is not enough to have a good hike. Complete your preparation by obtaining and carrying the Ten Essentials (a list developed by The Mountaineers) within your pack. Nobody plans to spend a night outdoors when they set out on a day

Enjoy splashes of silvery lupines along the banks of Budd Creek (Hike 63).

hike, but since the unimaginable can happen, the Ten Essentials will help protect you in the face of most trail disasters.

1. **Navigation (map and compass).** I suggest you bring a map and compass. Oh, and did I mention, bring a map and compass? And by the way: map and compass. It's also critical to spend some time learning how to use a map and compass—a valuable skill that will help ensure you don't get lost. Sure, you can probably get away with using a navigation application on your smartphone for some of the shorter hikes. But when hiking in the mountains, it's important to understand that tree cover, lack of reception, and any number of fluke occurrences can cause your applications to fail, which will leave you up poop creek without a paddle. A map and compass never run out of batteries, and they mean that you will spend less of your precious outdoor time staring at a glowing rectangle.

2. **Headlamp or flashlight.** Light sources come in extremely handy during early morning starts and late evening finishes. In emergency situations, a headlamp can help you during the long, dark Sierra night. Your smartphone flashlight is handy for a short duration, but you don't want your survival to hinge on your phone's battery life. It's also wise to carry extra batteries for your headlamp.

3. **Sun protection.** The brilliant Sierra sunshine can turn you into a lobster if you don't use adequate sun protection. The atmosphere is thinner at high elevations, so prepare for the unrelenting sunshine by wearing a wide-brimmed hat, applying sunscreen every two

hours, and wearing sunglasses to reduce the glare and UV radiation exposure on your sensitive retinas.

4. **First Aid.** Boo-boos happen, and they range from the trivial (blisters, splinters, minor cuts) to the severe (the boulder trapping your arm that all of your nonhiker friends will warn you about). No first-aid kit can manage a rare, catastrophic injury, but a decent one can help you tend to minor and even moderate injuries. Bandages, medical tape, ACE wraps, vitamin I (ibuprofen), moleskin, alcohol wipes, antibiotic ointments, and blister gel will help manage the minor stuff. And although it's not exactly a medical-grade item, a small roll of duct tape can solve an astonishing array of problems.

5. **A knife.** A knife comes in handy in countless scenarios, ranging from slicing the avocado for your turkey sandwich to performing maintenance on your gear. While a knife by itself is handy, a multitool provides even more uses, both in the backcountry and at camp when you need to open your post-hike beer.

6. **Firestarter.** The Sierra can get extremely cold at night, even during summer. Carry a lighter, or better yet, waterproof matches, as a means of creating a fire that will help you remain warm during emergency situations.

7. **Extra clothes.** On a warm day, it's tempting to head out in nothing but a T-shirt and shorts. However, that won't be enough to keep you warm in an emergency or should the weather unexpectedly turn from warm to cold. Carry additional clothing, including

A NOTE ABOUT SAFETY

Safety is an important concern in all outdoor activities. No guidebook can alert you to every hazard or anticipate the limitations of every reader. Therefore, the descriptions of roads, trails, routes, and natural features in this book are not representations that a particular place or excursion will be safe for you or your party. When you follow any of the routes described in this book, you assume responsibility for your own safety. Under normal conditions, such excursions require the usual attention to traffic, road and trail conditions, weather, terrain, the capabilities of your party, and other factors. Keeping informed on current conditions and exercising common sense are the keys to a safe, enjoyable outing.

—Mountaineers Books

additional layers of insulation and a jacket. On longer day hikes, consider bringing a light blanket or even a lightweight sleeping bag, which can double up as a comfortable insulation layer during breaks in the colder seasons.

8. **Shelter.** If you need to hunker down for the night, especially if there's stormy weather in the forecast, an emergency shelter will spare you the wrath of the elements. Lightweight backpacking tents or bivouac sacks are a good option, and some rain ponchos can become a makeshift shelter using string and trekking poles.

9. **Extra food.** Pack several calorically dense snacks beyond what you plan to eat on your day hike. This way, you will have a supply of food that will help get you through one or two extra nights. Even some extra granola bars and a few hunks of sweet, sweet chocolate may be enough to help you through an emergency situation.

10. **Bring extra water.** It's good practice to carry more water than you can drink, including a gallon or more on longer hikes, so that you're never in a situation where water scarcity becomes a concern. And because Yosemite has so much running water, a good, lightweight filtration system or microfilter will give you the option of quick, clean water at every water crossing.

ENJOY THE TRAIL

With hazards accounted for, and with all of your Ten Essentials stowed safely within your pack and on your person, you are now ready to experience the grandeur and life-altering beauty of Yosemite National Park. You are the next in a long line of mountain worshippers to seek out the park's legendary scenery, and to paraphrase John Muir, with every exploration into the park, you will undoubtedly receive far more than you seek. Go forth with care, exuberance, and a heart open to beauty and adventure, and receive Yosemite's good tidings.

How to Use This Book

Now that you've absorbed the information contained within the introduction and you've emerged triumphant with your treasured lodging reservations, it is time to hit the trail. I've personally hiked every trail in this guide, and I used GPS data and collaboration with the park to ensure that the information contained within is as accurate as possible. I've extrapolated all of that information into individual hike write-ups, and this section will guide you through understanding how that information is arranged.

THE INFORMATION BLOCK

At the beginning of each hike, you will find an information block containing the "nuts and bolts" information for each hike, beginning with **Trail Ratings**. There are two separate trail ratings: one for a subjective appraisal of a hike's values, and one for a more objective appraisal of a hike's **Difficulty**, which I list from 1 (the easiest) to 5 (for those with a masochistic streak). The subjective **Rating** operates on a scale of one star to five stars, with five stars being the most outstanding

El Capitan and the Cathedral Rocks from Valley View

hikes in the book. The information block also contains **Roundtrip distance, Elevation gain**, the trail's **High point**, and the optimal **Season** for hiking to a specific destination or destinations.

Below the information block, you'll find a reference to which **Maps** will aid you in routefinding for the trip. I include the relevant USGS topographic map quadrant as well as a supplementary map wherever appropriate. The **Contact** segment describes which visitor center is closest to the trailhead, which also will tell you where to pick up your wilderness permits if the

trail allows overnight camping. The **Notes** section includes specific information particular to the route, including whether there are restrooms, food storage lockers, winter travel routes, trail conditions, or any other important consideration you'll need to know in advance. Finally, the **GPS** section includes trailhead coordinates derived from WGS84 datum.

A Note on Ratings
As mentioned above, I include subjective appraisals on the scenic, historical, and physical conditions of any given trail.

LEGEND

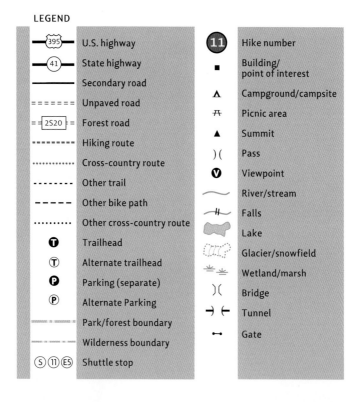

Although it is tempting to view these ratings as my hot take on what hikes are best, please note that the ratings are designed to help you to discern which trail offers what qualities. For instance, a five-star trail (Half Dome, for example) may be a highlight of the park experience, and for good reason. However, a five-star trail rating will also alert you to the high likelihood that the trail will be extremely crowded, which may be a turnoff for some hikers. A one-star trail may seem like a ho-hum experience in comparison to, say, the Mist Trail, but you can almost always count on solitude—a rare commodity for a park that may receive four million visitors over the course of any given year.

***** An iconic, even world-famous hiking experience. Any hike with five stars will likely be famous, and for good reason. The scenic values and memorability make these hikes essential while also making them exceptionally popular.

**** A top-notch trail experience with a memorable destination and other outstanding scenic qualities. Quite often, these routes are not world-famous, but their name carries a lot of resonance within hiking circles, thus attracting a lot of visitors.

*** A worthy experience with enjoyable scenery and reduced crowds. The destinations may not be as spectacular, although the scenery remains sublime. Fewer people hike these trails.

** A beautiful landscape with some memorable features and quite a bit more solitude than you'd get from the previous three ratings.

There may be some challenging trail conditions such as lack of maintenance or occasional downed trees.

* A great opportunity for solitude, although because these trails see a lot less visitation they may be a lot harder to travel. The destinations may not be as memorable, but in a place like Yosemite, even a "ho-hum" hike might be the most impressive hike in thousands of other places.

Other Components of the Information Block

Difficulty scores range from 1 to 5, with 1 being the easiest and 5 being something that will make you question your life choices. This number is a bit more objective than trail ratings, as it encompasses distance, elevation gain, rate of climbing, trail conditions (or lack thereof, in some cases), exposure, altitude, and an occasional unique feature—the Half Dome cables, for example. Please note that these ratings are designed to apply to the mythical "average hiker," a hypothetical creature who has some hiking experience, some level of fitness, and a certain amount of ambition. Many users of this book will fall on either side of average, and it is your job to consider this rating and extrapolate your own rating based on your fitness level. Uber-fit hikers will be able to complete a 5-rated trail with little to no trouble, whereas a novice or small child may struggle mightily with a 2-rated trail.

Roundtrip mileage provides the total distance to a specific destination, with some of the hikes offering more than one destination and thus including two separate distances. This mileage is gleaned from GPS data transposed onto CalTopo maps. Because of the inherent variability of GPS units and apps and the conditions under which they operate, your mileage may vary.

This guide counts **Elevation gain** cumulatively. This includes the elevation span from the lowest point on the trail to the highest point, and it also includes the elevation gain that accumulates from undulations throughout the hike. Note that elevations also may vary from recordings you may make with your own GPS applications or units. Without getting too far into the weeds, GPS technology is not an exact science, and the elevation gain numbers presented here are derived from a reasonably close approximation of how much you will end up climbing on a given hike.

The **High point** represents the highest elevation you will reach on a given hike. Most importantly, this number tells you what kind of altitude conditions you might face, which factors into your preparation. For instance, lower altitudes imply a higher likelihood of hot conditions during summer. Higher altitudes indicate potential cold and potential altitude sickness.

Season gives you an approximation on the best times to hike a given route based on climate data. Sometimes, the best time refers to the best conditions. For instance, you can hike up Upper Yosemite Fall any time of the year, but a hike during May when the weather is cool and the waterfall is roaring will be far more satisfying than the end of August when it's 90 degrees in the shade and there's no waterfall. In some cases, such as destinations along Tioga Road during winter, it is extremely difficult for hikers to access certain routes unless they are committing to multi-day cross-country skiing routes not described in this guide.

Following the information block, you will find a short **Summary** along with **Icons** that will alert you to key features on the route. These icons include:

🚶	Kid-friendly
🦴	Dog-friendly
💧	Exceptional waterfalls
🏠	Historical relevance
🗻	Exceptional geological features
🔭	Exceptional views
〰️	Lakes
🌲	Giant sequoias
🍁	Fall color
❄️	Winter route

Getting there gives you **driving** directions to the trailhead along with public transit options—called simply, **Transit**—where applicable. The **On the trail** section provides the Point A to Point B directions that will guide you through the hike. Finally, the **Extending your trip** section provides additional information on how to expand the hike to additional features not included within the primary hike.

Opposite: Towering sequoias and crimson dogwoods greet visitors on the Big Trees Trail (Hike 3).

wawona and
mariposa grove

Wawona has long served as a gathering place, first for the indigenous peoples who inhabited the area and later as a major stopping point for visitors traveling to Yosemite Valley from the Fresno area. As one of the primary entrances to Yosemite National Park, today's Wawona maintains its focus as a gathering place with a wealth of visitor services, lodging options, and quiet, wooded trails leading to waterfalls, meadows, and sequoias within the park's largest grove, Mariposa Grove. Legend has it that the name Wawona is itself an anglicization of the American Indian word "woh-woh'-nah," a word used to describe the giant sequoia.

Wawona's lodging options, including the Wawona Hotel and Wawona Campground, make fine base camps for local exploration, although the drive to and from Yosemite Valley is a bit far. There's plenty to see and do here without a trip to the Valley, and you can take advantage of extensive services, including a gas station, a market, a library, a visitor center, a history museum, and an art museum. This chapter also includes two routes south of Wawona within the Sierra National Forest, both included for their scenic, botanical, and historical value.

Corlieu Falls' main cascades swell with spring snowmelt.

1 Corlieu Falls

RATING/ DIFFICULTY	ROUNDTRIP	ELEV GAIN/ HIGH POINT	SEASON
**/1	2.4 miles	300 feet/ 3612 feet	Year-round

Maps: USGS 7.5-min White Chief Mountain, Fish Camp; **Contact:** Sierra National Forest, Bass Lake Ranger District; **Notes:** Day-use only. No restroom at trailhead. No food storage at trailhead; **GPS:** 37.4033, –119.6257

This jaunt along the Lewis Creek National Scenic Trail passes through a mixed-conifer and oak forest that sparkles with lush greenery and wildflowers during spring and colorful foliage in autumn. A series of cascades punctuates the peaceful creekside stroll, which culminates at a viewing platform showcasing cascading Corlieu Falls.

GETTING THERE

From the junction of State Route 41 and State Route 49 in the town of Oakhurst, drive

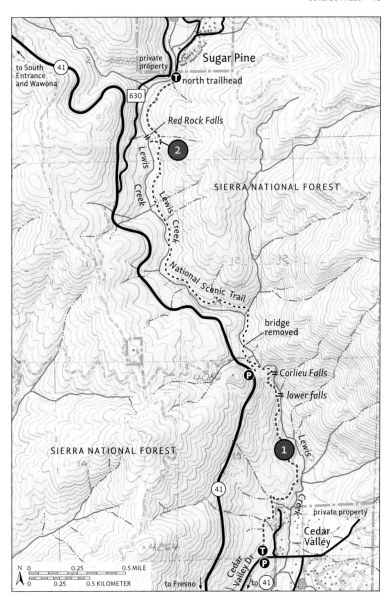

to South
Entrance
and Wawona

41

630

private
property

T north trailhead

Sugar Pine

Red Rock Falls

2

Lewis Creek

Lewis Creek

SIERRA NATIONAL FOREST

National Scenic Trail

bridge
removed

P

Corlieu Falls

lower falls

SIERRA NATIONAL FOREST

41

1

Lewis Creek

private property

Cedar
Valley

T
P

Cedar Valley Dr

to Fresno ↓

to 41

N

0	0.25	0.5 MILE
0	0.25	0.5 KILOMETER

north on SR 41 for 5.3 miles to Cedar Valley Drive. Turn right to follow Cedar Valley Drive north for another 1.1 mile to the unsigned southern trailhead for the Lewis Creek National Scenic Trail. Trailhead parking is on the south side of the road, and the trailhead is on the north side.

ON THE TRAIL

From the unmarked trailhead for the Lewis Creek National Scenic Trail, follow the wide path north into a forest of cedar, ponderosa pine, canyon live oak, black oak, and the occasional dogwood. This route follows an old flume grade used by the Sugar Pine Lumber Company to convey timber from Sugar Pine downhill to Madera. There's little evidence of the flume aside from the trail itself, which serves up smooth, easy walking for the first 0.4 mile of the hike.

After bending into and out of a gully at 0.4 mile, the narrowing trail passes through a fragrant carpet of mountain misery punctuated in spring by vibrant Indian pinks and delicate Hartweg's irises. Lewis Creek rumbles along on your right, sometimes near and sometimes far, as the trail undulates northward. At 0.9 mile, look for a steep, informal path that drops down to a broad pool fed by a raucous cascade. These lower falls are a picturesque appetizer to the main falls that lie 0.3 mile ahead.

The trail settles into a steep climb over the next 0.3 mile before reaching a wooden viewing platform granting a look at Corlieu Falls. Framed by oak trees, the falls spill over several bouldery tiers before emptying into another broad pool. The flow of the falls is strongest in April and May, but even the creek's diminished flow in autumn is a welcome sight—especially when the deciduous trees add fall color to the forest color palette.

The viewing platform is your turnaround point.

EXTENDING YOUR TRIP

You can continue farther uphill to the top of the falls to find the foundation of homesteader Charles Corlieu's cabin. Beyond that, the Lewis Creek National Scenic Trail connects to a parking area along SR 41 before coming to a crossing of Lewis Creek. A bridge used to span the creek before the Forest Service dismantled it due to safety concerns in 2015. A log now spans the creek, and if you don't mind a somewhat hair-raising crossing over the log, you can continue north to Red Rock Falls (see Hike 2) and the northern terminus of the Lewis Creek National Scenic Trail.

② Red Rock Falls

RATING/ DIFFICULTY	ROUNDTRIP	ELEV GAIN/ HIGH POINT	SEASON
**/1	1 mile	200 feet/ 4278 feet	Year-round

Map: USGS 7.5-min Fish Camp; **Contact:** Sierra National Forest, Bass Lake Ranger District; **Notes:** Day-use only. No restroom at trailhead. No food storage at trailhead; **GPS:** 37.4383, –119.6338

Satisfy your waterfall cravings in a hurry with this short jaunt on the Lewis Creek National Scenic Trail. A half mile from the trail's northern terminus, Lewis Creek spills over a 25-foot ledge into a beautiful pool shaded by alders, dogwoods, and conifers. Showy white dogwood blossoms brighten the forest in early May, providing a pleasing counterpoint to Lewis Creek's healthy springtime flow.

Red Rock Falls spills into an idyllic, alder-lined pool.

GETTING THERE

From the junction of State Route 41 and State Route 49 in the town of Oakhurst, drive north on SR 41 for 11 miles to Road 630; turn right. After 0.8 mile on Road 630, stay straight on Locust Road. After 100 yards on Locust Road, look for an unassuming sign marking the northern trailhead for the Lewis Creek National Scenic Trail. Several parking spots are just south of the trailhead.

ON THE TRAIL

After locating the unobtrusive trailhead sign on the east side of the road, follow the Lewis Creek National Scenic Trail south into dense coniferous forest with a lush understory of dogwoods. These dogwoods explode with a profusion of white blossoms every spring, and during October and November the foliage changes to yellow and red. The trail makes a short climb before settling into an even grade paralleling the creek as it makes a wide arc to the south. After a little over 0.4 mile, look for a spur trail on the right that will lead you through a somewhat overgrown corridor of trees to a large pool at the base of Red Rock Falls.

Unlike its cascading cousin Corlieu Falls downstream, Red Rock Falls spills in a wide sheet of water over a ledge into a pool shaded by conifers and alders. This appealing spot is a fine place to sit in quiet contemplation, and during the hot summer months when Lewis Creek's flow diminishes, you may be able to splash about in a handful of nice swimming holes. Be careful not to enter the creek if the water is high, since the swift current can sweep you away.

Enjoy the novelty of walking through the base of the California Tunnel Tree.

③ Grizzly Giant Loop

RATING/ DIFFICULTY	ROUNDTRIP	ELEV GAIN/ HIGH POINT	SEASON
***/2	2.1 miles	400 feet/ 5974 feet	May–Nov

Map: USGS 7.5-min Mariposa Grove; **Contact:** Wawona Visitor Center; **Notes:** Day-use only. Restroom at trailhead. Food storage at trailhead. Interpretive features; **GPS:** 37.5016, –119.6103

This family-friendly loop visits one of the most distinctive trees you will ever have the pleasure to meet—the Grizzly Giant Tree. Ol' Griz is the oldest tree in the grove with an estimated age of 1900 to 2400 years, and its size is second only to the grove's Washington Tree. This route also stops at the California Tunnel Tree before completing a meandering return loop back to the trailhead through mixed-conifer forest.

GETTING THERE

Driving: From the roundabout just north of the South Entrance on Wawona Road, turn right onto Mariposa Grove Road. Drive for 2 miles to the parking area. Please note that the shuttle is the preferred method of reaching the grove, as parking is limited.

Transit: The park offers a free shuttle from a parking area adjacent to the roundabout north of the South Entrance during the late spring, summer, and fall. The Mariposa Grove shuttle stop lies 50 feet to the west of the trailhead.

ON THE TRAIL

From the northeast end of the parking area, step onto the wide boardwalk trail that doubles as the Big Trees Loop. After 0.15 mile on the boardwalk, look to the left at a massive

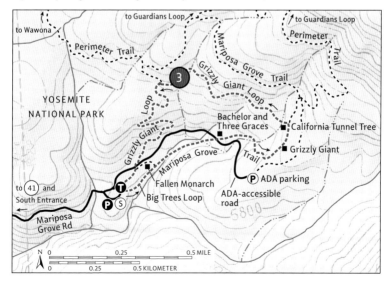

fallen sequoia known as the Fallen Monarch. Interpretive panels and photo opportunities await at the tree's enormous flared
root system, which is so massive as to defy
belief. Note that if you are hiking with very
small children, you can make a 0.3-mile loop
by keeping left at the Fallen Monarch on the
Big Trees Trail, which returns to the parking
area.

From the base of the Fallen Monarch,
keep to the right to commence climbing on
a wide trail marked occasionally by interpretive panels. After crossing a road leading
to an ADA-parking area at 0.4 mile, look to
the left to see the Bachelor and the Three
Graces, a cluster of trees with three growing
close together (the Graces) and one standing aloof from the trio (the Bachelor).

At 0.7 mile, the trail reaches a looping
path that encircles the base of the Grizzly Giant. Although somewhat squat for a
sequoia, the tree's thickness at the base
and its large, gnarled branches place it as
the 25th-largest sequoia on the planet. An
interpretive panel just to the north of Grizzly Giant details the tree's role in serving as
the backdrop for a historic meeting between
John Muir and President Theodore Roosevelt, which later led to the establishment of
Yosemite National Park.

Find a trail leading north from the Grizzly Giant and then make an immediate left
away from the Mariposa Grove Trail toward
the California Tunnel Tree. Like the fallen
Wawona Tunnel Tree deeper into the grove,
the tunnel carved into the tree served as
a tourist attraction to lure travelers to the
grove. You can still walk through the tree;
pass through it to follow the remainder of
the loop.

The rest of the hike passes through
a pleasant, but relatively unremarkable

section of mixed-conifer forest on a winding roadbed. A handful of medium-sized
sequoias seek aqueous sustenance in a
drainage at 1.3 miles, but those will be the
only sequoias you see until returning to the
Big Trees Loop at 2 miles. Turn right to finish
the hike with a 0.1-mile boardwalk stroll to
the parking area and shuttle stop.

4 Mariposa Grove Trail to Wawona Point

RATING/ DIFFICULTY	ROUNDTRIP	ELEV GAIN/ HIGH POINT	SEASON
****/3	7.2 miles	1200 feet/ 6910 feet	May–Nov

Map: USGS 7.5-min Mariposa Grove; **Contact:** Wawona Visitor Center; **Notes:** Day-use
only. Restroom at trailhead and near the Mariposa Tree. Food storage at trailhead. Interpretive features; **GPS:** 37.5016, –119.6103

*A comprehensive explo-
ration of Mariposa
Grove, this hike features most of the grove's
noteworthy trees and historic structures
capped off with memorable views from
Wawona Point. The wide, easily followed Mariposa Grove Trail (a dirt road still used by official vehicles) also doubles as a possible
snowshoeing route during winter, while a
looping return on the Guardians Loop Trail
features several impressive sequoia specimens and a visit to Galen Clark's old abode.*

GETTING THERE
Driving: From the roundabout just north
of the South Entrance on Wawona Road,
turn right onto Mariposa Grove Road. Drive
for 2 miles to the parking area. Please note
that the shuttle is the preferred method of

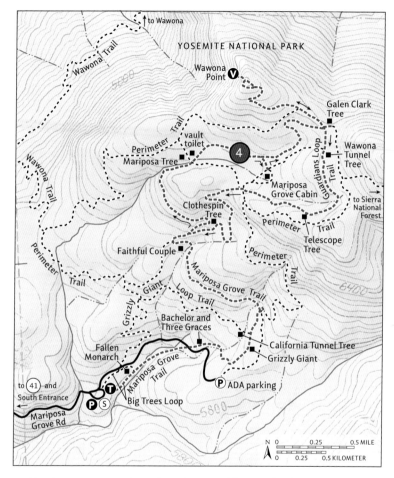

reaching the grove since parking is limited. Mariposa Grove Road closes during winter, so snowshoers will need to hike the road from the transit station near the roundabout to reach the trailhead, adding 4 miles roundtrip to the hike.

Transit: The park offers a free shuttle from a parking area adjacent to the roundabout north of the South Entrance during the late spring, summer, and fall. The Mariposa Grove shuttle stop lies 50 feet to the west of the trailhead.

ON THE TRAIL

From the northeast corner of the parking lot, find and follow a boardwalk marking the

Galen Clark's cabin sits in the heart of the upper reaches of Mariposa Grove.

beginning of the Big Trees Loop. At 0.15 mile, look to the left for a massive sequoia log with interpretive panels and photo opportunities. This tree, known as the Fallen Monarch, provides perspective on how enormous sequoia root systems can be. After admiring the Monarch, keep right on a dirt trail that veers away from the boardwalk on a moderate incline. Cross a road leading to a parking area, designated for ADA accessible use only, at 0.4 mile. Look to the left to find the Bachelor and the Three Graces before continuing uphill to the Grizzly Giant Tree at 0.7 mile (see Hike 3 for more on the Grizzly Giant).

Hiker traffic begins to peter out as you climb away from the Grizzly Giant Tree on the wide dirt road doubling as the Mariposa Grove Trail. Over the next 0.8 mile, the road climbs through mixed-conifer forests lacking in sequoias until arriving at the Faithful Couple at 1.5 miles. These two sequoias sprouted close to each other and eventually fused together with their roots deeply entwined. This strategy allows the two trees to share resources, but it also ensures that they will both topple and die at the same time. After a sharp switchback just past the Faithful Couple, the trail arrives at a second noteworthy tree, dubbed the Clothespin Tree thanks to its stilt-like base splitting apart like a clothespin. Note the junction with a trail that leads uphill to the Mariposa Grove Cabin. You will return to this spot via this path later in the hike.

At 2.2 miles, the Mariposa Grove Trail reaches the towering Mariposa Tree, namesake of the grove and herald of the largest and densest concentrations of sequoias in the area. A restroom marks this junction. At this point, the trail turns east and parallels a narrow, stream-fed meadow frequented by mule deer. Shortly after the restroom at 2.5 miles, look for the western leg of the Guardians Loop, which leads right to the Mariposa Grove Cabin. Turn right and take a short walk to the historic structure. This cabin once served as an office/home for Galen Clark, the park's first superintendent—then known as a "Guardian." Clark entertained and sheltered visitors to the grove in this house, and the structure remains as a monument to Clark's crucial role in advocating and protecting the Yosemite Grant during the park's early history.

Backtrack to the Mariposa Grove Trail and continue climbing past many fine sequoias to a junction with the Guardians Loop and Perimeter Trails at 3.1 miles. Turn left here and continue climbing on the dirt road as it leads you to Wawona Point. From Wawona Point, you can take in a panorama of Wawona Valley, with the town's buildings and jewel-like Wawona Meadow easily distinguished from the surrounding forest. Although the point serves modern visitors as a scenic lookout, the region's indigenous people used this spot to communicate by smoke signal, track wildlife, and observe comings and goings on adjacent trails.

Backtrack to the Guardians Loop Trail/Perimeter Trail junction and turn left on the Perimeter Trail. Walk a short distance to find a towering sequoia named after Galen Clark. Note that there's no sign marking the tree; you'll have to deduce its identity by its sheer size. This sequoia is reportedly the first sequoia Clark encountered upon reaching the grove for the first time. Backtrack to the junction once again, and turn left onto the wide, smooth Guardians Loop Trail. This trail will lead you to the shattered remains of the Wawona Tunnel Tree, a famous hollowed-out sequoia that served as a tourist attraction until a massive snowpack caused it to collapse.

Continuing beyond the Wawona Tunnel Tree, the Guardians Loop Trail curves around a drainage graced with numerous sequoias before returning to a junction with the trail back to the Clothespin Tree on the left and a connector to the Perimeter Trail on the right at 5 miles. Continue straight on the trail to the Clothespin Tree and follow it downhill to the Mariposa Grove Trail at 5.6 miles. From here, turn left to follow the trail downhill back to your starting point.

5 Wawona Meadow

RATING/ DIFFICULTY	ROUNDTRIP	ELEV GAIN/ HIGH POINT	SEASON
**/2	3.5 miles	250 feet/ 4212 feet	Year-round

Map: USGS 7.5-min Wawona; **Contact:** Wawona Visitor Center; **Notes:** Day-use only. Bikes allowed. No food storage lockers at trailheads. Restroom at adjacent visitor center; **GPS:** 37.5351, –119.6577

 *Wawona Meadow has served as a focal point for human activity in what is now southwestern Yosemite for 10,000 years. Known to the region's indigenous people as*

Pallahchun, meaning "a good place to stop," the meadow and surrounding environs have served as a site for lodging and visitor services, a partial golf course, a farm, a landing strip, and a grazing area, all while continuing to provide habitat for local wildlife. Follow this gentle loop around Wawona Meadow for a lovely evening walk that becomes all the lovelier in spring when the dogwoods are blooming.

GETTING THERE

From Yosemite National Park's South Entrance, drive north on Wawona Road for 4.7 miles to the Wawona Hotel. Turn left onto an access road heading south through the golf course. Shortly after turning left, look for the Wawona Meadow Trailhead on the left. If there is no parking available here, you can park across Wawona Road at the Wawona Hotel parking area.

ON THE TRAIL

Thanks in large part to the wide, easy-to-follow loop trail that makes up the bulk of this route, you can enjoy the Wawona Meadow Loop at any time and under virtually

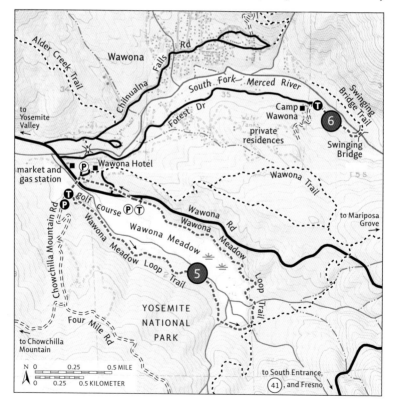

Ponderosa pines and a lush carpet of green awash in evening light

any condition. Snowshoeing is a fine option during winter, and this is one of the few trails in the park that allows both bike traffic and dog walking.

Head east from the Wawona Meadow Trailhead. The eastern end of a nine-hole golf course lies on the north side of the trail, but shouts of "fore!" will be a distant memory as you continue east through a cool forest of incense cedar, ponderosa pine, sugar pine, and bountiful mountain dogwood trees. The latter tree puts forth showy white blossoms at the beginning of May, which is perhaps the finest time to take this hike.

The loop continues through the forest, with the meadow frequently within view on the left. Occasional side paths sidle up to the meadow or lead to a handful of interpretive signs scattered along the route to educate and inform. Look to the east for a great view of Wawona Dome rising from the forest surrounding Wawona. Elevation gain accumulates slowly as you progress east, with the route reaching its halfway point (1.7 miles) where the trail doubles back to head west. As the trail completes this wide arc, cross a handful of streams that may require a bit of rock-hopping during spring and winter.

Once on the northern side of the meadow, the forest thins, creating favorable conditions for the impressive specimens of manzanita that compose the understory. The best meadow views occur around 2.4 miles as the trail approaches a parking area along Wawona Road at 3.2 miles; if you've parked here, you've now arrived at your vehicle. Otherwise, cross Wawona Road and follow a dirt path that leads west toward the Wawona

Hotel. The trail peters out at the handsome old structures on the Wawona Hotel's eastern end, and from here you will have to work your way across the lawn back to the parking area, if you parked here, or across Wawona Road to your vehicle at the trailhead to conclude the hike.

6 Wawona Swinging Bridge

RATING/ DIFFICULTY	ROUNDTRIP	ELEV GAIN/ HIGH POINT	SEASON
*/1	0.8 mile	100/4147 feet	Year-round

Maps: USGS 7.5-min Mariposa Grove, Wawona; **Contact:** Wawona Visitor Center; **Notes:** Day-use only. No restroom at trailhead. No food lockers at trailhead; **GPS:** 37.5431, –119.6278

A curious and satisfyingly bouncy wooden bridge forms the focal point for this family-friendly hike. A short hike through oak and conifer forest leads to the banks of the South Fork Merced River, spanned by a swinging bridge. During late summer when the river's flow recedes to safe levels, swimming holes adjacent to the bridge become a major attraction for families looking to make a splash.

GETTING THERE
From Yosemite National Park's South Entrance, drive north on Wawona Road for 4.7 miles to a junction with Forest Drive just past the Wawona Hotel. Turn right onto Forest Drive, and continue for 1.8 miles, first on paved road that transitions to smooth dirt road. Park just beyond Camp Wawona.

Opposite: *The satisfyingly bouncy Swinging Bridge spans the South Fork Merced River.*

ON THE TRAIL

Follow a wide former dirt road from the parking area through a gallery of pines, cedars, and oaks on a gentle incline. This is hiking at its easiest, which makes this a fine experience for children or even older hikers who are looking for a peaceful walk in the woods. After 0.4 mile, the trail turns to the left to approach the banks of the South Fork Merced River. Spanning the river lies the swinging bridge, which, unlike the more famous Swinging Bridge in Yosemite Valley, has some bounce and swing to it.

Walk across the bridge to enjoy pleasant views up and down the South Fork Merced River while admiring the craftsmanship of the bridge itself. During late summer, several waterfalls upstream become popular swimming destinations, especially for visitors to Camp Wawona. However, as with all watercourses in Yosemite, entering the river when water is high, especially during spring and early summer, carries an enormous risk of drowning and being swept away. Exercise caution and good judgment before entering the water, especially when children are involved.

7 Chilnualna Falls

RATING/ DIFFICULTY	ROUNDTRIP	ELEV GAIN/ HIGH POINT	SEASON
***/3	7.2 miles	2100 feet/ 6241 feet	Year-round

Maps: USGS 7.5-min Mariposa Grove, Wawona; **Contact:** Wawona Visitor Center; **Notes:** Day-use only. Food storage at trailhead. Vault toilets at trailhead; **GPS:** 37.5486, –119.6339

Here's a hike that's sure to please botany enthusiasts and waterfall fanatics alike. This beautifully engineered trail scales the northern wall of Wawona's valley to visit three separate falls fueled by Chilnualna Creek. A diverse forest of pine, cedar, oak, and mature, tree-sized manzanitas rising from a rich understory of wildflowers complements the falls, while the imposing form of Wawona Dome adds a touch of grandeur.

GETTING THERE

From Yosemite National Park's South Entrance, drive north on Wawona Road for 4.8 miles to a junction with Chilnualna Falls Road. Turn right to follow Chilnualna Falls Road for 1.7 miles. Look for a parking area on the right-hand (south) side of the road. After parking, return to the road and walk east for 0.1 mile to the signed Chilnualna Falls Trailhead on the left-hand (north) side of the road.

ON THE TRAIL

Spring's mild temperatures coupled with swollen watercourses fueled by a melting snowpack create the best conditions for enjoying this hike. Although the waterfalls are quietest in late October and early November, fall color produced by abundant black oaks along the route also makes for a fine hike. If you intend to hike this route during summer, get an early start, as the trail climbs a hot, south-facing slope that roasts beneath the midday sun.

After locating the trailhead, follow the Chilnualna Falls Trail north on a steep ascent. After 0.15 mile, keep right at a junction with a stock trail, which bypasses the steep, narrow stone staircase up ahead. This staircase

Opposite: *Upper Chilnualna Falls spills into a lush granitic basin.*

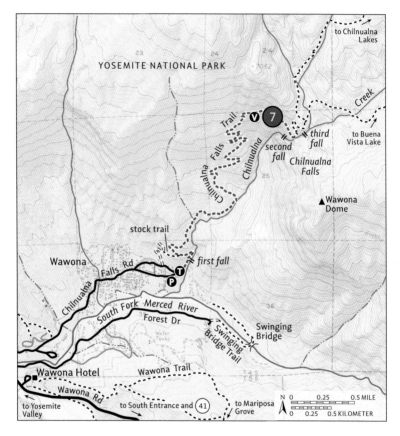

leads to a switchback at 0.2 mile adjacent to the first of the three falls on this route. The lower fall spills nearly 100 feet over several terraces through a shaded grotto, creating a splendid scene early in the hike. If you have neither time nor inclination for the full route, a quick hike to the first fall is still a satisfying venture.

After the first staircase, the trail's steep grade eases into a moderate incline. The botanically inclined will find a great deal to enjoy as the hike progresses; the warmer, south-facing slopes support a woodland of ponderosa pine, incense cedar, canyon live oak, black oak, and beautiful, tree-sized manzanitas rising from a fragrant carpet of mountain misery. A variety of flowers, including irises, penstemons, Indian pinks, wild hyacinths, larkspurs, and lupines add variety and color to the mountain misery carpet during spring. Frequent openings in the forest reveal views toward Wawona's signature granite feature, Wawona Dome, views of which improve as the trail climbs higher and higher.

After 1 mile of moderate climbing, the trail approaches the banks of Chilnualna Creek, which rumbles along to the south. Look for an informal path branching off on the right at 1.2 miles leading to a small cascade with an inviting pool of water. Shortly beyond this informal path, the trail turns north away from the creek to begin a prolonged series of switchbacks. For the next 1.7 miles you can expect to put in a fair amount of climbing. You'll have a variety of pleasant sights to distract you, including views across Wawona's forested valley, wildflowers, a lacy cascade at 2.9 miles, and views of the second of the three Chilnualna Falls from an outcrop at 3.1 miles.

Just beyond this view of the second fall, the switchbacks come to an end as the trail straightens out in an eastward direction. Forest cover thins and then disappears entirely as the trail passes through a rocky section. Here the trail evolves into a granite staircase; look for Sierra stonecrop, a pretty little succulent with showy, yellow flowers, blossoming in nooks and crannies in the granite wall on the left. At 3.6 miles, the trail rounds a bend in the trail and emerges atop a steep declivity into which pours the second fall.

Unfortunately, the second fall is not visible from above, and precipitous cliffs make any attempt to see the falls too dangerous. The only safe way to appreciate the second fall is from the viewpoint at 3.1 miles. Instead of messing around with the second fall, leave the trail and descend to the banks of the creek to discover the third and final fall rumbling into a lush grotto. The creek below the final fall nourishes thickets of fragrant Western azaleas and showy creek dogwoods. Several spacious granite flats appear custom-made to serve as lunch spots for weary hikers. Soak in the pleasant ambiance of the falls for as long as you like and then retrace your steps to return to the trailhead.

EXTENDING YOUR TRIP

By using the Chilnualna Falls Trail as a starting point, backpackers can fashion a 3-day trek that loops through a handful of lake basins. After turning right on a junction just after the last of the Chilnualna Falls, take a right turn at a Y-junction shortly after to continue east on the Chilnualna Falls Trail. After stops at Grouse Lake (8.3 miles), Crescent Lake (9.4 miles), and Johnson Lake (10.3 miles), turn north at 11.1 miles toward Buena Vista Pass and Buena Vista Lake; the latter destination makes a nice stopping point at 14.2 miles. At 14.6 miles, keep left on a trail leading to the Chilnualna Lakes and continue west to a connector trail at 19.5 miles. Turn left onto the connector trail, then right onto the Chilnualna Falls Trail to return to the trailhead (26.4 miles).

8 Alder Creek Falls

RATING/ DIFFICULTY	ROUNDTRIP	ELEV GAIN/ HIGH POINT	SEASON
**/3	7.2 miles	1000 feet/ 5811 feet	Apr–Nov

Map: USGS 7.5-min Wawona; **Contact:** Wawona Visitor Center; **Notes:** Suitable for backpacking (Alder Creek). Food storage locker at trailhead. No restroom at trailhead. Minor routefinding; **GPS:** 37.5750, –119.6797

 Not every waterfall in Yosemite comes with massive crowds and

high foot traffic. For solitude buffs who want to glimpse an impressive waterfall, the Alder Creek Trail satisfies on both counts as it treads a lightly traveled track to Alder Creek Falls spilling over 100 feet into a forested valley. A segment of this hike follows the original grade of the old Yosemite Sugar Pine Lumber Company railroad, where you will find ties, rails, and cables slowly melting into the encroaching habitat.

GETTING THERE

From Yosemite National Park's South Entrance, drive north on Wawona Road for 9.1 miles to the unassuming Mosquito Creek Trailhead on the right-hand side of the road. Parking, along with a set of food storage lockers, is on the left side of the road, which will require a very cautious U-turn to reach. After parking, cross the road on foot to find the trailhead on the south side of Wawona Road.

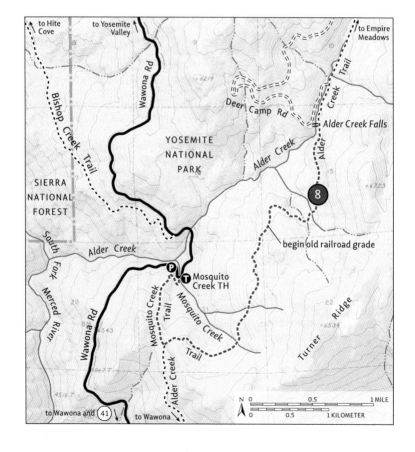

Alder Creek Falls offers a great opportunity to enjoy a roaring cascade in relative solitude.

ON THE TRAIL

Much of the habitat on this trail burned during a 2016 wildfire, resulting in numerous downed trees along the trail. The burn damage is particularly apparent over the first mile of the route as you climb up from the road to connect with the Alder Creek Trail. The downed trees necessitate minor routefinding where blowdowns obscure the trail. Future trail maintenance may clear up some of these blowdowns, but the trail's lightly traveled nature ensures that the trail receives only sporadic maintenance.

From the trailhead, begin a hearty climb through recovering forest toward the Alder Creek Trail. After gaining 600 feet in the span of 0.7 mile, the trail reaches a saddle and the junction with the Alder Creek Trail. A right turn leads downhill to Wawona, so be sure to turn left to begin an eventually northbound trek through sparse, recovering forest. The trail makes a wide, semi-circular arc across a handful of forks of Mosquito Creek before settling into a northbound groove along the western base of Turner Ridge (no relation to this author).

With the bulk of the climbing out of the way by the 2-mile mark, relax into an easy walk through the forest, which by now will have a less burnt-out appearance thanks to its cooler, damper north-facing aspect. Despite Wawona Road being less than a crow-flying mile to the west, the solitude is thick and delicious on this section. Hikers are unlikely to encounter many other souls on the trail, even on a spring weekend.

At 2.7 miles, the climbing ceases entirely as the trail joins the old railroad grade to begin a nearly flat traverse that leaves the burn area behind. Expect downed trees caused by heavy snow or high winds during the winter, which may create some mild navigation issues. In addition to downed tree trunks and branches, the detritus of the old railroad, including ties, rails, and cables litter the trail. Some of the ties are stacked neatly, while others continue to deteriorate slowly into the encroaching vegetation.

At 3.6 miles, the trail leaves the tree cover and the muffled roar of Alder Creek Falls suddenly becomes more defined. After 0.1 mile, the trail reaches a fitting turnaround spot with a good view from above of Alder Creek Falls. The waterfall spills into the valley below, conveying more water than one might expect. It may not be on par with the big valley showstoppers like Vernal Fall and Yosemite Falls, but you also never get to enjoy the showstoppers in relative solitude. After concluding your contemplations, retrace your steps and make your way back through the quiet forest to return to the trailhead.

Opposite: *World-famous views of Half Dome from Glacier Point*

glacier point road

Glacier Point Road provides the sole means of automobile access to one of Yosemite's most spectacular vista points, Glacier Point. The 11-mile road winds upward into the high country forming the southern ramparts of Yosemite Valley. Along the way the road connects several trailheads leading to a variety of hiking destinations, including valley viewpoints, lakes, meadows, and a pair of one-way traverses that sample some of the best scenery that Yosemite has to offer. A single campground, Bridalveil Creek Campground, provides the sole lodging option in this region.

Glacier Point Road closes in late fall and often remains snowbound until mid-May, during which time many of the region's popular trails go into hibernation. In winter, snow play, snowshoeing, and cross-country skiing become the dominant recreation modalities,

with the Badger Pass Ski Area catering to winter activities. Visitors can also take advantage of the Glacier Point Tour Bus, which departs from Yosemite Lodge and carries passengers to Glacier Point. This is a good way to see the sights without driving, but for hikers the bus serves as a shuttle from the valley floor up to Glacier Point to take advantage of the famed Panorama Trail.

9 Dewey Point Winter Route

RATING/ DIFFICULTY	ROUNDTRIP	ELEV GAIN/ HIGH POINT	SEASON
***/3	7.5 miles	650 feet/ 7577 feet	Dec–Mar

Maps: USGS 7.5-min El Capitan, Half Dome; **Contact:** Badger Pass Ski Area; **Notes:** Suitable for backpacking (Ridge Route 14;

Dewey Point serves up snow-coated views of the Yosemite high country.

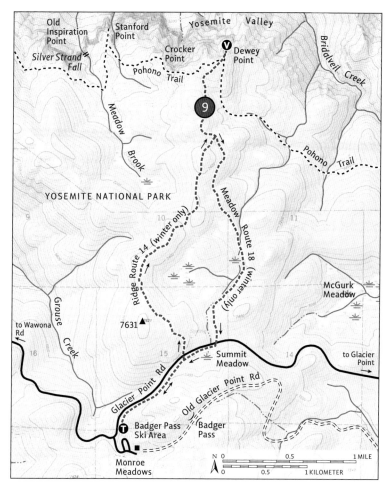

Meadow Route 18). Restroom adjacent to trailhead. **GPS:** 37.6647, –119.6634

![icons] Starting from the Badger Pass Ski Area, snow enthusiasts can follow several winter routes to explore the forests and viewpoints that

surround Glacier Point Road. Of these routes, the trek to Dewey Point stands out as the "can't miss" Yosemite winter experience. By way of Glacier Point Road and two separate winter routes marked by yellow, metallic blazes, snowshoers and cross-country skiers can enjoy a half day of exploration through *hushed, icy forests culminating in spectacular views of the snow-capped landmarks of Yosemite Valley.*

GETTING THERE

From the park's South Entrance near Wawona, head north on Wawona Road for 17 miles to a junction with Glacier Point Road and turn right. Follow Glacier Point Road for 5.2 miles to Badger Pass Ski Area, which is open from December through March. Turn right just before the road closure and find abundant parking south of the Badger Pass Ski Lodge. Note that Glacier Point Road closes through the winter at Badger Pass, and the only way to continue east beyond this point is under your own power. The trailhead begins at the north end of the parking area.

ON THE TRAIL

After locating the trailhead marked by an information sign, follow a short road segment connecting the Badger Pass Ski Area's parking lot to Glacier Point Road. During the ideal timeframe of this hike, this connecting road and Glacier Point Road itself are snowbound, and both roads receive frequent grooming to facilitate winter activities. Note a sign indicating the preferred etiquette for which part of the road that specific users—hikers, skiers, and snowshoers—should use. After a 50-yard walk on this road segment, turn right onto Glacier Point Road.

Once on Glacier Point Road, walk or snowshoe uphill above a ravine containing Grouse Creek. Continue uphill for 0.7 mile until you reach a sign indicating the Ridge Route 14 on the left side of the road. This is the beginning of the first of two possible approach routes to Dewey Point. You can hike either of these routes

as an out-and-back, but the most enjoyable option is a looping route beginning on Ridge Route 14 and returning on Meadow Route 18. To follow this route, look up to the trees for the blazes that mark the way. These blazes are usually yellow aluminum tags about 8 to 10 feet high on periodically spaced conifers.

Ridge Route 14 climbs toward a hill marked 7631 on the topo maps, and it keeps to the right of the summit before descending. Traveling north from blaze to blaze, the route rolls over a series of hills that crown a ridge dividing Grouse Creek to the west and the McGurk Meadow watershed to the east. At times, the forest cover opens to reveal some nice views west across the Merced River Gorge, but for the most part, the route consists of silent conifers caked in snow.

After 2.8 miles, Ridge Route 14 merges with Meadow Route 18 and continues due north over undulating terrain toward Dewey Point. Just before the 3.2-mile mark on the route, the first glimpses of Yosemite landmarks such as the Clark Range emerge to the east. Shortly beyond the signs indicating the Pohono Trail, which lies buried beneath the snow, continue 100 feet north to the icy promontory of Dewey Point.

Dewey Point surveys a beautiful panorama encompassing many of Yosemite's most famous sights. Many geographic icons are visible from here, including Half Dome, Clouds Rest, Sentinel Rock, North Dome, Yosemite Point, the Three Brothers, Mount Hoffmann, Cathedral Peak, and, most prominently, El Capitan. The spire-crowned valley immediately below the point, through which flows Bridalveil Creek before it spills over a crevice between the Leaning Tower and Cathedral Rocks, provides a fascinating counterpoint.

A ribbon of blue winds through Westfall Meadow's emerald fold.

For a looping return, retrace your steps south toward the merge between Ridge Route 14 and Meadow Route 18. Turn left onto Meadow Route 18 and continue south along the eastern base of the ridge you hiked in on. Meadow Route 18 has less undulating and climbing, which makes it an easier return route. About 0.5 mile before reaching Glacier Point Road, Meadow Route 18 passes through a long, linear meadow blanketed with snow. This pleasant section concludes at 6.1 miles, where the route returns to Glacier Point Road just north of Summit Meadow. Turn right to follow Glacier Point Road all the way back to Badger Pass Ski Area.

10 Westfall Meadow

RATING/ DIFFICULTY	ROUNDTRIP	ELEV GAIN/ HIGH POINT	SEASON
*/1	2.8 miles	225 feet/ 7090 feet	May–Oct

Maps: USGS 7.5-min El Capitan; **Contact:** Yosemite Valley Visitor Center; **Notes:** Day-use only. Food storage at trailhead; **GPS:** 37.6703, –119.6280

The forests surrounding Glacier Point Road harbor many jewel-like meadows rife with wildflowers and frequented by wildlife. This easy hike leads to one of the largest and most scenic, Westfall Meadow, which spans several football fields' worth of open, grassy space studded with wildflowers. Peaceful forest walking and solitude make this pleasant, family-friendly hike even more inviting.

GETTING THERE

From the park's South Entrance near Wawona, drive north on Wawona Road for 17 miles to a junction with Glacier Point Road and turn right. Follow Glacier Point Road for 7.5 miles to a parking area on the left-hand (north) side of the road just past the McGurk Meadow Trailhead. The Westfall Meadow Trailhead is unsigned and difficult to spot; walk west along the road shoulder from the parking area toward the signed McGurk Meadow Trailhead and cross to the south side of the road to find the unsigned Westfall Meadow Trailhead.

ON THE TRAIL

From the unsigned trailhead, follow the narrow path into dense forest heading due south. After cresting a small knoll, the trail begins a steady descent over the next 0.3 mile toward a Bridalveil Creek tributary. Carefully cross

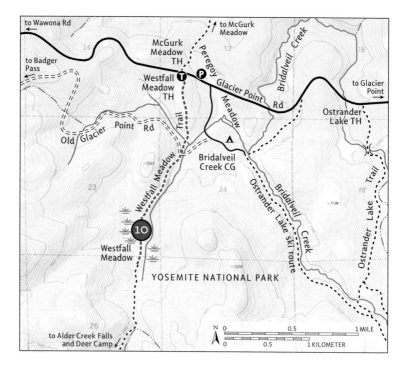

the creek and continue to a junction with an old alignment of Glacier Point Road. Continue across the road alignment and begin a steady ascent about 50 yards west from another Bridalveil Creek tributary that drains Westfall Meadow to the south.

At 1 mile, the climbing eases as the level path leads south through thick lodgepole forest. At the 1.4-mile mark, the trail emerges at the northern edge of Westfall Meadow. The meadow sprawls to the north and south here; early morning and late afternoon visitors may spy a variety of wildlife browsing for food. Wildflowers also bloom in profusion during June and July. You can cross the meadow if you want to continue to the saddle dividing the Bridalveil Creek and Alder Creek watersheds, but the meadow becomes marshy early in the season, making extended exploration a muddy affair.

EXTENDING YOUR TRIP

The trail continues beyond Westfall Meadow on a steady descent toward Deer Camp Road. The road connects to Deer Camp, an old California Conservation Corps (CCC) camp. CCC workers, some of whom operated out of Deer Camp during the New Deal heyday, are responsible for a great deal of the trails and original improvements across the park. Continuing to this historic site creates a much more substantial hike to the tune of 8.5 miles with 1300 feet of elevation gain.

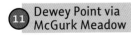

11 Dewey Point via McGurk Meadow

RATING/ DIFFICULTY	ROUNDTRIP	ELEV GAIN/ HIGH POINT	SEASON
***/3	7.6 miles	1400 feet/ 7337 feet	May–Oct

Maps: USGS 7.5-min El Capitan, Tom Harrison Maps Yosemite Valley; **Contact:** Yosemite Valley Visitor Center; **Notes:** Suitable for backpacking (McGurk Meadow). Food storage at trailhead; **GPS:** 37.6703, –119.6280

 From Dewey Point's lofty perch, hikers can survey most of Yosemite Valley and much of the Yosemite high country from an elevation 3300 feet above the valley floor. Sprawling McGurk Meadow and a surprisingly lush forest graced with wildflowers enliven the approach to the point's spectacular vistas. Backpackers can find several pleasant campsites along the rumbling waters of Bridalveil Creek a short walk east along the Pohono Trail.

GETTING THERE

From the park's South Entrance near Wawona, drive north on Wawona Road for 17 miles to a junction with Glacier Point Road and turn right. Follow Glacier Point Road for 7.5 miles to a small parking area on the left-hand (north) side of the road just past the McGurk Meadow Trailhead. Walk west along the road shoulder from the parking area toward the signed McGurk Meadow Trailhead on the north side of the road.

ON THE TRAIL

Head north on the McGurk Meadow Trail through a dense forest of lodgepole pines graced with a lush understory of grasses, corn lilies, and summer wildflowers. At 0.6 mile, the gently descending trail reaches a dilapidated old cabin, the seasonal home of James McGurk from 1895 to 1897. Shortly beyond the cabin, follow the trail across a bridge spanning McGurk Meadow at 0.7 mile. After crossing the meadow, the trail parallels the meadow's western edge for

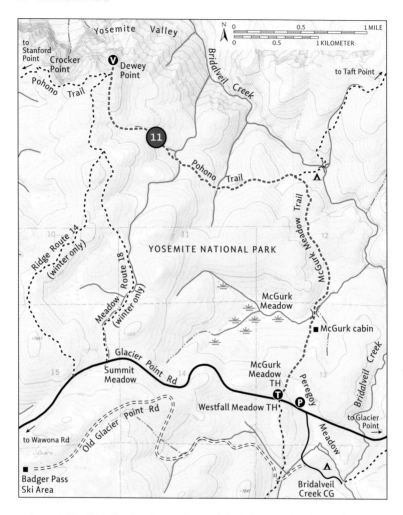

a pleasant 0.3 mile before bending to the north on a descent toward the Pohono Trail. At 1.9 miles, turn left on the Pohono Trail to begin the hike west toward Dewey Point. If you are backpacking, walk east for 0.3 mile to find a handful of nice campsites south of the Pohono Trail and west of Bridalveil Creek. Note that the park prohibits camping east of the Bridalveil Creek bridge.

After turning left on the Pohono Trail, begin an undulating traverse through vibrant forest laced with seasonal streams that nourish ribbon-like meadows. At 2.8 miles, the trail parallels a creek nourishing one such meadow, which signals the beginning of a prolonged climb gaining 450 feet over the next mile on the approach to Dewey Point. The ascent eases at 3.6 miles, at which point the forest cover thins enough to reveal hints of the views of Yosemite Valley and the Yosemite high country that await. At 3.75 miles, look for a metal trail sign and a

El Capitan, the world's largest hunk of granite, stands directly across from Dewey Point.

spur trail leading due north to a rocky promontory. Follow this short spur trail to reach Dewey Point at 3.8 miles.

From the apex of this rocky promontory, peer into the vastness of Yosemite Valley, which lies beyond Bridalveil Fall's complex drainage directly below. A map of the area will help you identify the Leaning Tower, the Cathedral Rocks, the Gunsight, and the Cathedral Spires in the rugged terrain beneath the point. Directly across the valley, the form of El Capitan dominates, while Half Dome plays peekaboo with Sentinel Dome's ridge to the east. Other landmarks include Clouds Rest, Eagle Peak, Mount Hoffmann, and the Cathedral Range in the distance. This inspired view merits at least an hour for full appreciation; save plenty of time to savor the scenery before returning to the McGurk Meadow Trailhead.

EXTENDING YOUR TRIP

For more stellar views, continue hiking west on the Pohono Trail past Dewey Point toward

Tranquil waters at Ostrander Lake ripple in the afternoon light.

Crocker and Stanford Points. Both points offer a variation on the views with an emphasis on Bridalveil Fall, which is not visible from Dewey Point. Crocker Point lies 0.6 mile west of Dewey Point, and Stanford Point is another 0.7 mile west of Crocker Point. This side trip adds a total of 2.6 miles with an additional 900 feet of elevation gain, mostly on the return from Crocker and Stanford Points.

12 Ostrander Lake

RATING/ DIFFICULTY	ROUNDTRIP	ELEV GAIN/ HIGH POINT	SEASON
***/4	12 miles	1700 feet/ 8615 feet	June–Oct

Maps: USGS 7.5-min Half Dome; **Contact:** Yosemite Valley Visitor Center; **Notes:** Suitable for backpacking (Ostrander/Lost Bear Meadow). Food storage at trailhead; **GPS:** 37.6669, –119.6039

This jewel of a lake perches high above Glacier Point Road in a basin tucked beneath Horse Ridge. Great as a day hike and even better as an overnight trip, the route to Ostrander Lake features a number of highlights in addition to the lake, including wildflowers, meadows, reliable bear sightings, and some killer views from a handful of spots along the aptly named Horizon Ridge.

GETTING THERE
From the park's South Entrance near Wawona, drive north on Wawona Road for 17 miles to a junction with Glacier Point Road. Turn right to follow Glacier Point Road for 9 miles to the Ostrander Lake Trailhead and parking area on the right (south) side of the road.

ON THE TRAIL
The trail sets off south from the parking area, and immediately you get the chance to enjoy that rarest of experiences in the Sierra Nevada: a long, flat walk. The initial section gains minimal elevation as it passes through a dense forest of lodgepole pines rising from an understory of grasses and wildflowers. After crossing a footbridge at 0.3 mile, the trail parallels a sluggish creek that feeds a pair of meadows at 0.8 mile and 1 mile. Bears are regular visitors at these meadows, and hikers report seeing them frequently throughout the day. If the thought of bears causes you unease, keep in mind that the three bears this author saw along this route all turned tail and ran like I was chasing them with a rocket launcher.

The route enters an expansive burn zone where the 2017 Empire Fire devastated the forest. This burn zone isn't uniform, and there are long stretches where the forest alternates between mature old growth and rapidly recovering saplings with a colorful understory of flowers. At 1.4 miles, keep left at a junction with a trail from Bridalveil Creek Campground. From here, the trail parallels Bridalveil Creek, which flows along quietly on the right. Most people know Bridalveil Creek as the creek fueling Bridalveil Fall. Ostrander Lake is the headwaters for Bridalveil Creek, which collects water from all corners of the broad valley through which you are walking. Every stream and rivulet you encounter along the way joins Bridalveil Creek eventually, and an hour or so later all of that water spills hundreds of feet over a cliff into Yosemite Valley.

At 2.7 miles, make a left turn at a second junction where a neglected, overgrown trail joins from Deer Camp. Decent campsites can be found by following this trail to an

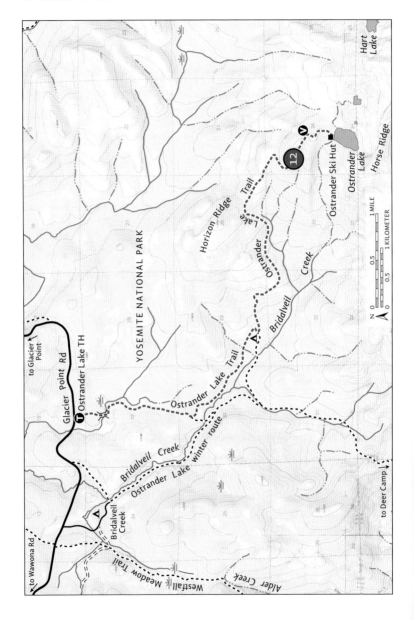

open flat about 100 yards to the west. If you are not camping, or you want to camp at the lake, keep left at the junction and continue east through the worst of the Empire Fire burn zone. Climbing begins shortly after this second junction. The trail gains nearly all of its elevation over the next 3 miles.

After ascending through a charred ghost forest, you reach Horizon Ridge at 4.4 miles. Here the trail turns to the southeast to climb over an open slope that offers up occasional snatches of views north toward Mount Starr King; see if you can also spot Half Dome peeking out above a forested ridge to the west of Mount Starr King. You'll have an even more impressive iteration of this view at 5.6 miles when the trail nears open forest on the crest of the ridge. Walk north a short distance from the main trail to view the Clark Range dominating the horizon to the east, along with other notable landmarks like Mount Hoffmann, the Cathedral Range, and Mount Starr King to the north.

After this viewpoint, the trail turns south to complete an undulating traverse to the banks of Ostrander Lake. The trail terminates at the base of the Ostrander Ski Hut, an overnight winter destination that visitors can reserve through Yosemite Conservancy. The hut closes during the summer, leaving overnight visitors to their ultralight tents and inflatable mattresses. The 80-year-old building possesses plenty of charm, and it fits right in with the pleasant scenery surrounding the lake. The nearly sheer wall of Horse Ridge bounds the southern banks of the lake, and the rest of the shore (near which you can find campsites if you're staying overnight) is cloaked in lodgepole pines and red firs. If you're day hiking, save an hour or two to explore the lake or to simply soak in the quiet lapping of waves against the shore punctuated by a trilling symphony of birdsong.

13 Mono Meadow

RATING/ DIFFICULTY	ROUNDTRIP	ELEV GAIN/ HIGH POINT	SEASON
**/2	3.7 miles	700 feet/ 7274 feet	May–Oct

Maps: USGS 7.5-min Half Dome, Tom Harrison Maps Yosemite Valley; **Contact:** Yosemite Valley Visitor Center; **Notes:** Day-use only, but trailhead does serve as a backcountry portal for extended hikes. Food storage at trailhead; **GPS:** 37.7123, –119.5863

For most hikers, the Mono Meadow Trailhead serves as a gateway to the lakes and peaks of the Clark Range in southern Yosemite. Although those destinations lie tantalizingly out of reach for casual visitors, day hikers can still catch a glimpse of the Clark Range from an unnamed viewpoint atop a ridge overlooking the Illilouette Gorge. A visit to lush Mono Meadow rounds out this quiet, off-the-beaten-path experience.

GETTING THERE
From the park's South Entrance near Wawona, drive north on Wawona Road for 17 miles to a junction with Glacier Point Road and turn right. Follow Glacier Point Road for 10.3 miles to the Mono Meadow Trailhead and parking, which are on the right-hand (east) side of the road.

ON THE TRAIL
Begin by following the Mono Meadow Trail on a steep descent that bottoms out at 0.6 mile at Mono Meadow. Although small compared to other meadows in the area,

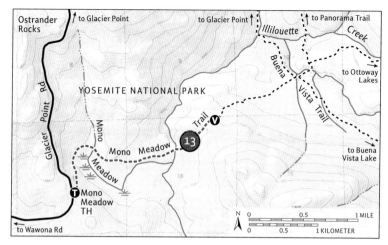

Mono Meadow ripples with life and colorful wildflowers during spring and early summer. Earlier in the season, the meadow also becomes boggy, especially where the trail crosses the creek.

Beyond the meadow, the trail continues east through dense lodgepole forest on a gentle descent to a second crossing over a much more robust creek. This creek can be tricky to cross at the beginning of the season, given that it drains a large area, but by summer the creek's flow dies down significantly.

After the crossing, the trail begins a gentle ascent over 0.5 mile to reach the crest of the ridge overlooking Illilouette Gorge and the Clark Range. Although you can gain similar views of these landmarks from Glacier Point and Washburn Point, those spots seldom offer much peace and quiet. If you visit this viewpoint early in the morning or in the late afternoon, dramatic lighting casts sharp relief on the glaciated crags of the Clark Range and Mount Starr King, creating a memorable scene enjoyed in relative solitude.

The viewpoint is your turnaround point. Backtrack to where you started, keeping in mind the steep climb back up to the trailhead.

EXTENDING YOUR TRIP

If you have two cars available, leave one car at Glacier Point to complete a one-way hike from Mono Meadow that takes in the full beauty of Illilouette Gorge. Follow the Mono Meadow Trail to the viewpoint and continue downhill to the Buena Vista Trail (2.7 miles). Turn left, and hike north along Illilouette Creek to a junction with the Panorama Trail at 5 miles. Follow the scenic opening stretch of the Panorama Trail uphill back to Glacier Point while enjoying spectacular views of Half Dome and the Merced River Gorge. This moderately strenuous hike covers 6.5 miles with 1400 feet of elevation gain.

Opposite: *Mono Meadow's lush environs are rife with wildflowers and wildlife.*

14 Taft Point

RATING/ DIFFICULTY	ROUNDTRIP	ELEV GAIN/ HIGH POINT	SEASON
****/2	2.4 miles	400 feet/ 7735 feet	May–Oct

Maps: USGS 7.5-min Half Dome, Tom Harrison Maps Yosemite Valley; **Contact:** Yosemite Valley Visitor Center; **Notes:** Day-use only. Food storage at trailhead. Vault toilets at trailhead; **GPS:** 37.7123, –119.5863

In 1909, long before Taft Point became the Instagram sensation it is today, President Howard Taft, accompanied by John Muir, visited the point as part of a three-day hiking trip from Glacier Point to Yosemite Valley. The flat shelf upon which Taft's party lunched became known as Taft Point in the President's honor. Of the experience, Taft stated, "While I am tired from the open air exercise, I feel greatly the better for it." Easy access from Glacier Point Road now removes some of the challenge of reaching Taft Point, allowing you to feel better for open air exercise without the attendant exhaustion.

GETTING THERE

From the park's South Entrance near Wawona, drive north on Wawona Road for 17 miles to a junction with Glacier Point Road and turn right. Follow Glacier Point Road for 13.6 miles to the Sentinel Dome Trailhead and parking area on the left (north) side of the road.

ON THE TRAIL

From the shared Taft Point/Sentinel Dome Trailhead, follow the path downhill to a T-junction where the Taft Point and Sentinel Dome Trails branch off in their respective directions. Turn left to hike southwest on a gently descending trail traversing sparse forest. The trail plunges into denser forest just before an unimproved crossing of Sentinel Creek at 0.2 mile. After crossing Sentinel

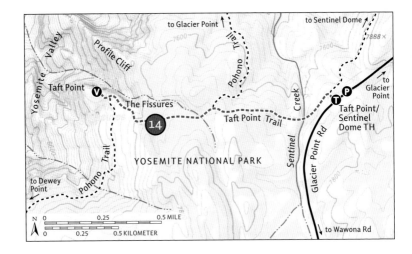

Taft Point protrudes from the rim of Yosemite Valley thousands of feet above the valley floor.

Creek, the trail undulates pleasantly before arriving at a junction with the Pohono Trail at 0.6 mile. Continue straight to merge onto the Pohono Trail as it continues due west toward Taft Point.

The Pohono Trail commences a 250-foot descent over the next 0.6 mile as it approaches the rim of Yosemite Valley. At 1 mile, the forest cover opens, revealing mild spoilers of the view across Yosemite Valley. Prior to reaching the rim of the valley, the trail bottoms out at a flat studded by Jeffrey pines and carpeted by mountain manzanita. Look to the right to find The Fissures, a series of naturally occurring fractures that are remarkably straight and deep. The trail continues past The Fissures until reaching a fenced viewpoint. The viewpoint takes in a large slice of Yosemite Valley ranging from El Capitan to Yosemite Falls. This viewpoint is a fantastic place to be in the evening on partly cloudy days when the low angle of light makes it impossible to take a bad picture.

The true Taft Point lies a short distance to the northwest from the viewpoint; you can identify it as a flat rock protruding from the valley's rim. This has become a popular spot for photography, often of the selfie variety. Take that selfie, but exercise great caution. People have fallen to their deaths from Taft Point, which does not feature any guard rails to protect from catastrophic free falls.

EXTENDING YOUR TRIP
You can loop Taft Point and Sentinel Dome together by way of the Pohono Trail. On the return route, turn left onto the Pohono Trail, and follow it east toward a junction with the

trail to Sentinel Dome at 3.6 miles. Follow that trail straight up the spine of Sentinel Dome. Follow the return route described in Hike 15 (Sentinel Dome) back to the trailhead for a 5-mile hike. Note that the hike gains a considerable amount of elevation from Sentinel Creek to Sentinel Dome, giving the full route a total of nearly 1600 feet of elevation gain and loss.

15 Sentinel Dome

RATING/ DIFFICULTY	ROUNDTRIP	ELEV GAIN/ HIGH POINT	SEASON
****/2	2.2 miles	500 feet/ 8122 feet	May–Oct

Maps: USGS 7.5-min Half Dome, Tom Harrison Maps Yosemite Valley; **Contact:** Yosemite Valley Visitor Center; **Notes:** Day-use only. Food storage at trailhead. Vault toilets at trailhead; **GPS:** 37.7123, –119.5863

The highlights of this moderate hike to Sentinel Dome are spectacular views and inspiring sunsets. Made famous decades ago by Ansel Adams's photographs of a gnarled Jeffrey pine, Sentinel Dome remains a beacon for photographers and sunset-chasers, many of whom line up on the summit at dusk to immortalize magical moments spent with friends new and old.

A trio of hikers admires the Clark Range and Mount Starr King from Sentinel Dome.

GETTING THERE

From the park's South Entrance near Wawona, head north on Wawona Road for 17 miles to a junction with Glacier Point Road and turn right. Follow Glacier Point Road for 13.6 miles to the Sentinel Dome Trailhead and parking on the left (north) side of the road.

ON THE TRAIL

After snagging a coveted parking spot, follow the unsigned path downhill to a junction where the Taft Point Trail and the Sentinel Dome Trail split. Turn right to hike north toward Sentinel Dome through a spacious forest of red and white firs. The well-traveled trail passes over a rocky section along the base of a knoll before next traversing a rocky outcrop dotted with several picturesque Jeffrey pines. Merge with an old dirt road at 0.75 mile to continue heading north.

The dirt road wraps around the eastern base of Sentinel Dome to reach the summit trail at 0.9 mile. Make a hairpin turn to the south to follow a steep, bare granite slope that rises to the summit of Sentinel Dome at 1.1 miles.

The summit views encompass a generous swath of Yosemite high country to the east as well as a substantial portion of Yosemite Valley to the west. El Capitan and Half Dome

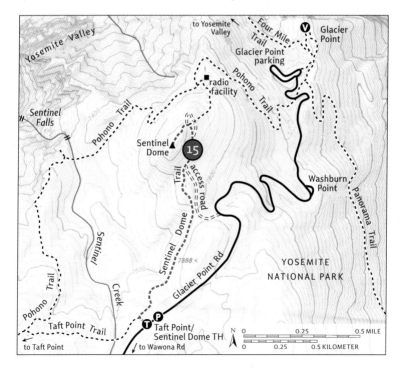

are prominent figures in this panorama, and astute hikers armed with a regional map will also be able to pick out the Three Brothers topped by Eagle Peak, Yosemite Falls, North Dome, Tenaya Canyon, Clouds Rest, Mount Watkins, Mount Hoffmann, Tenaya Peak, and even Mount Conness and White Mountain crowning the Sierra Crest. Sunset views are among the best that you can enjoy in the park, but it is wise to get here early to snag a prime boulder. During summer, the summit becomes congested with photographers and other hikers angling to get those sweet sunset shots.

16 Taft-Sentinel Circuit

RATING/ DIFFICULTY	ROUNDTRIP	ELEV GAIN/ HIGH POINT	SEASON
****/3	7.2 miles	1600 feet/ 8122 feet	June–Oct

Maps: USGS 7.5-min Half Dome, El Capitan; **Contact:** Yosemite Valley Visitor Center; **Notes:** Day-use only. Food storage at trailhead. Vault toilets at trailhead; **GPS:** Glacier Point: 37.7275, –119.5741

This lovely bit of hiking stitches together two enticing destinations by way of a marvelous segment of the Pohono Trail. In addition to the exceptional views on Taft Point and Sentinel Dome, several spots along the Pohono Trail feature equally outstanding views but without the huge crowds. Complementing those views are miles of beautiful mixed-conifer forests imbued with a sense of peace and grandeur.

GETTING THERE

From the park's South Entrance, drive north on Wawona Road for 17 miles to a junction

with Glacier Point Road and turn right. Follow Glacier Point Road for 16 miles to the parking area for Glacier Point. Follow the paved path to Glacier Point for about 50 feet; look for the combined Pohono and Panorama Trailheads on the right for your start point.

ON THE TRAIL

The Pohono Trail departs from the paved Glacier Point Trail a short distance from the parking area. But while here, you might as well follow the Glacier Point Trail north to Glacier Point itself (an extra 0.5 mile); the views are worth it. Return to the combined Panorama/Pohono Trailhead and follow the combined trail briefly east. Turn right on the Pohono Trail to ascend toward Sentinel Dome. After crossing Glacier Point Road at 0.2 mile, the trail switches back to the northwest on a steady climb toward Sentinel Dome's northern ridge. Upon reaching this ridge—the first unofficial viewpoint at 0.9 mile—be sure to turn back to admire a different look at Half Dome, Clouds Rest, the Clark Range, and the rest of the Yosemite high country.

After crossing over Sentinel Dome's north ridge, the trail enters a dense forest of red fir and sugar pine as it descends along the base of Sentinel Dome. Occasional glimpses through the trees toward Yosemite Falls hint at the views to come, but for now enjoy the cool shade cast by towering trees and the symphony of birdsong in the branches above. At 1.5 miles, look for a spur trail on the right that leads away to the second unofficial viewpoint. The second viewpoint peers straight down and directly across at Yosemite Falls, revealing the entirety of the 2650-foot waterfall as it spills into the valley below.

Return to the trail and resume westward hiking on a gradual descent. At 1.9 miles, look for a well-defined spur trail on the right that follows the east bank of Sentinel Creek to the third unofficial viewpoint on the trail—a cliff just above Sentinel Falls. This view also surveys Yosemite Falls while offering the first unobstructed views west toward the dominant form of El Capitan.

Return to the Pohono Trail, then turn right to cross Sentinel Creek. Once on the other side of the creek, the trail climbs

An unnamed viewpoint serves up scenery and solitude along the Pohono Trail.

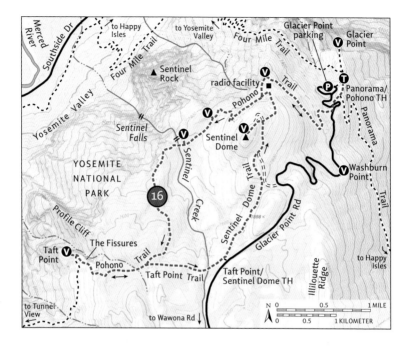

away from the rim of the valley on a steady incline toward a junction with the Taft Point Trail at 3 miles. Keep right to remain on the Pohono Trail to travel due west toward Taft Point. After passing The Fissures, a series of deep cuts in the cliffs east of Taft Point, turn right on a spur trail at 3.2 miles leading to the Taft Point overlook. Here you can enjoy the most impressive views yet of Yosemite Falls and many other highlights on the north side of the valley, including Eagle Peak; the Three Brothers; El Capitan; Leidig, Sentinel, and Cooks Meadows; and high above it all, Mount Hoffmann.

After enjoying the views at Taft Point, retrace your steps on the Pohono Trail to the Taft Point Trail junction at 4 miles. Keep right on the Taft Point Trail and follow it

back almost all the way to the Taft Point/ Sentinel Dome Trailhead. Instead of walking to the parking area, keep left at the Sentinel Dome Trail Junction at 4.5 miles. Follow that trail to a junction at 5.4 miles with the start of a short cross-country climb to the top of Sentinel Dome. Turn south to climb to the summit of Sentinel Dome, which provides a grand finale of outstanding scenery to round out the hike. From here, you can enjoy views similar to those at Glacier Point, albeit from a perspective 800 feet higher. Return to the Sentinel Dome Trail, then follow the access road north, keeping to the left of the radio facility at 6 miles to reach the Pohono Trail shortly beyond the facility. Turn right here to return to Glacier Point at 7 miles.

17 Pohono Trail

RATING/ DIFFICULTY	ROUNDTRIP	ELEV GAIN/ HIGH POINT	SEASON
****/4	12.8 miles one-way	1800 feet/ 7756 feet	June–Oct

Maps: USGS 7.5-min Half Dome, El Capitan; **Contact:** Yosemite Valley Visitor Center; **Notes:** One-way route is suitable for backpacking. Pohono Trail to Taft Point is day-use only. Food storage at Glacier Point. Vault toilets at Glacier Point; **GPS:** Glacier Point: 37.7275, –119.5741; Tunnel View: 37.7151, –119.6766

This spectacular one-way route traverses Yosemite Valley's southern rim for a scenic experience with enough jaw dropping and breath taking to leave any hiker dumbfounded. Along the way, the Pohono Trail visits no fewer than seven named viewpoints along with countless other unnamed spots surveying Yosemite Valley from several thousand feet above. Hikers with the logistical means to leave cars at both Glacier Point and Tunnel View can enjoy the full trail from top to bottom.

GETTING THERE

Note that this is a one-way shuttle hike designed to start at Glacier Point and end at Tunnel View. Start by parking a car at Tunnel View near the Pohono Trailhead. Drive the second car to Glacier Point, park, and then hike. At the end, you will need to drive back to Glacier Point to retrieve your car.

Tunnel View Trailhead: From Yosemite National Park's South Entrance, drive north on Wawona Road for 24.6 miles to the Tunnel View parking area. The western trailhead for the Pohono Trail, which leads to both

Inspiration Point and Artist Point, is at the edge of the southern parking lot.

Glacier Point Trailhead: From Tunnel View, head south on Wawona Road for 7.6 miles to a junction with Glacier Point Road and turn left onto Glacier Point Road. Follow Glacier Point Road for 16 miles to the parking area for Glacier Point.

ON THE TRAIL

Locate the Pohono Trail by following the paved path to Glacier Point from the parking area. After about 50 feet, look for a signed trailhead for the Panorama Trail and Pohono Trail on the right. Turn right onto the Panorama/Pohono Trail and travel south for another 100 feet. Make the next right where the Pohono Trail diverges from the Panorama Trail. After crossing Glacier Point Road at 0.2 mile, the trail begins a steep climb through a dense forest of sugar pine, Jeffrey pine, and white fir and leads northwest along the base of Sentinel Dome. Your first clear views on the hike—assuming you didn't stop at Glacier Point first—occur 0.9 mile and 500 feet of climbing beyond the trailhead at a spot where the tree cover recedes, opening up spectacular vistas surveying Half Dome and Yosemite's high country. Before moving along, say farewell to Half Dome, Clouds Rest, the Clark Range, and other points east, as the Pohono Trail's views will focus exclusively on Yosemite Valley for the remainder of the hike.

From the first viewpoint, the trail descends toward a junction at 1.1 miles with an access road serving a nearby radio facility. Keep right at this junction to continue hiking west through cool, shady forest. At 1.5 miles, look for a spur trail that leads north to the rim of Yosemite Valley for the first unobstructed view of Yosemite Falls in its full splendor. A third option for great views at another unnamed viewpoint occurs just before the Sentinel Creek crossing at 1.9 miles. Before crossing the creek, turn right onto an unmarked spur trail, which leads to a rocky outcrop with similar views of Yosemite Falls and additional views looking west toward El Capitan and western Yosemite Valley.

After a careful crossing of Sentinel Creek, the trail veers away from the rim of the valley on an uphill climb to a junction with the Taft Point Trail at 3 miles. Keep right here to begin a moderate descent over the next 0.5 mile to Taft Point. As you approach, keep an eye out for The Fissures, a series of deep crevices in the cliffside on your right. A spur trail leads to the viewpoint, while informal trails lead farther west to the true Taft Point. The abundance of informal trails may cause some confusion as you return from the viewpoint. Look for a sign marking the Pohono Trail where a hairpin turn steers the trail due south through an open forest of Jeffrey pines that rise from a thick carpet of manzanita and chinquapin.

After 0.4 mile of southbound travel through this open forest, the Pohono Trail plunges back into a dense mix of red fir and white fir as it begins a prolonged descent to Bridalveil Creek—the approximate halfway point of the hike. A spring-fed meadow at 4.4 miles provides a minor scenic highlight on the gentle trek through cool, dense forest to the footbridge over Bridalveil Creek at 5.6 miles. If you are backpacking this route, you will find your first legal and viable campsites on the west side of the bridge just south from the Pohono Trail; note that the park restricts camping east of the Bridalveil Creek Bridge. Bridalveil Creek is also the most reliable source of water on the trail, which makes this area an ideal place to camp if you are taking this route as an overnight trip. Even if you plan on camping farther west, Bridalveil Creek will be your most reliable spot to fill up on water.

Once across the creek, the Pohono Trail begins a climb toward Dewey Point. At first, the ascent is gentle, with a few undulations into various tributary streams nourishing lush ribbon meadows rife with corn lilies and lupines. The climb becomes steeper at 6.8 miles as the trail begins the final approach to Dewey Point itself. Shortly before the spur trail to the point, the forest cover clears, revealing glimpses toward the Clark Range and the Cathedral Range. A short climb up to a rocky knoll leads to the apex of Dewey Point, from which you can enjoy a unique vantage across the Cathedral Rocks toward Yosemite Valley.

Except for a short climb after crossing Meadow Brook, the remainder of the Pohono Trail descends from Dewey Point to Tunnel View. After 0.6 mile of easy downhill walking from Dewey Point, the trail reaches Crocker Point. Crocker Point and the next two points, Stanford and Old Inspiration, do not have any formal signs marking their location. Instead, the park marks Crocker and Stanford with the traditional Yosemite metal trail signs indicating distance to the next destination. When you encounter these signs, look for spur trails leading away on the right; those spur trails will lead to the viewpoint. Such is the case with Crocker Point, where a short spur trail leads to a rocky knoll from which you can peer down into the valley. The primary difference between Crocker and Dewey Point is that Crocker Point affords a view of Bridalveil Fall, which is obscured at Dewey Point.

From Crocker Point, the Pohono Trail descends to the next destination, Stanford

Point. At 9 miles, look for another set of signs along with another spur trail leading away on the right. To find the best view at Stanford Point, head downhill and then cut over to the left to a set of boulders near the edge of the point; this spot offers the clearest views of Bridalveil Fall 2500 feet below.

Return to the Pohono Trail and begin one final climb to a crossing of Meadow Brook (a possible water source early in the season) at 9.5 miles before the final descent commences. One more viewpoint awaits at Old Inspiration Point. The obscure spur trail—long abandoned by the Park—can be difficult to find because there are no signs to mark it. At 10.1 miles, look for an overgrown spur trail branching off to the right at a pronounced switchback. This neglected

Yosemite Falls is an omnipresent landmark on the eastern half of the Pohono Trail.

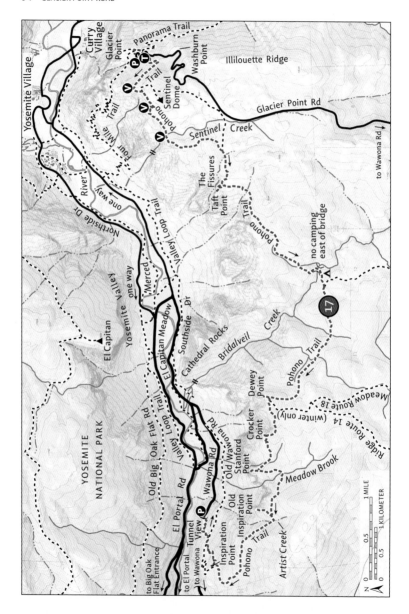

trail descends, first through forest and then through chaparral, to an isolated promontory jutting out into the valley. The view here is far more dramatic than what you will find at "new" Inspiration Point, which lies downhill from this spot.

The final segment of the Pohono Trail descends from the Old Inspiration Point spur trail on a steep track through dense forest to a junction with Old Wawona Road at 11.6 miles. Adjacent to this junction, find an ancient stone structure marking the location of Inspiration Point. The park abandoned this Inspiration Point years ago, and cedar trees now obscure the viewpoint. You can find equivalent views at an informal "new" Inspiration Point that lies downhill and to the northwest via a spur trail. This is the last viewpoint on the route, although there are plenty of spots on the final 1.2-mile descent down to Tunnel View from which to regard Yosemite Valley. Continue along the steep, rocky, downhill trail, crossing Old Wawona Road one more time at 12.2 miles. The Pohono Trail terminates at the Tunnel View parking area 0.6 mile from the last Old Wawona Road crossing, signaling the end of the hike.

⑱ Panorama Trail

RATING/ DIFFICULTY	ROUNDTRIP	ELEV GAIN/ HIGH POINT	SEASON
****/3	8.8 miles one-way	900 feet/ 7286 feet	May–Oct

Maps: USGS 7.5-min Half Dome, Tom Harrison Maps Yosemite Valley; **Contacts**: Yosemite Valley Visitor Center; **Notes:** Day-use only. Restrooms at both trailheads. Shuttle required. Food storage lockers

at Glacier Point Trailhead; **GPS:** 37.7275, –119.5741

 With a bit of advance planning and the use of the Glacier Point Tour Bus, you can access this classic Yosemite adventure through a litany of Yosemite's famous geological and hydrological features. On the descent, the Panorama Trail features great views of Half Dome, the Yosemite high country, and Illilouette, Nevada, and Vernal Falls before following the opening segment of the John Muir Trail back to Happy Isles.

GETTING THERE

Driving: From the Arch Rock Entrance east of El Portal, head east on El Portal Road for 5.5 miles until the road splits into Northside Drive and Southside Drive. Keep right to follow Southside Drive and continue driving east for another 5.1 miles. Turn left onto Sentinel Drive, which you will follow for 0.3 mile until you reach Northside Drive. Turn left again to continue for 1 mile to Yosemite Valley Lodge.

Transit: From Yosemite Valley Lodge, take a one-way trip on the Glacier Point Tour Bus (see Appendix II for contact information), and exit at Glacier Point. After completing your hike, take the Valley Shuttle back to Yosemite Valley Lodge or to wherever you may be staying inside the valley.

ON THE TRAIL

After exiting the Glacier Point Tour Bus, walk south from the parking area toward Glacier Point and make an immediate right onto the Panorama Trail. As it peels away from the bustle of Glacier Point, the Panorama Trail descends obliquely along a slope dotted with chaparral and punctuated with open pine forest that allows brilliant views east toward Half Dome, Nevada Fall, Vernal Fall, and Little Yosemite Valley. After 1.7 miles of view-packed, downhill walking, turn left at a junction with the Buena Vista Trail to remain on the Panorama Trail, which commences a series of descending switchbacks that take you to the banks of Illilouette Creek. At the 2.2-mile mark before reaching the creek, look for a spot just off the left side of the trail where you can see Illilouette Falls—one of the only spots in the park where you can admire this impressive cascade in its entirety.

You'll reach Illilouette Creek at 2.5 miles, where spacious granite slabs along the conifer-shaded banks provide a great opportunity to relax and enjoy the rumbling

orchestra of water music as the creek rushes toward its 450-foot fall about 0.1 mile downstream. Cross the creek via a footbridge to begin this hike's only section of significant climbing, moving away from the creek via another set of switchbacks to Panorama Point at 3.2 miles. An informal, unmarked trail through manzanita leads north to the point, from which you can peer down into the Merced River Gorge and beyond into Yosemite Valley.

Beyond Panorama Point, the trail bends toward the east with another 0.7 mile of moderate climbing. As the trail progresses east high above the Merced River Gorge, views across the gorge evolve, with Half Dome becoming less prominent and the gray monolith of Liberty Cap becoming the dominant feature. The rumble of Vernal and Nevada Falls drifts up from below, teasing the highlights at the end of the hike. At 4.5 miles, keep left at a junction with the Mono Meadow Trail, which leads south to the Ottoway Lakes. You'll soon begin another series of tight switchbacks that drop down to a junction with the John Muir Trail (JMT) at 5.4 miles. Before following the JMT back to Happy Isles, turn right to take a short diversion to the footbridge crossing the Merced River just above Nevada Fall.

After returning to the JMT junction, follow the JMT west toward Happy Isles. The trail descends to Clark Point at 6.6 miles, where you can get another good look back at Nevada Fall. Continue on the John Muir Trail, which takes a hairpin turn at Clark Point and heads west, and follow one final set of descending switchbacks that deposits you along the banks of the Merced River at a junction with the Mist Trail at 7.7 miles. Turn left here and within a few hundred yards, cross the Merced River on a footbridge to follow the JMT as it parallels the river on a westward and later northward course toward the JMT trailhead. Walk west across the Happy Isles Bridge, where you can jump on the Yosemite Valley Shuttle back to Yosemite Valley Lodge.

Views rarely get more iconic than those on the opening stretch of the Panorama Trail.

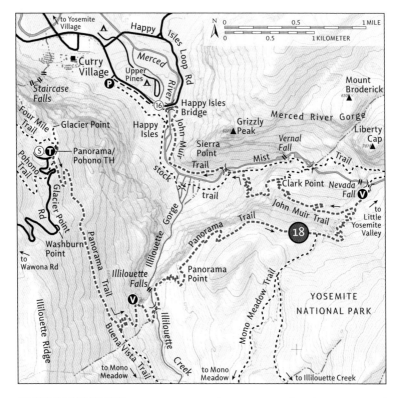

EXTENDING YOUR TRIP

Skip the shuttle with a full-day odyssey combining the Panorama Trail, Valley Loop Trail, and Four Mile Trail. Take the Four Mile Trail (Hike 24) from the valley floor to Glacier Point. Complete the Panorama Trail described above. Follow the Valley Loop Trail west from Happy Isles to the Four Mile Trail parking area. This epic route covers 16.25 miles with 4000 feet of elevation.

Opposite: Yosemite Falls rages on a brilliant spring day (Hike 25).

yosemite valley

When it comes to introducing one of the most iconic landscapes on the planet, John Muir sums up the Valley best, saying, "Between every two pines stood the door to the world's greatest cathedral." As you wander along the valley floor or perhaps away from the valley floor on a steep, winding footpath, you will find countless opportunities to affirm Muir's observation through a litany of unforgettable sights and sounds. Waterfalls thunder. Granite formations soar and gleam. Crystalline Sierra sunshine bathes everything in its brilliant clarity. And the contrast between quiet intimacy and impossible grandeur confounds and overwhelms the senses.

Given this stupendous beauty, it should come as no surprise that Yosemite Valley is a popular place. Many of the park's millions of annual visitors come seeking waterfalls, rivers, and world-famous vistas, and thus it is unreasonable to expect a quiet wilderness experience unless you visit during winter. Hotels, a quartet of campgrounds, tent cabins, markets, restaurants, exhibits, a visitor center, a chapel, a museum, several bustling roads and parking areas, employee residences, and a helpful shuttle system coexist surprisingly well with the meadows, forests, and the Merced River. The valley can get very congested, especially during spring and summer, which may frustrate some visitors. Parking comes at a premium for anybody who doesn't start their day before sunrise, and therefore it's wisest to rely on the shuttle system throughout the year.

Half Dome on a fall evening from Turtleback Dome

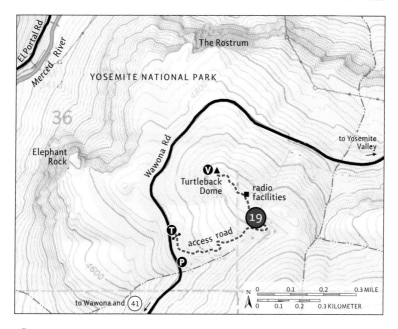

19 Turtleback Dome

RATING/ DIFFICULTY	ROUNDTRIP	ELEV GAIN/ HIGH POINT	SEASON
*/1	1.2 miles	350 feet/ 5283 feet	Year- round

Map: USGS 7.5-min El Capitan; **Contact:** Yosemite Valley Visitor Center; **Notes:** Day-use only. No restroom at trailhead. No food storage at trailhead; **GPS:** 37.710995, –119.708729

This rounded granite outcrop rising over the mouth of Yosemite Valley yields some fine sunsets and equally impressive views east toward El Capitan and Half Dome. The effort to reach this spot is minimal, and the dome's relative obscurity ensures that sunset chasers might get to enjoy this view-packed perch in solitude.

GETTING THERE

From the park's South Entrance near Wawona, drive north on Wawona Road for 22.5 miles to an unsigned and gated paved access road that leads to the top of Turtleback Dome. Look for a pullout on the right (east) side of Wawona Road about 50 yards before the gated road. Park here and carefully walk north along the shoulder of Wawona Road to begin the hike.

ON THE TRAIL

The route starts from a gated paved road that accesses some communications structures atop the dome. Though this route does take you by the structures, they don't hinder

With a rainbow added to the scene, Pohono Trail is just showing off.

the great views. Follow the paved road uphill and east through a forest of incense cedar, black oak, and live oak as it ascends alongside a ravine to the south of Turtleback Dome. After 0.35 mile and a few switchbacks, the road turns north to reach the complex of antennae and service buildings. Where the road ends at this complex, at 0.45 mile, look for an informal path that extends northwest along the crest of the dome. This path will lead away from the structures to a jumble of large boulders. These boulders mark a great spot to hunker down and enjoy the setting sun and the softly fading light.

Look west, and you can follow the winding course of the Merced River as it meanders past El Portal toward Lake McClure. The setting sun puts on an impressive display of color and warmth, especially on partly cloudy evenings. Look east for a partial view into Yosemite Valley. El Capitan and Half Dome dominate this scene, but you will also be able to pick out Sentinel Dome on the south side of the valley. Turtleback Dome is also one of the only accessible spots in the park where you can take in the entirety of the Cascades to the north, which most visitors only ever see from a picnic area near the Arch Rock Entrance.

20 Inspiration Point

RATING/ DIFFICULTY	ROUNDTRIP	ELEV GAIN/ HIGH POINT	SEASON
***/3	2.3 miles	950 feet/ 5403 feet	Year-round

Maps: USGS 7.5-min El Capitan, Tom Harrison Maps Yosemite Valley; **Contact:** Yosemite Valley Visitor Center; **Notes:** Day-use only. Food storage lockers at trailhead. Vault toilets at trailhead; **GPS:** 37.7151, –119.6766

🏠 🧭 *As you mill about with the throngs of visitors soaking in the revelatory vistas at Tunnel View, the hiker in you might wonder whether there's a way to not only improve upon the view, but also to have the same kind of vista all to yourself. For the price of a short, steep climb, you can attain a viewpoint that lives up to its name with classic views of Yosemite Valley.*

GETTING THERE

From Yosemite National Park's South Entrance on State Route 41 (Wawona Road), drive north for 24.6 miles to the Tunnel View parking area. The western trailhead for the Pohono Trail, which leads to both Inspiration Point and Artist Point, is at the edge of the southern parking lot.

ON THE TRAIL

First locate the western trailhead for the Pohono Trail, which lies on the south side of Wawona Road. Within minutes of hiking away from the parking area, the Pohono Trail performs an astonishing magic trick: the tumult and hubbub of visitors flocking to the Tunnel View lookout vanish like an ice cube in El Portal during August. Sure, the steep grade picks up nearly 1000 feet over the next 1.1 miles, but for hikers this gift yields the same phenomenal views

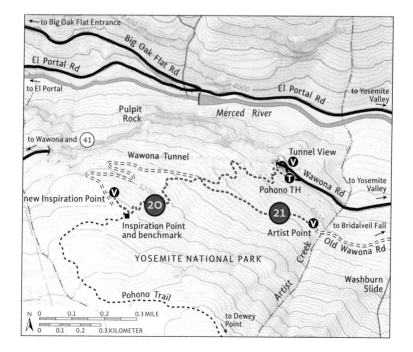

accompanied by peaceful forest sounds instead of the sounds of tour buses.

As you progress upward over numerous rocky switchbacks, the dense forest cover of pine, cedar, Douglas fir, and live oaks occasionally opens to reveal glimpses up Yosemite Valley. El Capitan and Bridalveil Fall are only the most obvious focal points in this vista; many other famous landmarks, including the Cathedral Rocks, Sentinel Rock, Half Dome, and a slice of Clouds Rest lie beyond. Continue straight ahead when you come to a junction with Old Wawona Road at 0.5 mile. A left turn on the old road will take you downhill toward Artist Point, which is a possible side trip if you have the energy.

The switchbacking climb continues past Old Wawona Road for another 0.6 mile to

The pyramid of Clouds Rest takes center stage from Artist Point.

the site of Inspiration Point, marked by a dilapidated stone marker. Inspiration Point, with its various iterations, is one of the more confusing landmarks in Yosemite Valley. This Inspiration Point was abandoned long ago, and a copse of cedar trees obscures the views in front of the stone marker and benchmark. From the marker, find an informal path running downhill to the current iteration of Inspiration Point, or "new" Inspiration Point. If that's not confusing enough for you, there's an Old Inspiration Point another 1.4 miles along the Pohono Trail. From the "new" Inspiration Point, you can enjoy the brilliant view up-valley from a perch nearly 1000 feet higher than Tunnel View. The exceptional scenery and relative peace and quiet make this an ideal location from which to regard one of the most famous landscapes in the United States.

21 Artist Point

RATING/ DIFFICULTY	ROUNDTRIP	ELEV GAIN/ HIGH POINT	SEASON
**/2	1.8 mile	700 feet/ 4903 feet	Year-round

Maps: USGS 7.5-min El Capitan, Tom Harrison Maps Yosemite Valley; **Contact:** Yosemite Valley Visitor Center; **Notes:** Day-use only. Food storage lockers. Vault toilets at trailhead; **GPS:** 37.7151, –119.6766

 For over fifty years from its completion in 1875, the Old Wawona Road conveyed stagecoach and motor traffic into Yosemite Valley. Along the way, the road stopped at a handful of jaw-dropping viewpoints that are the predecessors of today's Tunnel View. Artist Point, so

named for the numerous artists who set up their easels here, bears an air of forgottenness today, but the views remain as remarkable as ever.

GETTING THERE
From Yosemite National Park's South Entrance on State Route 41 (Wawona Road), drive north for 24.6 miles to the Tunnel View parking area. The western trailhead for the Pohono Trail, which leads to both Inspiration Point and Artist Point, lies at the edge of the southern parking lot.

ON THE TRAIL
This slightly shorter and gentler alternative to the Inspiration Point hike (Hike 20) follows the same opening segment of the Pohono Trail on a rocky, uphill grade that picks up a breathless 500 feet of elevation over 0.5 mile of climbing. After this first half-mile segment, the trail reaches a junction with the Old Wawona Road. Turn left here and begin a descent along a much gentler grade, which passes through a dense forest of Douglas fir, incense cedar, and ponderosa pine casting shade over moss-covered boulders. This largely forgotten roadbed may have downed trees blocking portions of the path, but the roadbed is wide enough that these obstacles should be easy to navigate.

After 0.4 mile and about 200 feet of descending, Old Wawona Road comes to an obvious clearing at a bend in the road. This unmarked clearing is Artist Point, which peers into Yosemite Valley from an elevated vantage similar to Tunnel View. Yosemite's most famous formations all tower over a carpet of cedar and pine lining the valley floor. Following winter and spring storms, mists fill the valley and splash against the austere granite walls of the canyon.

For a quick diversion from the iconic views into Yosemite Valley, continue about 30 yards down Old Wawona Road to a crossing of Artist Creek. The creek spills melodiously over a series of granite outcrops, proving more musical than artisanal.

22 Old Inspiration Point and Stanford Point

RATING/ DIFFICULTY	ROUNDTRIP	ELEV GAIN/ HIGH POINT	SEASON
***/4	7 miles	2600 feet/ 6969 feet	May–Oct

Map: USGS 7.5-min El Capitan; **Contact:** Yosemite Valley Visitor Center; **Notes:** Day-use only. Food storage lockers. Vault toilets at trailhead; **GPS:** 37.7151, –119.6766

Although there are less strenuous methods of reaching Stanford Point, there is something special about a vigorous climb through dense forest before finally reaching a precipitous cliffside surveying jaw-dropping views of Yosemite Valley. The work involved in accomplishing this climb is anything but trivial, but the scenic rewards and sense of accomplishment are significant. Tack on a visit to hard-to-find, historic Old Inspiration Point to admire the same views from which the early Yosemite visitors took their inspiration.

GETTING THERE
From Yosemite National Park's South Entrance on State Route 41 (Wawona Road), drive north for 24.6 miles to the Tunnel View parking area. The western trailhead for the Pohono Trail, which leads to both Inspiration Point and Artist Point, is at the edge of the southern parking lot.

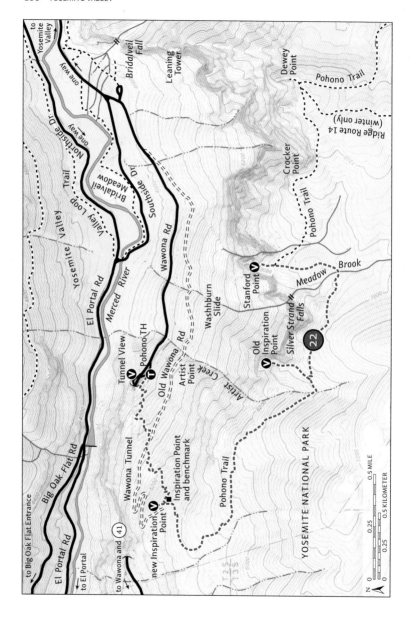

Yosemite Valley dazzles from Stanford Point.

ON THE TRAIL

Not one to delay the inevitable, the Pohono Trail begins an immediate steep incline away from the trailhead at the Tunnel View parking area south of Wawona Road. On the climb up, a slightly elevated variation of the classic Tunnel View vista emerges, although a dense forest of oak, pine, and cedar partially obscures that view for much of the initial climb. Cross Old Wawona Road at 0.5 mile, then continue the steep climb for another 0.6 mile to Inspiration Point.

By the time you reach Inspiration Point, you will have gained 1000 feet over 1.1 miles. The Inspiration Point marked by an ancient stone monument is now obscured by cedars; to find the "new" Inspiration Point, follow a short spur trail downhill from the monument to a clearing that reveals a further elevated perspective of Yosemite Valley that is similar but superior to Tunnel View. Yes, I know it is confusing with all of these Inspiration Points; for those keeping score, the "new" Inspiration Point lies downhill from Inspiration Point, which lies downhill from the Old Inspiration Point. So, basically the higher you climb, the older the Inspiration Points get. Inspiring? Confusing? Exhausting? Anyway, back to the hike.

Return to the Pohono Trail to resume the stiff climb. At 1.3 miles, the Pohono Trail bends to the southeast as it continues its relentless ascent through pine and fir forest. Views largely remain obscured by the dense forest through which you climb, which helps create a sense of anticipation regarding how the valley views will expand and evolve by the time you reach Stanford Point. The only significant event between here and the spur trail to Old Inspiration Point is a crossing of Artist Creek at 2.4 miles, which also serves as a cue to begin searching for the difficult-to-find spur trail to Old Inspiration Point.

To find this spur trail, continue beyond Artist Creek for 0.1 mile. At 2.55 miles, the trail makes a sharp switchback. At this switchback, look to the left for a faint path that may be barred by logs and branches. This is the only evidence you will find of the spur trail from the Pohono Trail; there are no signs or other indications, which attests to the trail's decades of abandonment. Turn left onto the rough trail, which may have several downed trees presenting minor navigational obstacles. The rough path threads its way downhill, first through dense forest and soon through chaparral for 0.3 mile until ascending slightly to a prominent knoll extending into the airy expanses of Yosemite Valley. The views from the point are sublime, taking in a vantage similar to Tunnel View and the "new" Inspiration Point but from over 1000 feet higher. Look directly down and to the west to see if you can spot the distant Tunnel View parking area where your car now appears no larger than an aphid on an understory shrub. Next, look to the southeast to enjoy an up-close view of Silver Strand Falls, which can be difficult to spot from the valley floor.

Backtrack to the Pohono Trail along the spur trail. From here, you can turn right to hike down the way you came back to Tunnel View. If you want to continue to Stanford Point, turn left and continue climbing a bit longer until the trail crests at 2.9 miles. From this crest, the trail descends, crossing

Meadow Brook at 3.2 miles. The trail sidles up to the edge of the valley at 3.5 miles. Look for a spur trail leading away on the left to Stanford Point; a pair of trail signs indicating distances to other features are the only markers. This spur trail will lead you downhill through boulders and shrubs to the edge of a cliff. To find the best view, continue a short distance west to a set of boulders that reveals a full view of Bridalveil Fall below. The view here is similar to Old Inspiration Point, but given that Old Inspiration can be difficult to find, Stanford Point is a suitable destination with revelatory views that are a fit reward for all of the hard work you put in on the climb from Tunnel View.

EXTENDING YOUR TRIP

Up the ante on epic views by continuing east on the Pohono Trail to Crocker Point (4.1 miles from Tunnel View) and Dewey Point (4.7 miles from Tunnel View). The extension to Crocker Point adds 350 feet of elevation gain. The extension to Dewey Point adds another 300 feet of elevation up from Crocker Point.

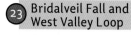

23 Bridalveil Fall and West Valley Loop

RATING/ DIFFICULTY	ROUNDTRIP	ELEV GAIN/ HIGH POINT	SEASON
**/3	6.5 miles	550 feet/ 4073 feet	Year-round

Maps: USGS 7.5-min El Capitan, Half Dome, Tom Harrison Maps Yosemite Valley; **Contact:** Yosemite Valley Visitor Center; **Notes:** Day-use only. Food storage lockers at trailhead. Vault toilets at trailhead; **GPS:** 37.7167, −119.6510

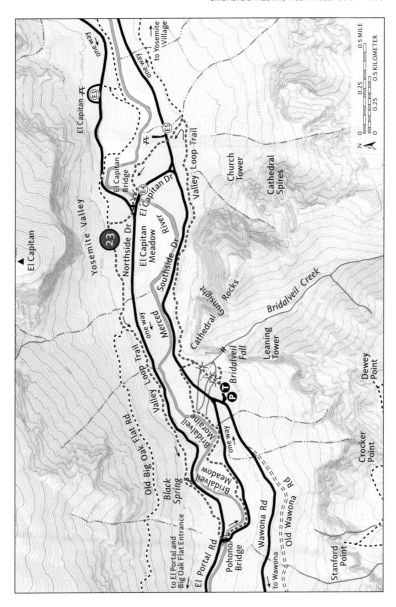

The Valley Loop Trail traces the length of Yosemite Valley from Bridalveil Fall to Happy Isles on both the north and south sides of the Merced River. While the trail does not ascend to great heights or offer many iconic views, there are countless spots along the loop from which you can admire the valley's spectacular granite cliffs, spacious meadows, and famous waterfalls. The western segment of the loop encircles Bridalveil Fall, El Capitan Meadow, and Bridalveil Meadow for a peaceful half-day ramble. Fall color can be outstanding on this segment thanks to abundant dogwoods, maples, and black oaks.

GETTING THERE

From the Arch Rock Entrance east of El Portal, follow El Portal Road east for 5.6 miles. Keep right to stay on Southside Drive, which you will follow east for 0.9 mile to a junction with Wawona Road. Turn right onto Wawona Road, then after 100 yards turn left into the Bridalveil Fall parking area.

ON THE TRAIL

Starting from the Bridalveil Fall Trailhead, walk northeast on the Valley Loop Trail to a junction with the Bridalveil Fall Trail. To stop at the fall, turn right for the 0.4-mile roundtrip spur trail to the base of the fall. To begin the West Valley Loop hike, return to the Valley Loop Trail and turn right to cross a series of picturesque bridges spanning the forks of Bridalveil Creek. Beyond the bridges, the trail enters a forest of ponderosa pine, incense cedar, black oak, and bigleaf maple as it traces the base of the Cathedral Rocks for 1.7 miles. The periodic rumbling of cars passing by on Southside

Drive to your left punctures the peace of the forest on occasion, but otherwise you can expect a generous amount of quiet as you wander through the trees.

At 1.7 miles, turn left onto a connecting path that leads north across Southside Drive. Follow this path along the southern banks of the Merced River, perhaps following a handful of informal paths to the northern banks at 2.1 miles. Beyond these informal paths, the trail reaches El Capitan Drive just east of the El Capitan Bridge at 2.3 miles. Turn right here to cross the bridge that spans the Merced River.

Once across the bridge, continue along the shoulder of the road along the north edge of El Capitan Meadow. As you progress, look up at the massive form of El Capitan to spot climbers scaling the massive granite block's sheer vertical southern face. El Capitan Meadow lies to your left, and its sprawling, grassy environs yield to a forest of ponderosa pine and black oak punctuated by the Cathedral Rocks rising thousands of feet above the valley floor. After 2.5 miles, look for a connecting path that leads away from the road to reach the northern branch of the Valley Loop Trail. Turn left onto the Valley Loop Trail to work your way through a few vaguely signed junctions with other connecting trails. Continue past Old Big Oak Flat Road at 3.2 miles (a possible side trip; see Hike 36) before passing through a lush corridor of mountain dogwoods leading to the Pohono Bridge. Cross the bridge on a sidewalk to pick up a continuation of the Valley Loop Trail that heads east to the Bridalveil Fall parking area.

The final leg of the hike travels east along Southside Drive through more dense

Opposite: *The Cathedral Rocks rise above the tranquil Merced River on a November afternoon.*

corridors of maple and dogwood. After skirting the southern edge of Bridalveil Meadow, the trail makes a brief climb up and over Bridalveil Moraine. Beyond the moraine, you will have to navigate a confusing stretch where the forks of Bridalveil Creek have washed out portions of the trail. During summer and fall, it should not be too difficult to hop across the creek, but springtime flooding may oblige you to follow the shoulder of the road back to Bridalveil Fall.

If the creek is passable, follow the Valley Loop Trail east to the 6-mile mark. From there, cross Southside Drive via connector trail, and turn right onto the Valley Loop Trail once again. Follow the short 0.2-mile segment across the stone bridges spanning Bridalveil Creek back to the trailhead.

24 Four Mile Trail

RATING/ DIFFICULTY	ROUNDTRIP	ELEV GAIN/ HIGH POINT	SEASON
****/4	9.4 miles	3200 feet/ 7214 feet	Late spring– early fall

Maps: USGS 7.5-min Half Dome, Tom Harrison Maps Yosemite Valley; **Contact:** Yosemite Valley Visitor Center; **Notes:** Day-use only. Trail closes following first snowfall and reopens after snow melts from upper elevations. No food storage at trailhead. Vault toilets at Glacier Point parking area; **GPS:** 37.7339, –119.6018

The Four Mile Trail boasts the distinction of being one of the fastest and steepest routes out of Yosemite Valley, ascending from the valley floor to Glacier Point. Constantly evolving views running the length of Yosemite Valley provide the principal highlights, while a distinct transition from oak woodland to coniferous forest will satisfy the botanically curious. Glacier Point's famous views are the cherry topping on this satisfying full-day hike.

GETTING THERE

Driving: From the Arch Rock Entrance east of El Portal, follow El Portal Road east for 5.6 miles. Keep right to stay on Southside Drive, and continue east for another 4.2 miles to the Four Mile Trailhead. Parking, available on both sides of the road, is limited, so be the early bird.

Transit: During the summer when the El Capitan Shuttle is running, take the shuttle to stop E6 to reach the Four Mile Trail. If the El Capitan Shuttle is not running, the closest Valley Shuttle stop is stop 7 at Yosemite Lodge. From there, you can follow a paved path south along the east edge of Leidig Meadow for 0.4 mile to Southside Drive. Turn right onto the bike path or the Valley Loop Trail and walk west for another 0.25 mile to the Four Mile Trailhead.

ON THE TRAIL

Step onto the Four Mile Trail from the signed trailhead departing from Southside Drive and follow it south on a mellow incline through a spacious forest of incense cedars, ponderosa pines, and black oaks. After 0.3 mile, the trail's initially gentle ascent becomes a distant memory as the trail begins climbing at a rate of 750 to 850 feet per mile. A dense forest of canyon live oak, black oak, and bigleaf maple mostly obscures views across the valley toward El Capitan and the Three Brothers until 0.9 mile when the density of

Opposite: Sentinel Rock and El Capitan dominate the view on the Four Mile Trail.

the forest decreases. After the trail straightens out to head northeast along the base of Sentinel Rock, hop over an unnamed creek at 1.1 miles. Next reach a second series of tight switchbacks that ascend a prominent ridge rising to Union Point.

Both the views and the habitat make a dramatic transition as the trail rounds a bend at 2.5 miles. Through gaps in the trees, enjoy the first views up Tenaya Canyon toward Half Dome, North Dome, and Clouds Rest. The flora also changes at this point, with towering Douglas firs thriving on the cooler, shadier northeast-facing slopes. Switchbacks remain your constant companion, however, as the trail doggedly incinerates calories en route to a junction with the Union Point spur trail at 3 miles. Although the views from Union Point are somewhat obstructed by vegetation, consider the side trip if only for the opportunity to stop, catch your breath, and eat a sandwich.

Another tight series of switchbacks awaits beyond Union Point. With each step, views west toward Yosemite Valley become increasingly spectacular. El Capitan and

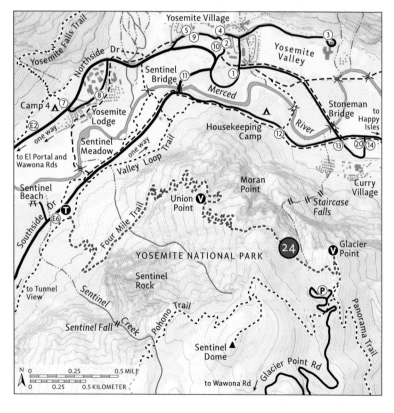

Sentinel Rock figure prominently in this scene, and careful observers will also spot the Three Brothers, Cathedral Rocks, Dewey Point, and several of the valley's meadows, including El Capitan and Bridalveil.

The switchbacks come to a merciful end at 3.7 miles as the Four Mile Trail makes its final approach to Glacier Point through a dense forest of white fir, red fir, Jeffrey pine, and sugar pine. The Four Mile Trail terminates at a busy, paved footpath connecting Glacier Point to the Glacier Point parking area. Turn left and walk an additional 0.1 mile to Glacier Point, where you can soak in the famous views of Half Dome and the Yosemite high country. Revel in the glory of this view for as long as you can before you must face the knee-rattling descent back to the valley floor.

EXTENDING YOUR TRIP

You can combine the Four Mile Trail with the Panorama Trail (see Hike 18) for a 16.25-mile trek from the Four Mile Trailhead to Happy Isles. From there, follow the Valley Loop Trail west to the Four Mile Trailhead to finish the hike.

 *This easy loop meanders its way through Cooks and Sentinel Meadows, showcasing world-famous views of Yosemite Falls, Half Dome, North Dome, and Sentinel Rock while staying firmly rooted to the valley floor. A combination of dirt trail, boardwalk, and paved bike path traverses an appealing mixture of grassy meadows, stately deciduous trees, and the Merced River, creating a can't-miss experience for hikers of every ability.*

GETTING THERE

Driving: From the Arch Rock Entrance east of El Portal, follow El Portal Road east for 5.6 miles. Keep right to stay on Southside Drive and continue east for another 4.2 miles to Sentinel Drive. Turn left on Sentinel Drive to drive 100 yards north to the Sentinel Bridge parking area and the Cooks Meadow Trailhead on the left.

Transit: Take the Valley Shuttle to stop 11, which lies adjacent to the Sentinel Bridge parking area. From the shuttle stop, walk west through the parking area to the trailhead.

ON THE TRAIL

As with most trails on the Yosemite Valley floor, you will get the most out of the hike if you take it either during the spring or during the fall. In spring, Yosemite Falls thunders over its 2650-foot precipice to the north, while the Merced thunders along, swollen with snowmelt. In the fall, the cottonwoods and black oaks lining the meadow turn shades of yellow and orange, casting a golden glow across the scene. Ratchet up the beauty a few more notches by hiking during late afternoon when the sun's low

25 Cooks and Sentinel Meadows

RATING/ DIFFICULTY	ROUNDTRIP	ELEV GAIN/ HIGH POINT	SEASON
***/1	2.6 miles	Negligible/ 3993 feet	Year-round

Maps: USGS 7.5-min Half Dome, Tom Harrison Maps Yosemite Valley; **Contact:** Yosemite Valley Visitor Center; **Notes:** Day-use only. Food storage at trailhead. Restroom at trailhead; **GPS:** 37.7441, –119.5900

angle casts beautiful light across lush, pillowy meadows.

Find the Cooks Meadow Loop Trailhead on the west side of the parking lot and then head west on a flat path that's part-paved, and part-boardwalk. When the waterfalls are flowing, Yosemite Falls to the north will demand your immediate attention as it thunders nearly half a vertical mile down to the valley floor. After 0.2 mile, turn left at a junction to head south toward the Superintendents Bridge. On the approach to the

A peaceful scene where the Swinging Bridge crosses the Merced River

bridge, look to the southwest to observe Sentinel Rock, a towering pillar of granite that stands apart from the south wall of Yosemite Valley.

Just beyond the Superintendents Bridge at 0.3 mile, turn right at another junction onto a dirt path that follows the course of the Merced River and the northern edge of Sentinel Meadow. After another 0.3 mile of pleasant wandering along the river beneath the occasional shade of cottonwoods, the path meets a short stretch of wooden boardwalk. Continue straight across the boardwalk to pick up a spur trail that leads to a particularly nice stretch of beach along the Merced at 0.9 mile.

Backtrack to the boardwalk after a visit to the Merced River, turn right, and follow a continuation of the boardwalk toward the bike path that parallels Southside Drive.

Turn right onto the bike path and continue hiking west to the Swinging Bridge parking area. The Swinging Bridge, with its famous views of Yosemite Falls, spans the Merced on the right and is well worth a quick side trip. Once you've enjoyed the scenery at Swinging Bridge, cross Southside Drive to pick up the Valley Loop Trail at 1.5 miles and turn left.

This section of the Valley Loop Trail passes through a cathedral-like forest of ponderosa pine, incense cedar, black oak, and bigleaf maple casting deep pools of shade along the park-like path. After 0.5 mile of pleasant strolling through the forest, turn left and follow a short connecting trail to the picturesque Yosemite Valley Chapel. Originally built in 1879 and relocated in 1901, the chapel continues to offer services, including weddings.

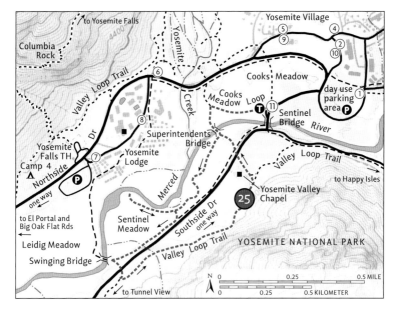

Cross Southside Drive once again to continue north on a connecting trail that leads back to the Superintendents Bridge at 2.25 miles. Cross the bridge and make a right turn onto the Cooks Meadow Loop Trail to return to the parking area.

26 East Valley Loop

RATING/ DIFFICULTY	ROUNDTRIP	ELEV GAIN/ HIGH POINT	SEASON
**/3	6.4 miles	500 feet/ 4164 feet	Year-round

Maps: USGS 7.5-min Yosemite Falls, Half Dome; Tom Harrison Maps Yosemite Valley; **Contact:** Yosemite Valley Visitor Center; **Notes:** Day-use only. No food storage at trailhead. No toilets at trailhead, but several bathroom opportunities along the route; **GPS:** 37.7442, –119.5895

Valley congestion got you down? Is that traffic making your head ache? Consider this rambling exploration of the eastern third of Yosemite Valley as a means of getting around bipedally, as a tour of the eastern valley's famous landmarks, and as a jumping off point for extended explorations. Beyond this route's utility as an alternative to driving or to the occasional mosh pits that form to get on the shuttle buses, this route showcases numerous views of valley highlights while yielding a few surprises of its own.

GETTING THERE
Driving: From the Arch Rock Entrance on State Route 140, drive east on SR 140/El Portal Road. After 5.6 miles, keep right onto one-way Southside Drive. Follow Southside Drive for 4.2 miles to Sentinel Drive. Drive 100 yards north to the Sentinel Bridge parking area on the left.

Transit: Take the Yosemite Valley Shuttle to stop 11, which lies adjacent to the Sentinel Bridge parking area. Walk to the north side of the parking area to find a trailhead accessing the boardwalk traveling north across Cooks Meadow.

ON THE TRAIL
This hike opens with one of the most gob-smacking views found anywhere in the valley. Head north from the parking area through a small copse of ponderosa pines, and step onto the wooden boardwalk heading northbound across Cooks Meadow. Directly ahead, Yosemite Falls roars over a 2650-foot cliff framed by Eagle Tower and Yosemite Point. Cooks Meadow itself is a picture-perfect foreground for such a scene, especially in spring and fall when seasonal color adds brilliant hues to the austere granite spectacle. Photographers take note.

Take the boardwalk to reach Northside Drive then cross the road and make a left onto the paved path just beyond the road that goes to Yosemite Village. The paved path parallels Northside Drive for about 100 yards before reaching the eastern branch of the Lower Yosemite Fall Trail at 0.4 mile. Turn right here, and progress uphill to a spur trail leading west to the Galen Clark Memorial Bench where you will also find a plaque commemorating the site of John Muir's residence. Backtrack on the spur to the Lower Yosemite Fall Trail and turn left. Two hundred yards north of the spur trail, turn right at a junction with the Valley Loop Trail. If you

Opposite: Half Dome towers above the cottonwood cloister in Ahwahnee Meadow.

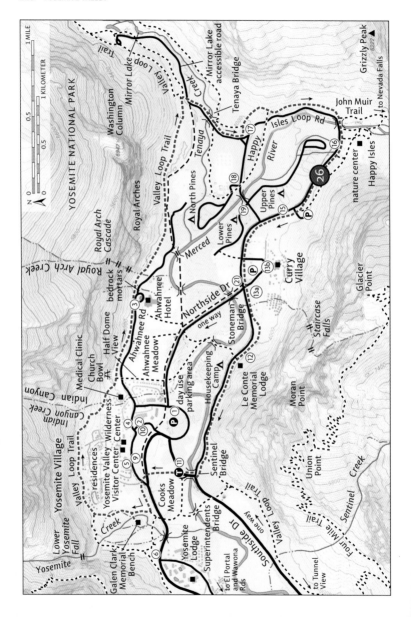

have time, you can turn left for a quick visit to Lower Yosemite Fall (see Hike 32).

Immediately, the bustle melts away as the trail climbs through a dense forest on an arcing route behind Yosemite Village. The trail reaches its high point at 1.2 miles before descending across Indian Canyon Creek en route to the Church Bowl picnic area on the northwest edge of Ahwahnee Meadow. For a short diversion and a fantastic view of Half Dome, head south on the paved path traversing the west end of the meadow. A copse of cottonwoods stands in the heart of the meadow, providing a focal point for photographers.

Returning to the Church Bowl picnic area, continue east as the Valley Loop Trail parallels the road that ends at the Ahwahnee Hotel at 1.9 miles. The hotel itself is worth a stop if only to admire the architecture and setting. Continue beyond the Ahwahnee Hotel on the Valley Loop Trail, and keep your eyes peeled for a large panel of bedrock mortars, which testify to this site's former use by the Ahwahneechee people. The mortars are a series of circular depressions that the Ahwahneechee used to grind certain staple foods, including acorns and seeds, into meal used to make cakes and porridges. Beyond the Ahwahnee Hotel, the trail passes through one of the most peaceful corners of the valley before meeting a junction with the bike path at 2.4 miles. Continue straight through the junction, heading east to another set of junctions at 2.9 miles. Turn right onto a connecting trail that leads south across the bike path before reaching the Tenaya Bridge. From that same junction, the Valley Loop Trail continues east toward Mirror Lake and Tenaya Canyon—another side trip if you have the time. Otherwise, cross the Tenaya Bridge and find a continuation of the Valley Loop Trail leading south toward Happy Isles.

Now heading south, the trail parallels Happy Isles Loop Road on an approach to the John Muir Trailhead and Happy Isles. Once at the Happy Isles Bridge at 4 miles, you have the option to join the John Muir Trail/Mist Trail for a 1.7-mile optional diversion to the footbridge spanning the Merced River. From here, you can glimpse Vernal Fall to double your waterfall viewing pleasure. Otherwise, cross the Happy Isles Bridge to begin hiking west on the Valley Loop Trail's final segment back to the trailhead.

This last stretch brings you back to the hectic activity emanating from sprawling Upper Pines Campground and surrounding Curry Village at 5.1 miles. The latter offers restrooms, a market, and a decent lunch spot. From here, the Valley Loop Trail sticks close to the road, making routefinding simple as you return to the Sentinel Bridge parking area. At 6.3 miles, turn right to cross over Sentinel Bridge for one final photo opportunity—Half Dome rising above the Merced River—before returning to the beginning.

27 Happy Isles

RATING/ DIFFICULTY	ROUNDTRIP	ELEV GAIN/ HIGH POINT	SEASON
**/1	1.6 miles	0 feet/ 4073 feet	Year-round

Maps: USGS 7.5-min Half Dome, Tom Harrison Maps Yosemite Valley; **Contact:** Yosemite Valley Visitor Center; **Notes:** Day-use only. Restroom near trailhead. Interpretive features; **GPS:** 37.7325, –119.5593

 This short and sweet exploration samples the scenic delights of

Happy Isles. The titular "Isles" refer to a pair of islands splitting the Merced River that are accessible by way of a wooded trail and a pair of bridges. Stops on the back half of the route include interpretive features detailing a 1996 rockfall, a trip indoors for some naturalist education at the Happy Isles Nature Center, and a short diversion over a wooden boardwalk to a marshy meadow dubbed "the Fen."

GETTING THERE

Driving: From the Arch Rock Entrance on State Route 140, drive east on SR 140/El Portal Road. After 5.6 miles, keep right onto one-way Southside Drive. Follow Southside Drive for 6.1 miles to a junction with Happy Isles Loop Road and turn right. After 0.6 mile, turn right into the dirt parking area. Note that this parking area can fill up early in the

North Dome framed by trees above the snowmelt-swollen Merced River

morning during the summer, in which case you may have better luck using the Yosemite Shuttle. Walk 0.4 mile from the parking area to the beginning of the route at the Happy Isles shuttle stop.

Transit: Take the Yosemite Valley Shuttle to stop 16, which services Happy Isles. The route begins here.

ON THE TRAIL

If starting from the parking area, follow the bike path east to the Happy Isles shuttle stop, which is where the route begins. Note that taking the shuttle shaves about 1 mile of walking from the route. From the Happy Isles shuttle stop, walk south on a dirt path hugging the banks of the Merced River that leads toward a wooden bridge spanning the Merced. Cross the bridge to the island and follow the well-marked path as it winds through cedars and oaks covering the small island. The two isles here owe their existence to rocky obstructions in the riverbed that,

over time, accumulated enough soil to form islands and support pines, cedars, oaks, and alders. Cross a second bridge leading to the second isle and follow the trail to the isle's southern tip. Here you can relax while enjoying the sights and sounds of the river along with an impressive view downstream toward North Dome.

Backtrack across the two isles to the main path and turn left toward an interpretive plaque describing a 1996 rockfall that wiped out the original Happy Isles Nature Center. The new nature center lies 20 yards to the north from this plaque, and you can bypass the center by staying right, or you can pass directly through the nature center to get a naturalist's education on Yosemite Valley's forest and meadow habitats along with their resident wildlife.

As you leave the center and continue north toward the shuttle stop, take a left onto a path marked for the Fen. After crossing an ADA-accessibile parking area, find and

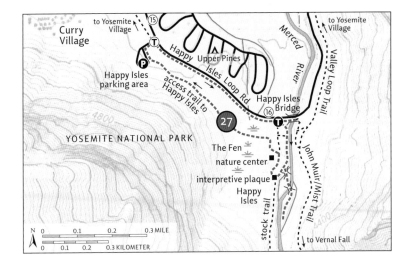

follow a wooden boardwalk west across a marshy meadow known as the Fen. This lush habitat ripples with life, and if you visit early or late in the day, you may spot a black bear foraging for food.

If you took the shuttle to Happy Isles, backtrack toward the nature center, and turn left toward Happy Isles Loop Road. If you parked at the parking area, continue west across the Fen's boardwalk on a well-defined path that connects to the parking area.

28 Mist Trail to Nevada Fall

RATING/ DIFFICULTY	ROUNDTRIP	ELEV GAIN/ HIGH POINT	SEASON
*****/3	6 miles	2000 feet/ 6016 feet	Year-round

Maps: USGS 7.5-min Half Dome, Tom Harrison Maps Yosemite Valley; **Contact:** Yosemite Valley Visitor Center; **Notes:** Day hiking only. Food storage at trailhead parking. Restrooms near Happy Isles, the first footbridge, at Emerald Pool, and above Nevada Fall; **GPS:** 37.7328, –119.5578

 *This remarkable hike follows the Mist Trail to two of Yosemite's most celebrated waterfalls: Vernal and Nevada. The roar of the mighty Merced River accompanies a vigorous climb over a beautifully engineered granite staircase that, at least during spring, becomes thoroughly soaked by Vernal Fall's prodigious mist. A looping return route along the opening segment of the fabled John Muir Trail provides an elevated perspective of the scenic highlights above the Merced River Gorge, including both waterfalls, Half Dome, Mount Broderick, and Liberty Cap.*

GETTING THERE

Driving: From the Arch Rock Entrance, drive east on State Route 140/El Portal Road. After 5.6 miles, turn right onto one-way Southside Drive. Follow Southside Drive for 6.1 miles to a junction with Happy Isles Loop Road and turn right. After 0.6 mile, turn right into the dirt parking area. Note that this parking area can fill up early in the morning during the summer. Walk 0.5 mile from the parking area to the Mist Trail/John Muir Trailhead, which lies on the east side of the Happy Isles Bridge.

Transit: Yosemite Shuttle stop 16 services Happy Isles. From this stop, walk 100 yards across the Happy Isles Bridge to the Mist Trail/John Muir Trailhead to begin the hike.

ON THE TRAIL

Whether you're hopping off of the shuttle at Happy Isles or walking from the parking area, make your way east across the Happy Isles Bridge to find the signed trailhead for the combined John Muir Trail (JMT) and Mist Trail; all hike distances begin from this point. Begin hiking south on the wide, well-traveled path along the eastern bank of the Merced River. Be sure to introduce yourself cordially to the Merced, as it will accompany you for the next 5 to 8 hours as you hike through some of Yosemite's most remarkable terrain.

The trail quickly transitions from dirt to pavement, which also signals the beginning of a prolonged climb beneath the thick shade of canyon live oaks and big-leaf maples. At a bend in the trail and river, look to the south through gaps in the trees to get a rare glimpse at Illilouette Fall rumbling high within its namesake gorge, which remains obscured from most viewpoints. The hearty climb continues until a brief pause at a wooden footbridge spanning the

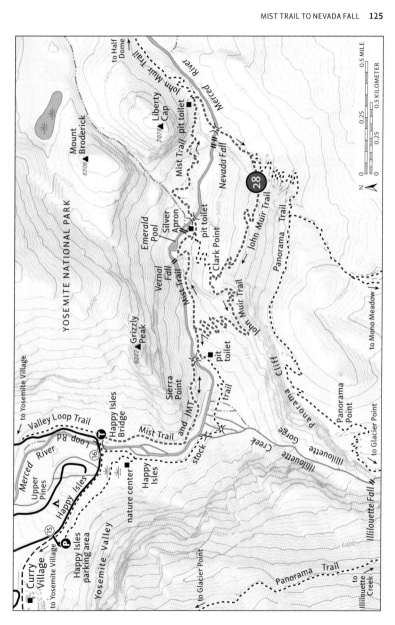

to Half
Dome

to Yosemite Village

Liberty
Cap
7076

John Muir Trail

Merced River

Mist Trail / pit toilet

Mount
Broderick
6706

Nevada Fall

YOSEMITE NATIONAL PARK

Emerald
Pool
Silver
Apron

pit toilet

Clark Point

28

John Muir Trail

Panorama Trail

Vernal
Fall

Mist Trail

Grizzly
Peak
6222

John Muir Trail

pit toilet

to Mono Meadow

Sierra
Point

Panorama Cliff

to Yosemite Village

Valley Loop Trail

Loop Rd.

Happy Isles
Bridge

Mist Trail and JMT

stock trail

Panorama Point

to Glacier Point

Merced River

16

Happy Isles

nature center

Illilouette Gorge

Illilouette Creek

Upper
Pines

Happy Isles

15

Happy Isles
parking area

Illilouette Fall

Curry
Village

to Yosemite Village

Yosemite Valley

to Glacier Point

Panorama Trail

to
Illilouette
Creek

N

0   0.25   0.5 MILE

0   0.25   0.5 KILOMETER

Merced River at 0.8 mile. From this spot, you can look up and down the river while catching a partial glimpse of Vernal Fall. A nearby drinking fountain and a pit toilet adjacent to a junction with a trail leading north to Happy Isles provide an opportunity to rest and refresh.

Keep left at the junction beyond the bridge to continue the steady, steep incline on the Mist Trail. At 1 mile, continue straight at a junction where the JMT branches away on the right—this will be your return route—and keep hiking to the base of a granite staircase at 1.2 miles. If you're hiking during spring, you'll quickly figure out why they call it the Mist Trail; Vernal Fall kicks up a prodigious amount of mist, which will soak you to the bone if you don't have some kind of water-resistant outer layer. If the angle of the sun is right, the mist produces impressive rainbows. Note that this section closes during the winter due to the formation of a formidable ice shelf that makes travel treacherous.

This memorable section comes to an end with a steep climb up more stairs followed by a sharp bend to the north along a precipitous stretch of trail protected by a guardrail. This section reaches the top of Vernal Fall (1.4 miles), where a fence stands between hikers and the raging Merced River mere feet before it drops into the rocky gorge below. Exercise good judgment and keep well back from the edge.

The Mist Trail turns east to parallel the Merced River along the southern edge of Emerald Pool and the Silver Apron. If the sound of running water is giving your bladder an uncomfortable nudge, stop by the pit toilets along the trail at 1.5 miles; otherwise continue east across a second footbridge spanning the Merced River just above the Silver Apron. Once on the north side of the river, the trail grade eases as the path winds through forest. At just shy of the 2-mile mark, carefully make your way toward the edge of the river. Although no ruins remain, this is the site of La Casa Nevada, a chalet operated by the Snow family from the 1860s to 1880s. From the edge of the river, revel in a first look at Nevada Fall where the Merced leaps over a 600-foot cliff into a rocky basin. Like Vernal Fall, Nevada Fall kicks up quite a bit of mist, which also creates rainbows when the light is right.

Return to the trail and resume the steep climb through a ravine that offers a variety of viewpoints from which to consider Nevada Fall. This climb continues for another 0.6 mile until topping out at a junction with the JMT. Yet another restroom sits adjacent to this junction, giving you an opportunity to heed nature's call. Keep right at this junction and follow the John Muir Trail southwest a short distance to a final footbridge spanning the Merced River—this time just above the top of Nevada Fall. Exposed granite outcrops on either side of the footbridge provide great lunch spots from which you can consider the stellar views down-canyon toward Glacier Point as well as the towering forms of Liberty Cap and Mount Broderick just above the falls.

Because the Mist Trail is so narrow in some spots, to return, it's best to avoid working against the flow of heavy hiker traffic by looping back on the JMT by way of Clark Point. Continue across the bridge above Nevada Fall and climb toward a memorable section of the JMT that traverses a cliffside laced with small waterfalls. Spectacular views from this section include Nevada Fall,

A chilled hiker on a spring morning discovers why it's called the Mist Trail.

Liberty Cap, Mount Broderick, and the massive backside of Half Dome.

After darting back into the cover of forest, keep right at a junction with the Panorama Trail, and begin a prolonged, switchbacking descent toward Clark Point at 3.8 miles. Keep left here for another prolonged descent down to the footbridge you first crossed that spans the Merced. Avoid turning left on a stock trail just before the junction with the Mist Trail, which you will return to at the 4.9-mile mark. Cross the footbridge with the views upstream toward Vernal Fall and continue west and then north back to the trailhead to finish the hike.

ALTERNATIVE WINTER ROUTE

Despite winter closures on the Mist Trail, you can hike a version of this route by turning right onto the JMT after the first footbridge (1 mile). From there, climb up to Clark Point (2.1 miles), and keep left to descend to the Mist Trail near the Silver Apron (2.6 miles). From here, turn right onto the Mist Trail and follow it to the top of Nevada Fall. The section of the John Muir Trail that leads back to Clark Point also closes during winter, so you will have to retrace your steps back to the trailhead for an out-and-back hike.

29 Half Dome

RATING/ DIFFICULTY	ROUNDTRIP	ELEV GAIN/ HIGH POINT	SEASON
*****/5	14.6 miles	5000 feet/ 8836 feet	June–early Oct

Maps: USGS 7.5-min Half Dome, Tom Harrison Maps Half Dome, Yosemite Valley; **Contact:** Yosemite Valley Visitor Center; **Notes:** Suitable for backpacking (Happy Isles to Little Yosemite Valley). Restrooms at Happy Isles. Vault toilets at Mist Trail Junction, Silver Apron, the top of Nevada Fall, and Little Yosemite Valley. Food storage at parking area and Little Yosemite Valley. Permit required for the cables section; **GPS:** 37.7328, –119.5578

 This legendary hiking route ascends from the valley floor to the top of Yosemite's signature landmark, Half Dome. The strenuous, full-day adventure follows the Mist Trail to Little Yosemite Valley, from which point hikers climb to the famous Half Dome cables. A breathtaking (or heart-stopping, depending on your feelings about heights) final ascent requires that hikers pull themselves up Half Dome's east slope by using a set of steel cables before arriving atop the dome's rounded summit to feast on exceptional views and bask in a sense of accomplishment.

GETTING THERE

Driving: From the Arch Rock Entrance, drive east on State Route 140/El Portal Road. After 5.6 miles, keep right to merge onto one-way Southside Drive. Follow Southside Drive for 6.1 miles to a junction with Happy Isles Loop Road and turn right. After 0.6 mile, turn right into the dirt parking area. Note that this parking area can fill up early in the morning during the summer. Also note that you will need to walk an additional 0.5 mile from the parking area to the Mist Trail/John Muir Trailhead, which lies on the east side of the Happy Isles Bridge.

Transit: Yosemite Shuttle stop 16 services Happy Isles. From this stop, walk 100 yards across the Happy Isles Bridge to the Mist Trail/John Muir Trailhead to begin the hike.

ON THE TRAIL

This is the only hike in the park that requires a day-use permit, which the park issues according to a strict quota. For more on the permit system, review the Fees, Permits, and Regulations section in the Introduction. The permit allows you to follow the cables

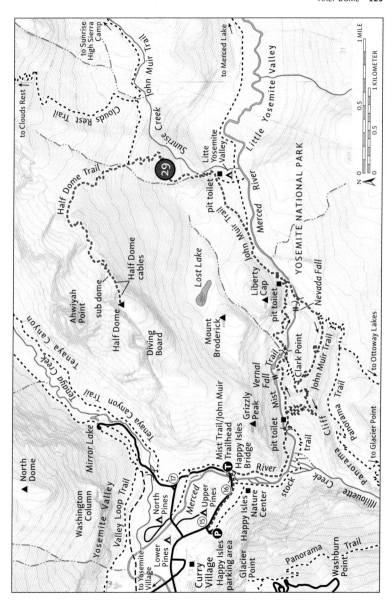

to Clouds Rest

to Sunrise High Sierra Camp

John Muir Trail

Clouds Rest Trail

Sunrise Creek

to Merced Lake

Little Yosemite Valley

29

Half Dome Trail

Litte Yosemite Valley

pit toilet

Merced River

YOSEMITE NATIONAL PARK

Half Dome cables

sub dome

Ahwiyah Point

Lost Lake

John Muir Trail

Liberty Cap

Nevada Fall

pit toilet

Half Dome

Diving Board

Mount Broderick

Tenaya Canyon

Tenaya Creek

Clark Point

John Muir Trail

to Ottoway Lakes

North Dome

Washington Column

Mirror Lake

Vernal Fall

Mist Trail

Grizzly Peak

Cliff Trail

Panorama Trail

to Glacier Point

Valley Loop Trail

Yosemite Valley

17

North Pines

Merced

Happy Isles

Mist Trail/John Muir Trailhead

Happy Isles Bridge

pit toilet

trail

stock trail

Illilouette Creek

to Yosemite Village

Lower Pines

Upper Pines

16

15

River

Happy Isles Nature Center

Glacier Point

Panorama Trail

Curry Village

Happy Isles parking area

Washburn Point

Panorama Trail

Washburn Trail

N

0   0.5   1 KILOMETER

0   0.5   1 MILE

to the summit of Half Dome, which is only about 0.15 mile of hiking. You can follow this route all the way to the sub dome without a permit, which may feel like a bit of a cheat without the final stretch. However, the sub dome itself is a phenomenal spot that would receive top billing if not for the presence of Half Dome.

The first 2.6 miles of this route follow the John Muir Trail (JMT) and Mist Trail (Hike 28). After a steady climb over the first 0.9 mile on the JMT, cross the Merced River via footbridge, and turn left onto the Mist Trail. This section of trail ascends via a picturesque stone staircase through heavy springtime mist produced by Vernal Fall up to a second footbridge crossing the Merced at 1.7 miles. The climb continues through Nevada Fall's granite amphitheater before topping out at a junction with the JMT at 2.6 miles. Turn left onto the JMT, heading northeast toward Little Yosemite Valley.

A short section of gently ascending trail skirts the base of Liberty Cap until flattening out at the mouth of Little Yosemite Valley. This flat, forested valley provides a welcome reprieve from the unrelenting climb from Happy Isles, and for the next 0.8 mile the trail gains minimal elevation while approaching the Little Yosemite Valley camping area. Keep left where the trail forks at 3.2 miles. This trail leads to the north end of the camping area and the continuation of the Half Dome route. If you are backpacking this route, pitch your tent at the camping area, which features a pit toilet and food storage lockers.

At 3.7 miles, keep left at the junction just north of the camping area to begin a grueling climb that initially parallels Sunrise Creek

before veering north on a switchbacking track to the shoulder of Half Dome. The best that can be said about this relentless 1800-foot climb is that it features a lot of shade, and you can expect a welcome sense of relief and excitement when the forest recedes atop Half Dome's ridge at the 6-mile mark.

Excitement floods the weary hiker, restoring a bit of pep to your step as the first hints of stellar views across Tenaya Canyon to the north and the Clark Range toward the south reward your efforts. After a flat stretch along the view-packed ridge, the trail arrives at the base of the sub dome at 6.4 miles. The sub dome is a delightful appetizer to the cable ascent, and the steep, switchbacking route carved ingeniously into the granite yields ever-more-impressive views as you climb. At 6.7 miles, the trail reaches the top of the sub dome, which reveals Half Dome and the awe-inspiring cable route in its full glory. Note that the sub dome is as far as you can go without a permit. Rangers patrol the sub dome, checking for permits, and they will turn you around if you did not secure one of the 300 daily permits allotted by the park's wilderness office.

All that's left to do now is to follow the cables. Although the distance is short (0.15 mile), you gain 400 feet as you pull yourself up the slick granite surface of the dome. The cables can tear the skin on your hands to shreds, so it's wise to pick up a pair of sturdy work or gardening gloves specifically for this section. It's also crucial to wear shoes with strong grip; the granite surface within the cables has been worn slick from foot traffic, and insufficient tread will leave you terrified that you could slip and fall. Finally, avoid

Opposite: *The Half Dome Cables: stairway to heaven—or an acrophobe's worst nightmare?*

this section if there is any chance it might rain. Moisture on the slick surfaces makes it nearly impossible to maintain traction, and numerous people have fallen to their deaths under these conditions.

The painstaking climb comes to an end as the rounded summit flattens out. There's no one spot to get a full 360-degree view down into the depths of Yosemite Valley, Tenaya Canyon, and Little Yosemite Valley, so a bit of wandering to get the full experience is in order. Many people will congregate at an overhanging rock outcrop that juts out over Half Dome's north face. Many people seek out the opportunity for a death-defying photo op from this spot, so consider this rock outcrop your turnaround point.

Note that the descent down the cables requires just as much care and caution as the ascent. You will undoubtedly encounter dozens of hikers on their way up, and making space for hikers when you're standing between two steel cables on a slick, steep slope is easier said than done. After making your way down the cables, retrace your steps back to Little Yosemite Valley and finally to the top of Nevada Fall. At this point, keep left to follow the JMT across a footbridge crossing the top of the fall at 11.4 miles. Continue straight on the JMT, and keep right at a junction with the Panorama Trail at 11.6 miles. The JMT descends at a steep grade toward Clark Point, where you keep left to complete the steep, winding descent down to the Mist Trail at 13.6 miles. Turn left at the Mist Trail junction, and then keep right to cross the footbridge over the Merced River. From here, there's only 0.9 mile left before you arrive at the Mist Trail/John Muir Trailhead feeling exhausted, depleted, and utterly satisfied.

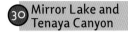

30 Mirror Lake and Tenaya Canyon

Mirror Lake

RATING/ DIFFICULTY	ROUNDTRIP	ELEV GAIN/ HIGH POINT	SEASON
****/1	1.8 miles	200 feet/ 4128 feet	Year-round

Tenaya Canyon

RATING/ DIFFICULTY	ROUNDTRIP	ELEV GAIN/ HIGH POINT	SEASON
***/2	4.6 miles	350 feet/ 4199 feet	Year-round

Maps: USGS 7.5-min Half Dome, Yosemite Falls, Tom Harrison Maps Yosemite Valley; **Contact:** Yosemite Valley Visitor Center; **Notes:** Day-use only. Restroom near Mirror Lake. Accessible trail; **GPS:** 37.7394, –119.5598

For the quintessential Yosemite experience of exquisitely sculpted granite cliffs held in perfect reflection on the surface of tranquil pools, consider the hike to Mirror Lake. Technically, the lake is one of a trio of large pools where Tenaya Creek collects before rushing to meet the Merced River. On a clear, cool spring day, visitors can soak up the spectacular, spacious confines of Tenaya Canyon reflected in impossibly clear, still waters.

GETTING THERE

Driving: From the Arch Rock Entrance, drive east on El Portal Road for 5.6 miles and keep right on Southside Drive. After 5.1 miles on Southside Drive, turn left onto Sentinel Drive.

After 0.3 mile, turn right into the Yosemite Village day-use parking area. Because there is no parking lot immediately adjacent to the start of the route, your best bet will be to park at the Village day-use parking area and take the Yosemite Valley Shuttle from stop 11 to stop 17 where the hike begins.

Transit: Take the Yosemite Valley Shuttle to stop 17, which doubles as the starting point on the hike.

ON THE TRAIL

As you gather your bearings after exiting the shuttle, look for the paved road heading north toward Mirror Lake. This paved road allows access for handicapped individuals, and it will also serve as the opening segment of the route. After 0.4 mile of walking on the road and over the Tenaya Bridge, look for a dirt path that splits from the road on the left. Turn onto the path and continue at a gentle incline heading northeast through forest composed of pine, cedar, oak, and maple.

At 0.8 mile, the trail reaches the trio of large pools where Tenaya Creek's waters collect. Turn right onto a short loop trail featuring interpretive panels that detail several aspects of Mirror Lake's history. From about December to June, you can count on finding at least some water holding a perfect mirror image of Half Dome, Mount Watkins, and Ahwiyah Point, but the pools dry up during summer and early fall. Numerous spots along the pools offer great places to take a break and soak in the memorable scenery. Late summer and fall

Mount Watkins rises above a partially frozen Mirror Lake.

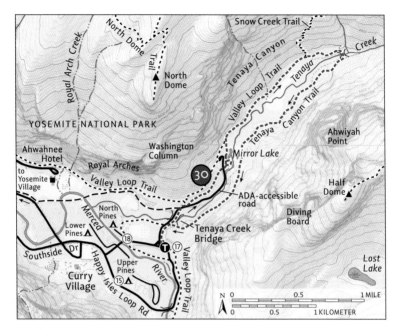

visitors may walk away disappointed, since Tenaya Creek often runs dry during these seasons.

If you intend to visit only Mirror Lake, turn left at the end of the loop where it joins with the trail you hiked in on to return to shuttle stop 17. For a longer exploration, turn right at this junction to follow the Valley Loop Trail northeast through Tenaya Canyon. The trail undulates gently through dense forest that mostly precludes the sort of views you enjoyed from the lake. However, only a small fraction of the crowd from Mirror Lake continues this far, so the solitude compensates for the lack of vistas.

The Valley Loop Trail reaches a junction with the Snow Creek Trail (Hike 31) at 2 miles. Keep right here and continue for another 0.4 mile to a picturesque wooden bridge spanning Tenaya Creek, which doubles as the route's midpoint. After the bridge, the trail—now dubbed Tenaya Canyon Trail—heads southwest back toward Mirror Lake. The forest on the canyon's eastern side is denser, cooler, and wetter thanks to the sheltering influence of the Half Dome massif. Several marshy sections harbor mosquitos during the warmer months, so be prepared to bring the hurt for the bloodsuckers. At 3.5 miles, the trail skirts eastern banks of the Mirror Lake pools before continuing on a quiet dirt path along the banks of Tenaya Creek all the way back to shuttle stop 17. Be sure to keep right at the junction just before the shuttle stop to avoid inadvertently following the Valley Loop Trail toward Happy Isles—an easy mistake to make.

31 Snow Creek Trail

RATING/ DIFFICULTY	ROUNDTRIP	ELEV GAIN/ HIGH POINT	SEASON
****/4	9 miles	2900 feet/ 4128 feet	Year- round

Maps: USGS 7.5-min Half Dome, Yosemite Falls, Tom Harrison Maps Yosemite Valley; **Contact:** Yosemite Valley Visitor Center;

Notes: Suitable for backpacking (Mirror Lake to Snow Creek); camping is not allowed south of the Snow Creek Trail footbridge. Vault toilets near Mirror Lake; **GPS:** 37.7394, –119.5598

Hikers with no aversion to putting in some breathless uphill work will enjoy a wonderful hiking experience loaded with

Classic Yosemite trail stonework with Basket Dome in the background

spectacular scenery on the Snow Creek Trail. This no-nonsense, magnificently constructed footpath gains 2700 feet of elevation over 1.6 miles of climbing from the floor of Tenaya Canyon to the mouth of a forested valley separating Indian Ridge from Mount Watkins. Day hikers can set their sights on two possible destinations: a footbridge spanning the tranquil, bubbling waters of Snow Creek and a view-packed promontory rising high above Tenaya Canyon.

GETTING THERE

Driving: From the Arch Rock Entrance, drive east on El Portal Road for 5.5 miles and keep right on Southside Drive. After 5.1 miles on Southside Drive, turn left onto Sentinel Drive. After 0.3 mile, turn right into the day-use parking area. Although there is possible parking closer to the trailhead, your best bet is to park and take the Yosemite Valley Shuttle to stop 17 where the hike begins.

Transit: Take the Yosemite Valley Shuttle to stop 17.

ON THE TRAIL

A few cautions apply to hikers attempting the Snow Creek Trail. First, the trail receives direct sun exposure thanks to its south-facing slope, and there are long stretches of steeply ascending trail that receive the full brunt of the sun. During hot summer days, hikers will benefit from getting a very early start to avoid a good roasting. The upside is that the trail is often clear of snow and ice during the winter since the sun melts snow away much faster. Backpackers should also note that the area south of the Snow Creek footbridge is closed to camping because of a particularly clever and persistent black bear known for going to great lengths to break into food supplies.

To begin, find and follow a segment of the Valley Loop Trail paralleling the east side of an ADA-accessible road that leads to Mirror Lake. At 0.2 mile, cut across that road, and continue north across the Tenaya Creek Bridge. Just beyond the bridge, find a trail on the left side that connects to the northern branch of the Valley Loop Trail shortly after crossing the bike path at 0.3 mile. Upon reaching the Valley Loop Trail, turn right and commence a gently ascending trek northeast through a garden of house-sized boulders shaded by live oaks, maples, pines, and cedars.

This pleasant woods-walking continues for another 0.9 mile to a junction with a trail on the right leading to Mirror Lake. Make a quick stop at the lake if there's time, but otherwise continue northeast into the depths of Tenaya Canyon. Glimpses of Half Dome, massive and imposing from this perspective, hint at the scenery that awaits on the Snow Creek Trail, which lies ahead after 1.1 miles of mellow hiking through the forest. Turn left onto the Snow Creek Trail at 2 miles.

At first, the hike climbs steeply through deep tree cover until emerging from the trees at 2.2 miles. The view of the landmarks above Tenaya Canyon offers a touch of the sublime with the first clear looks at Half Dome, the Quarter Domes, Clouds Rest, Mount Watkins, and Basket Dome. Closer afoot, be sure to stop periodically to enjoy the classic cobbled stonework characteristic of many of Yosemite's greatest hiking trails. The trail re-enters the tree cover at the 2.9-mile mark after 1100 feet of climbing from the floor of Tenaya Canyon. The trail continues its steep ascent for another 0.7 mile and *1600 feet* (yes, you read that correctly) until the trail mercifully begins to level out within dense forest. The rest of the walking from this point to either the bridge or the viewpoint will be blissfully flat.

If you wish to stop at the bridge, continue north for 0.4 mile beyond the end of the climb, keeping right at a junction with a pack trail leading toward Indian Ridge and North Dome just before the bridge. The footbridge spans the creek, and several pools harbor trout during the summer.

For the viewpoint, cut cross-country heading southeast from the 3.9-mile mark of the Snow Creek Trail. After 0.2 mile of hiking,

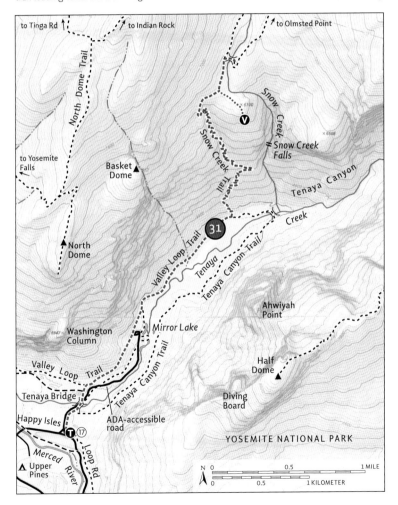

stop at the edge of a promontory just south of Peak 6700. From the edge of this promontory, peer deep into Tenaya Canyon while also marveling at great views of Tenaya Canyon landmarks. Half Dome is particularly impressive here: from this vantage you can see the full 4800 feet of sheer cliffs spanning the summit of the dome to the base of Tenaya Canyon.

Exercise patience on the steep descent as you make the return journey. To counter gravity's enthusiastic downhill influence, consider using trekking poles to slow your momentum and to take pressure off your joints from the relentless downhill pounding.

32 Lower Yosemite Fall

RATING/ DIFFICULTY	ROUNDTRIP	ELEV GAIN/ HIGH POINT	SEASON
****/1	1.2 miles	100 feet/ 4009 feet	Year-round

Maps: USGS 7.5-min Yosemite Falls, Tom Harrison Maps Yosemite Valley; **Contact:** Yosemite Valley Visitor Center; **Notes:** Day-use only. Restroom near trailhead. No food storage at trailhead; **GPS:** 37.7456, –119.5956

Yosemite's signature waterfall, Yosemite Falls, divides into three distinct sections: upper, middle, and lower. Unlike the eye-popping upper and middle sections, the lower fall possesses a more intimate quality as it spills into a shady grotto. Follow this short, paved trail to Lower Yosemite Fall while enjoying stops at the site of John Muir's old living quarters along the way.

GETTING THERE

Driving: From the Arch Rock Entrance, head east on El Portal Road for 5.5 miles and keep right to remain on Southside Drive. Follow Southside Drive for another 5.1 miles and make a left onto Sentinel Drive. After 0.3 mile on Sentinel Drive, turn left onto Northside Drive. Follow Northside Drive for 0.5 mile to reach roadside parking adjacent to the Lower Yosemite Falls Trailhead. Note that parking fills quickly; consider the Yosemite Shuttle as an option for reaching the trailhead.

Transit: Exit at shuttle stop 6 on the Yosemite Valley Shuttle line, which also doubles as the trailhead for the Lower Yosemite Falls Trail.

ON THE TRAIL

Depending on where you parked or whether you took the shuttle, you can hop onto the looping, paved trail at a handful of connecting paths. Assuming a start from the shuttle stop, walk north on the brief connecting trail. Turn left to follow the looping trail clockwise, which affords iconic views of the entirety of Yosemite Falls framed by towering ponderosa pines. The trail splits at a loop at 0.15 mile, with the right fork leading to an interpretive display showing Yosemite Falls in relief. The loop closes shortly after with the trail continuing north to a footbridge spanning Yosemite Creek just below Lower Yosemite Fall at 0.35 mile.

Although the lower fall represents only a 215-foot fraction of the overall falls, the intimate setting makes this scene as memorable as views of the full falls. There are several spots from which to regard the fall, but resist the temptation to scramble on the rocks. Hikers have slipped, fallen, and even

Opposite: A rare view of Lower Yosemite Fall without a single tourist

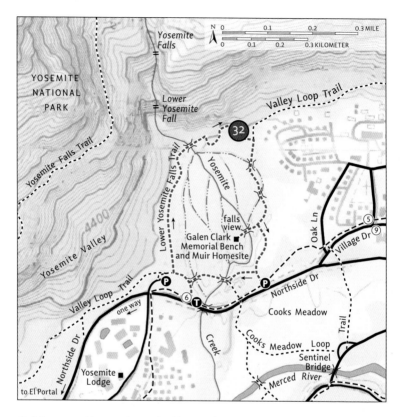

died from scrambling on the wet boulders below the fall.

Once across the bridge, the trail bends to the east to a junction with the Valley Loop Trail at 0.5 mile. Turn right to head south along the paved path through a tranquil forest of oaks, pines, and cedars. Be sure to turn right onto the spur trail to the Galen Clark Memorial Bench at 0.7 mile. The bench is dedicated to Yosemite's first superintendent, and there's also a nearby plaque commemorating Yosemite's most famous early denizen, John Muir. Muir resided here

during a stint as a woodcutter for an early era Yosemite hotel. Throughout his employment, his wild and eloquent love affair with Yosemite deepened, ultimately leading to the valley's preservation and the birth of the national park system. Look to the north to discover that Muir's choice for a homesite was no accident. A pine-framed view of Lower Yosemite Fall would have been Muir's companion for those rare moments when he sat still.

Return to the main trail and turn right to continue south toward Northside Drive. Turn right again at 0.95 mile to head west across a pair of bridges spanning two forks of Yosemite Creek. After the second bridge, the trail returns to the starting point of the loop next to the shuttle stop.

33 Upper Yosemite Fall and Yosemite Point

RATING/ DIFFICULTY	ROUNDTRIP	ELEV GAIN/ HIGH POINT	SEASON
*****/4	7.6 miles	4000 feet/ 6974 feet	Year-round

Maps: USGS 7.5-min Yosemite Falls, Tom Harrison Maps Yosemite Valley; **Contact:** Yosemite Valley Visitor Center; **Notes:** Suitable for backpacking (Yosemite Falls), restroom adjacent to trailhead in Camp 4, food storage lockers at trailhead parking; **GPS:** 37.7423, −119.6021

This challenging odyssey from the valley floor to the windswept heights of Yosemite Point delivers both fabulous scenery and ever-more-creative ways to punish your quadriceps. Yosemite Falls, America's tallest waterfall and the centerpiece of this outstanding adventure, keeps you company along the way, occasionally even drenching you when the flow is heavy and the wind blows just right. Even a truncated excursion on the route that ends at either Columbia Rock or just beyond at the first view of the falls will be sure to leave a lasting impression.

GETTING THERE

Driving: From the Arch Rock Entrance, head east on El Portal Road for 5.5 miles and keep right to remain on Southside Drive. Follow Southside Drive for another 5.1 miles and make a left onto Sentinel Drive. After 0.3 mile

on Sentinel Drive, turn left onto Northside Drive. Follow Northside Drive for 1.1 miles to the Yosemite Falls parking area. Turn left into the parking lot, which you can expect to fill up by mid-morning during spring and summer.

Transit: Exit at shuttle stop 7 on the Yosemite Valley Shuttle line, which lies about 50 feet east of the parking area. Cross Northside Drive and walk through the Camp 4 parking area to find the Yosemite Falls Trailhead on the northwest side of the Camp 4 parking area.

ON THE TRAIL

Let's not mince words. This is a grueling hike. Not only does the average elevation gain on this hike exceed 1000 feet per mile, but exposure to the full brunt of mountain sunshine on the toughest parts of the climb ensure that it will also be a hot, sweaty affair. It will behoove hikers to get an early start, especially during summer. Bring more water than you think you can drink, and be sure to wear sturdy footwear with good tread.

From the Yosemite Falls parking area, cross Northside Drive and make your way through the Camp 4 parking area. Look for the Yosemite Falls Trailhead on the northwest side of the parking area and follow it north through a junction with the Valley Loop Trail and into a canopy of canyon live oaks. Immediately, the trail begins a steep climb over tight switchbacks that will suck the oxygen right out of your lungs. The best way to tackle this cardiosaurus is to adopt the philosophy of the sloth: You'll get there when you get there, and there's nothing to be gained from rushing.

Slowly and deliberately, reach the top of the first set of switchbacks, which signals a brief reprieve from climbing. Cross over a seasonal stream and continue east toward the route's second set of switchbacks leading to Columbia Rock. From Columbia Rock, glimpse a stellar view across the valley toward Half Dome, which pairs nicely with a quick break to catch your breath. Although Columbia Rock is only 1 mile from the trailhead, the trail gains 1200 feet of elevation getting here. Clearly, not all miles are created equal, so be sure to charge your batteries for the next stage of the journey.

After a short, steep climb from Columbia Rock, the trail crests just after bending to the north to reveal an awe-inspiring sight: Yosemite Falls. Although the falls seem to be omnipresent throughout the valley, seeing them (and hearing them) up close is a powerful experience. It may also be very wet from the spray coming off the falls, so bring a rain poncho to avoid getting soaked during the peak runoff season.

From this crest, the trail starts a descent, losing 200 feet as it travels north toward the falls. Soak in the spectacular views of the falls and the valley beyond while simultaneously enjoying the only gently graded section of trail on the route. This mellow segment ends abruptly at 1.6 miles at a set of switchbacks that wind upward through an often-damp forest of cedars, live oaks, and bewilderingly fragrant bay laurel trees. These switchbacks will lead to a ravine shielded from the falls by a ridge, and the sound and sight of Yosemite Falls recedes as the final and most challenging segment of the climb begins.

Over the next mile, the trail gains 1500 feet on a mostly exposed trail that bakes under the summer sun. Keeping a sloth's pace, make steady, deliberate progress up the switchbacks, stopping wherever shade is available, until reaching a junction with

Round a bend to come face-to-face with the full force of Yosemite Falls.

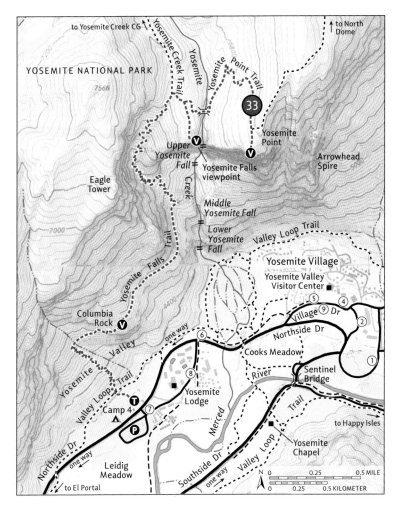

the Yosemite Creek Trail, which leads north, and the Yosemite Point Trail leading east at 2.6 miles. Turn right to begin a short climb to another junction with the Yosemite Point Trail (left) and a spur trail leading to the top of Yosemite Falls (right).

Follow the spur trail south for 0.2 mile to the rim of the valley. The spur trail leads to a beautiful viewpoint, where you'll see Glacier Point and Sentinel Dome rising from the valley directly to the south. If you have even the slightest hint of acrophobia, this may be as far as you want to go. But if you want the experience of viewing Yosemite Falls from the top, begin a short, sharp descent on a creatively engineered trail to a viewpoint. Pass a few sketchy, exposed sections, where a guide rail anchored into the rock is your best defense from a fall, before bottoming out at a rocky shelf. From this shelf, peer over a second guide rail to see the full extent of Yosemite Falls spilling into the valley below.

If there's energy left after the long climb, consider tacking on a quick trip to Yosemite Point. Backtrack 0.2 mile north and turn right at the junction. This trail will lead you downhill to a bridge crossing Yosemite Creek. Cross the bridge and continue north along the banks of the creek until reaching one final set of switchbacks leading south to Yosemite Point. The views of the western half of the valley resemble the views from the top of the falls, but a quick scramble to the eastern side of the point reveals outstanding views of Half Dome and the Yosemite high country beyond.

Be prepared for a deceptively difficult return journey. Gravity is your friend again, but the steep grade and irresistible downhill momentum can wreak havoc on knee and ankle joints if you move too fast. Trekking poles and footwear with good tread will be of great use, especially since the trail can be slippery at times. Take a slow, deliberate approach on the way down, and eventually, painstakingly, you will find yourself back at Camp 4 with a story to tell.

34 Eagle Peak

RATING/ DIFFICULTY	ROUNDTRIP	ELEV GAIN/ HIGH POINT	SEASON
*****/5	10.8 miles	4700 feet/ 7738 feet	Apr–Nov

Maps: USGS 7.5-min Yosemite Falls, Tom Harrison Maps Yosemite Valley; **Contact:** Yosemite Valley Visitor Center; **Notes:** Suitable for backpacking (Yosemite Falls). Restroom adjacent to trailhead in Camp 4. Food storage lockers at trailhead parking; **GPS:** 37.7423, –119.6021

 If you read the trail description for Upper Yosemite Fall and thought, "Hmm, sounds nice, but I wish it were harder," your wish is granted. The route to Eagle Peak, a peak which also moonlights as the third of the Three Brothers, follows the Yosemite Falls Trail and then continues beyond to the soaring heights of Eagle Peak. Stellar views await those who crave a bit of truly strenuous uphill work.

GETTING THERE

Driving: From the Arch Rock Entrance, head east on El Portal Road for 5.5 miles and keep right to remain on Southside Drive. Follow Southside Drive for another 5.1 miles, then make a left onto Sentinel Drive. After 0.3 mile on Sentinel Drive, turn left onto Northside Drive. Follow Northside Drive for 1.1 miles to the Yosemite Falls parking area. Turn left into the parking lot, which you can expect to fill up by mid-morning during spring and summer.

Transit: Exit at shuttle stop 7 on the Yosemite Valley Shuttle line, which lies about 50 feet east of the parking area. Cross Northside Drive and walk through the Camp 4 parking area to find the Yosemite Falls Trailhead on the northwest side of the Camp 4 parking area.

ON THE TRAIL

The initial segment of this route follows the Yosemite Falls Trail from Camp 4 up to a junction with the Yosemite Creek Trail. This steep, winding trail yields the most up-close and personal views of Yosemite Falls in the park, and the sweeping views of Yosemite Valley, crowned by Half Dome, are exceptional as well. The Yosemite Falls Trail is also mostly exposed to the sun, and thus an early start on this route is key if you want to avoid getting roasted by the sun during summer. This portion of the route is world-class on its own, and you can find more detail on it in Hike 33.

After 2.7 miles and 2700 feet of climbing, the Yosemite Falls Trail reaches a junction with the Yosemite Creek Trail. Turn left here to begin a much more moderate ascent along the banks of Yosemite Creek, which rages during spring and whispers during fall. This nearly flat stretch of hiking provides a welcome reprieve from climbing over the next 0.6 mile, but that reprieve comes to a premature end after you turn left onto the Eagle Peak Trail at 3.3 miles.

The Eagle Peak Trail begins a switch-backing ascent away from the Yosemite Creek Trail, gaining elevation at a moderate clip as it climbs to a small, wooded, hidden valley containing Eagle Peak Meadows. The trail skirts the western edge of the meadows as it travels south to a junction with the El Capitan Trail at 4.8 miles. Turn left to stay on the Eagle Peak Trail and begin climbing. At exactly 5 miles, backpackers should keep an eye out for a faint spur trail that leads north to a rocky but generally flat knoll where there is a set of spectacular campsites featuring stellar views east toward Half Dome.

Half Dome is majestic no matter your vantage point, but the view from Eagle Peak tops them all.

The climb and the trail both terminate below the summit of Eagle Peak at 5.4 miles. A short scramble leads to the summit. Although you've had a taste of the views east across Yosemite Valley toward Half Dome and beyond, the earlier iterations pale in comparison to the bird's-eye views from the top. The views from the east are particularly shocking, with a nearly sheer drop from the summit to the valley floor below. These views merit at least an hour, preferably two, for full appreciation. If you're backpacking,

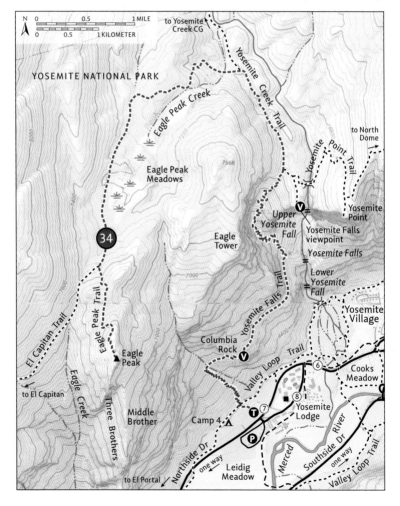

the sunsets can be phenomenal. If you are day hiking, be sure to save plenty of time for the long, grueling descent back to the Yosemite Falls Trailhead.

35 Middle Valley Loop

RATING/ DIFFICULTY	ROUNDTRIP	ELEV GAIN/ HIGH POINT	SEASON
**/3	6 miles	150 feet/ 4056 feet	Year- round

Maps: USGS 7.5-min Yosemite Falls, Tom Harrison Maps Yosemite Valley; **Contact:** Yosemite Valley Visitor Center; **Notes:** Day-use only. No food storage at trailhead. No restroom at trailhead, but bathrooms are located within Camp 4 near the trailhead; **GPS:** 37.7423, –119.6021

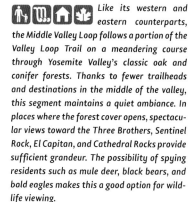 *Like its western and eastern counterparts, the Middle Valley Loop follows a portion of the Valley Loop Trail on a meandering course through Yosemite Valley's classic oak and conifer forests. Thanks to fewer trailheads and destinations in the middle of the valley, this segment maintains a quiet ambiance. In places where the forest cover opens, spectacular views toward the Three Brothers, Sentinel Rock, El Capitan, and Cathedral Rocks provide sufficient grandeur. The possibility of spying residents such as mule deer, black bears, and bald eagles makes this a good option for wildlife viewing.*

GETTING THERE
Driving: From the Arch Rock Entrance, drive east on El Portal Road for 5.5 miles and keep right to remain on Southside Drive. Follow Southside Drive for another 5.1 miles, then make a left onto Sentinel Drive. After 0.3 mile

on Sentinel Drive, turn left onto Northside Drive. Follow Northside Drive for 1.1 miles to the Yosemite Falls parking area. Turn left into the parking lot, which you can expect to fill up by mid-morning during spring and summer.

Transit: Exit at shuttle stop 7 on the Yosemite Valley Shuttle line, which lies about 50 feet east of the parking area. Cross Northside Drive and walk through the Camp 4 parking area to find the Yosemite Falls Trailhead on the northwest side of the Camp 4 parking area.

ON THE TRAIL
To locate the trailhead, cross Northside Drive from the parking area and continue through the Camp 4 parking area. The Yosemite Falls Trailhead lies on the northwest corner of the parking area. After following the Yosemite Falls Trail for about 100 feet, turn left at a junction marked for the Valley Loop Trail and follow it west along a slope above Camp 4. Several house-sized boulders, which are popular with climbing enthusiasts, lie along the trail.

At 0.3 mile, the trail cuts south around a demonstration site where descendants of the Ahwahneechee have constructed traditional lodges made from incense cedar. Shortly afterward, the trail crosses Northside Drive and continues west along the northwestern edge of Leidig Meadow. Although traffic noise detracts somewhat from the scenery, the views across Leidig Meadow and the Merced River toward Sentinel Rock are outstanding. By the 0.7-mile mark, the trail closely parallels the Merced River before crossing Eagle Creek and entering an extended section of pine, cedar, and oak forest with occasional views north toward the Three Brothers.

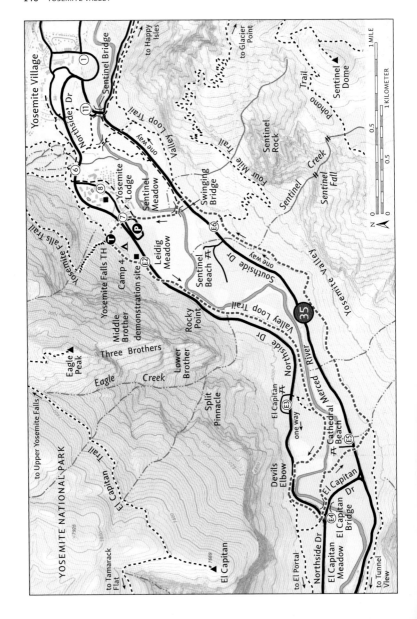

The loveliest stretch of the route begins at 2 miles when the trail takes a wide bend away from the road and enters a spacious meadow. The imposing form of El Capitan dominates this meadow, and the photographically inclined may find good positioning in this area to photograph Horsetail Falls in mid-February when the setting sun makes it glow like a true "firefall." The trail again approaches Northside Drive at 2.3 miles, and it hugs the road around the "Devils Elbow," a pronounced bend in the Merced River. Keep left to follow the shoulder of Northside Drive toward the El Capitan Bridge. Immediately

The Valley Loop Trail leads to a meadow offering superb views of El Capitan.

after crossing the El Capitan Bridge (2.7 miles), look to the left for a connecting trail that connects to the southern half of the Valley Loop Trail.

The connecting trail crosses Southside Drive at 3.2 miles. At 3.3 miles, turn left to follow the Valley Loop Trail east through tranquil forest dominated by black oaks and cedar. Cross Sentinel Creek at 4.7 miles to continue through a junction with the Four Mile Trail at 5 miles. Continue straight to the 5.2-mile mark and cross Southside Drive to reach the parking area for the Swinging Bridge—not to be confused with the Swinging Bridge in Wawona. Cross the road at the crosswalk, and then cross the bridge, which features renowned views toward Yosemite Falls. After the bridge, a paved trail skirts the eastern edge of Leidig Meadow, leading you back to the parking area at 6 miles.

36 Old Big Oak Flat Road

RATING/ DIFFICULTY	ROUNDTRIP	ELEV GAIN/ HIGH POINT	SEASON
*/2	2.4 miles	650 feet/ 4489 feet	Year-round

Map: USGS El Capitan; **Contact:** Yosemite Valley Visitor Center; **Notes:** Day-use only. Minor routefinding required. Moderately difficult terrain. No restroom or food storage at trailhead; **GPS:** 37.7244, –119.6408

Back in the day—150 years ago, to be precise—when Yosemite Valley was a sleepy destination a week's journey from the nearest population center, visitors rode in on horse-led wagons along the valley's first access road, Old Big Oak Flat Road. Although segments of the historic roadbed have been obliterated by rockfall, hikers can still follow a section of the old road to glimpse the same spectacular views that early park visitors reveled in upon their arrival.

GETTING THERE

From the Arch Rock Entrance, drive east for 5.5 miles on El Portal Road to a junction with Southside Drive. Bear right to remain on Southside Drive and continue east for another 2.3 miles to El Capitan Drive. Turn left, then turn left again after 0.4 mile onto Northside Drive. Drive for another 0.4 mile to the west end of El Capitan Meadow. Park in an unmarked parking area rimmed by large boulders on the right side of Northside Drive. You can also park along the road wherever space is available.

ON THE TRAIL

Look for an unmarked, partially paved path that leads northeast from the parking area. Follow this path for 0.1 mile, then make a left turn onto the Valley Loop Trail. The Valley Loop Trail heads west through a scraggly forest of oaks and ponderosa pines, crossing Ribbon Creek at 0.25 mile. At 0.4 mile, the Valley Loop Trail briefly joins Old Big Oak Flat Road. Turn right here to begin ascending on the old roadbed.

Initial progress on the roadbed takes you through a dense, occasionally overgrown forest that reinforces the wild, forgotten character of this route. At the first gap in this forest cover, look to the south for a revelatory view of Bridalveil Fall. Although views of the waterfall from this angle were common for early park visitors, most modern visitors never see the fall from this aspect. You will see the waterfall several more times as you progress, and occasionally, the moss-covered branches of live oaks and fragrant bay laurels frame the view for the photographically inclined.

At 0.75 mile, a rockfall requires a bit of routefinding. Carefully scramble over a short section of rubble to find the continuation of the roadbed. Beyond this point, the rockfalls occur more frequently, and the vegetation encroaches onto the roadbed more persistently until the road reaches an open, sunny spot at 1.2 miles that provides the best view on the roadbed to this point. Bridalveil Fall and the Cathedral Rocks figure prominently, but it's the imposing presence of El Capitan that carries so much gravity in the scene. Project your imagination back in time to hear echoes of the thrill that these views assuredly inspired in early visitors reaching the end of their long journeys.

Because the rockfalls and vegetation overgrowth become increasingly tedious from this point, this is a good turnaround

The domineering form of El Capitan looks much the same as it did to visitors in 1875.

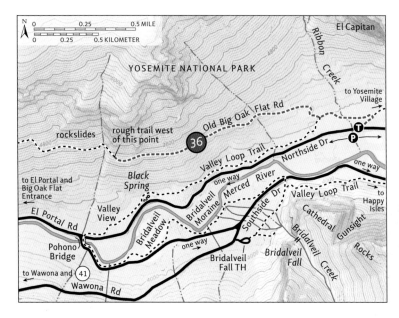

N
0   0.25   0.5 MILE
0   0.25   0.5 KILOMETER

El Capitan

Ribbon Creek

YOSEMITE NATIONAL PARK

to Yosemite Village

rocklides

rough trail west of this point

Old Big Oak Flat Rd

36

Valley Loop Trail

Northside Dr

T
P

one way

to El Portal and Big Oak Flat Entrance

Black Spring

one way

Merced River

Bridalveil Moraine

Southside Dr

Valley Loop Trail

to Happy Isles

El Portal Rd

Valley View

Bridalveil Meadow

Cathedral

Gunsight

Pohono Bridge

one way

Bridalveil Fall TH

Bridalveil Fall

Bridalveil Creek

Rocks

to Wawona and 41

Wawona Rd

spot. You can continue to Rainbow Point and even beyond toward a junction with the Cascade Creek Trail (Hike 39) and the El Capitan Trail (Hike 42), but the going is anything but easy. The toughest rockfall to negotiate occurs at 2 miles; it took out a set of switchbacks on the roadbed, which means hikers must scramble up the rockfall to locate the continuation of the roadbed that leads to Rainbow Point at 2.3 miles.

Opposite: *Half Dome and El Capitan peeking above Big Meadows (Hike 38)*

big oak flat road

Extending from El Portal to the Big Oak Flat Entrance, Big Oak Flat Road serves primarily as a travel artery connecting Yosemite Valley, Tioga Road, and the Big Oak Flat Entrance and Information Station. Given that most people use Big Oak Flat Road to reach other destinations, the trailheads along the road receive less attention than other famous destinations, but the attractions are well worth visiting.

Hikers seeking solitude may enjoy several hikes to wonders including sequoia groves, waterfalls, historic routes, and sweeping views. In addition to the scenic destinations along the road, this area features a wealth of early park history along an older alignment of Big Oak Flat Road and the nearby, nearly forgotten Coulterville Road.

In addition to the entrance station and the information station on Big Oak Flat Road, there are two major campgrounds along the road: Crane Flat and Hodgdon Meadow. A small, first-come, first-served campground along with a trailhead connecting to Old Big Oak Flat Road can be found at Tamarack Flat, reached via an access road departing from Tioga Road just east of Crane Flat.

One of the two gas stations in the park can be found at Crane Flat, although there are no additional services in the area. Crane Flat also doubles as a snow play area during the winter, provided the roads are clear enough for travel. Finally, the historic town of Foresta houses a tiny community within the park boundaries. Foresta offers no visitor services; however, there are two routes following historic road alignments leading to a pair of unassuming, but pretty waterfalls.

37 Foresta Falls

RATING/ DIFFICULTY	ROUNDTRIP	ELEV GAIN/ HIGH POINT	SEASON
**/2	2.3 miles	400 feet/ 4319 feet	Year- round

Map: USGS 7.5-min El Portal; **Contact:** Big Oak Flat Information Station; **Notes:** Day-use only. No restroom at trailhead. No food storage at trailhead; **GPS:** 37.7030, –119.7529

A little-known but impressive waterfall cascades and crashes over a 60-foot granite ledge just south of the village of Foresta. This short walk along Foresta Road (closed to traffic) leads to the base of the falls, which you can have to yourself in a way that is never possible with the big Yosemite Valley showstoppers.

GETTING THERE
From the Big Oak Flat Entrance on State Route 120, head south on Big Oak Flat Road/SR 120 toward Yosemite Valley. After 13.8 miles, turn right onto Yosemite National Park Road/Old Coulterville Road. Continue heading west on Yosemite National Park Road/Old Coulterville Road for 1.7 miles, then turn left onto Foresta Road. Follow Foresta Road through Foresta, and find a handful of parking spots where the pavement ends just past Lyell Way.

ON THE TRAIL
This route begins in the tiny community of Foresta, which is one of a handful of private property inholdings within Yosemite National Park. Originally a homestead

Opposite: *This hidden gem thunders over a cliff just below the village of Foresta.*

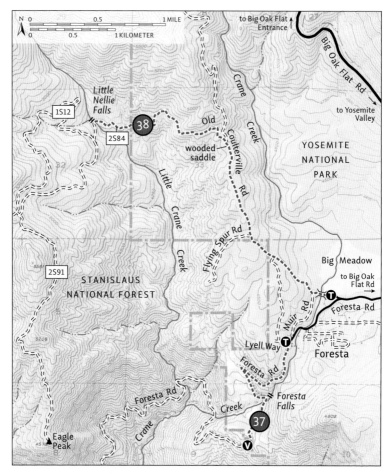

centered around Big Meadow, which itself was the site of an American Indian village, this community evolved into a small hamlet of private residences with ambitions toward becoming a hub of connectivity for Yosemite visitors. Developers constructed the Foresta Road—the same road this route follows to the falls—to facilitate travel between Foresta and El Portal. However, various man-made catastrophes, including World Wars, the Great Depression, and lack of real estate sales kept the community small and obscure.

From the parking area at the end of the pavement, follow Foresta Road downhill along the banks of Crane Creek, which cascades over granite slabs on your left. A

1990 fire burned through this area, and twenty-eight years later, the Ferguson Fire reburned much of the habitat, leaving a swath of destruction and recovering forest in its wake. The upside of this devastation is that, for several years at least, wildflowers will bloom in profusion on the hillsides.

After bending to the northwest away from the creek, Foresta Road makes a sharp switchback to the southeast to descend toward the falls. Views across a grassy pasture where mules graze add a nice scenic note as you progress. At 0.7 mile, the trail rounds a bend, revealing the falls directly ahead. Continue across the bridge to stare face to face with Foresta Falls, which rages in impressive fashion during peak runoff in May.

You can turn back at the waterfall, but if you fancy a peek into the depths of the Merced River Gorge, continue walking south from the waterfall toward the rim of the gorge. At 1.1 miles, the trail crests this rim, which reveals a view of the Merced River snaking its way through its rugged canyon several thousand feet below. Make this viewpoint your turnaround point since the road continues descending all the way down to El Portal.

38 Little Nellie Falls

RATING/ DIFFICULTY	ROUNDTRIP	ELEV GAIN/ HIGH POINT	SEASON
*/2	5.4 miles	800 feet/ 4816 feet	Year-round

Map: USGS 7.5-min El Portal; **Contact:** Big Oak Flat Information Station; **Notes:** Day-use only. No restroom at trailhead. No food storage at trailhead; **GPS:** 37.7031, –119.7533

 Tucked deep into Little Crane Creek's canyon, Little Nellie Falls spills 20 feet over a granite ledge beneath the shade of conifers and alders. Few visitors to the park venture out to witness this peaceful scene, ensuring an abundance of solitude. Springtime visitors will also be rewarded by a surprisingly rich wildflower display enlivening the habitat along historic Old Coulterville Road.

GETTING THERE

From the Big Oak Flat Entrance on State Route 120, head south on Big Oak Flat Road/SR 120 toward Yosemite Valley. After 13.8 miles, turn right onto Yosemite National Park Road. Continue heading west on Yosemite National Park Road, which becomes Old Coulterville Road after 0.7 mile. After another mile, keep right to remain on Old Coulterville Road/Forest Route 2S84. Park at the end of the road just before a closed, dilapidated bridge crossing Crane Creek.

ON THE TRAIL

During the late 1800s when various interests within and without Yosemite were seeking to increase visitor access, competition between the local gateway communities of Coulterville, Big Oak Flat (now Groveland), and Mariposa raged over who could construct the first road into the valley. Construction of Coulterville Road occurred in fits and starts from 1870 until its completion in 1874, and for one short month before Old Big Oak Flat Road opened and became the preferred route into the park, it was the only road into Yosemite Valley. Old Big Oak Flat Road quickly replaced Coulterville Road, which fell into disrepair. Today, it sees only occasional foot traffic on the route to Little

The route to Little Nellie Falls comes alive with wildflowers in the spring: a tiger swallowtail enjoys a wild hyacinth.

Nellie Falls and at the hike down to Merced Grove (Hike 43).

Park and then walk over the bridge to continue onto the unpaved roadbed of Old Coulterville Road. Once across the bridge, turn right to remain on Old Coulterville Road, which ascends along the spine of a broad ridge dividing Crane Creek to the east and Little Crane Creek to the west. The habitat here has burned a couple of times over the past four decades, and much of the forest that once covered the ridge continues to recover. The lack of tree cover allows unique views toward Yosemite Valley, where El Capitan, Half Dome, and Sentinel Dome loom above Big Meadow and the pine-studded ridges to the east. Copious wildflowers, including yerba santa, lupines, mountain misery, mariposa lilies, wild hyacinths, brodiaeas, and clarkias brighten the habitat along the northbound road.

Follow the road uphill, keeping right at a dirt road at 0.5 mile, and right again at Flying Spur Road at 0.7 mile. At 1.4 miles, Old Coulterville Road reaches a wooded saddle and a Y junction with a road that continues north along Crane Creek all the way to Crane Flat. Keep left to remain on Old Coulterville Road as it begins a descent along a sunny hillside speckled with flowers. At 2.4 miles, after about a mile of moderate descent, the road passes into Stanislaus National Forest, at which point the road's designation changes to Forest Route 2S84. Shortly beyond the national forest boundary, the trail nears the banks of Little Crane Creek.

Upon reaching the banks of Little Crane Creek, look for an unmarked spur trail that leads to the base of Little Nellie Falls. Little Nellie is not remarkable by Yosemite Valley standards, but its intimate, isolated setting gives it a special charm all its own. Look for a picnic bench on the other side of the creek if you want to enjoy lunch in the shade of pines and cedars before you begin the return journey to your vehicle.

39 Cascade Creek

RATING/ DIFFICULTY	ROUNDTRIP	ELEV GAIN/ HIGH POINT	SEASON
**/3	8.2 miles	1500 feet/ 6066 feet	Year-round

Map: USGS 7.5-min El Portal; **Contact:** Big Oak Flat Information Station; **Notes:** Suitable for backpacking. Unimproved creek crossings. Food storage at trailhead; **GPS:** 37.7145, –119.7362

If you're looking for a quiet hiking experience with some nice views, quiet forest, and rumbling watercourses, the oft-overlooked Old Big Oak Flat Road Trail meets all criteria. Spring may be the best time for this route thanks to copious wildflowers blossoming on the first segment of the route, but be warned that spring runoff makes crossings at Tamarack Creek dangerous or even fatal.

GETTING THERE
From the Big Oak Flat Road Entrance Station on State Route 120 (Big Oak Flat Road), drive 13.5 miles south on Big Oak Flat Road/SR 120 to the Old Big Oak Flat Road Trailhead parking area on the right (south) side of the road.

The trail begins on the opposite side of the road from the parking area.

ON THE TRAIL
After carefully crossing Big Oak Flat Road, follow the Old Big Oak Flat Road Trail east on a moderately steep, switchbacking incline through a garden of shrubs recovering from the 2009 Big Meadow Fire. Views west across Foresta and El Portal improve as you climb, and if you can time your return descent around sunset, evening light draws out the beauty of this scene.

At 0.6 mile, the trail crests a ridge, revealing a partial view of Yosemite Valley. The trail turns to the north, traversing a sunny hillside bedecked with recovering vegetation. The square block of granite towering above to the north is the Devils Dance Floor. At 0.8 mile, the initial climb eases, and a gentle descent toward Wildcat Creek begins. Cross this small creek and its even smaller tributary at 1.5 miles to follow the trail as it bends to the east and resumes a modest climb. The perimeter of the Big Meadow Fire just beyond Wildcat Creek also marks the welcome beginning of travel through unburnt forest. After the creek, the trail wraps around the slope 1500 feet below the Devils Dance Floor.

At 2.4 miles, the trail dips into Tamarack Creek's densely wooded ravine before reaching the creek's rocky banks. Between April and June, Tamarack Creek roars with snowmelt from the high country around Tamarack Flat Campground, which makes this unimproved crossing treacherous. The crossing proves safer during summer, fall, and winter, but even in low water it is difficult not to get wet as you cross. If the water is high, the banks of Tamarack Creek, which

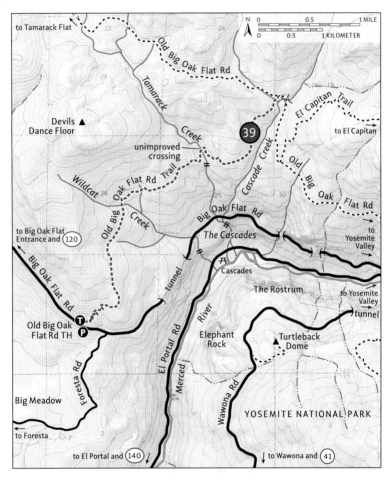

feature a few picturesque cascades, is about as far as it is advisable to go.

If the creek is passable, cross it and continue following the trail uphill. Trees partially obscure the view south toward Henness Ridge and Pinoche Peak as you progress eastward, but following a northward bend in the trail, the trees recede enough to reveal an appreciable panorama. Following the bend north, the trail dips into a densely wooded hollow before reaching a tributary creek at 3.7 miles. This tributary spills over granite slabs, creating a small but picturesque waterfall.

Shortly after crossing the tributary, turn right onto Old Big Oak Flat Road's deteriorating roadbed. A 0.2-mile descent leads to a wooden footbridge spanning Cascade Creek. Although most people experience Cascade Creek as a roadside waterfall beyond the Arch Rock Entrance, this segment of the creek rushes and roars over boulders through a broad ravine. This pleasant destination marks your turnaround point. Retrace your steps to conclude your hike.

EXTENDING YOUR HIKE
You can continue from the Cascade Creek Bridge along the route to El Capitan for an extremely challenging day hike, or perhaps more realistically, an overnight excursion. The full out-and-back route from the trailhead on Big Oak Flat Road runs 19.6 miles with 5000 feet of elevation gain. Difficult though this route is, it presents a possible alternative approach for times when Tamarack Flat Campground is closed.

40 Clark Range View

RATING/ DIFFICULTY	ROUNDTRIP	ELEV GAIN/ HIGH POINT	SEASON
*/1	3 miles	150 feet/ 6298 feet	Dec–Apr

Map: USGS 7.5-min El Portal; **Contact:** Big Oak Flat Information Station; **Notes:** Suitable for snowshoeing. Restroom adjacent to trailhead during summer; **GPS:** 37.7457, –119.8009

Although unremarkable for most of the year, this unassuming route to a pleasing viewpoint is at its best during the winter months when a blanket of snow lies upon a hushed forest floor. The ease of following this route makes it a fine introductory snowshoeing or cross-country ski excursion, and the views across El Portal and the Clark Range provide a nice reward.

GETTING THERE
From the Big Oak Flat Entrance and Information Station on State Route 120, head south for 7.5 miles to Crane Flat Campground and turn right. Follow the campground road for a half mile. During the winter, the road ends at a designated snow play area, and you can park along the road before commencing the hike along an old logging road.

ON THE TRAIL
Follow an old logging road departing from Crane Flat Campground that heads first east and then south on a moderate grade through

Whether snowbound or graced with wild azaleas, Cascade Creek's rumbling waters are a worthwhile destination.

The winter snowpack transforms an old logging route into a winter wonderland.

a shady forest. Sugar pines, incense cedars, ponderosa pines, white firs, and black oaks populate the forest. If you visit following a winter storm, the forest evokes a sense of quiet wonder as winter's soft light casts deep shadows across fresh snow.

The road winds gently south to its terminus. This flat spot yields nice views south across El Portal and east across the upper reaches of Yosemite Valley and beyond toward the Clark Range. Although none of the views here are remarkable by Yosemite

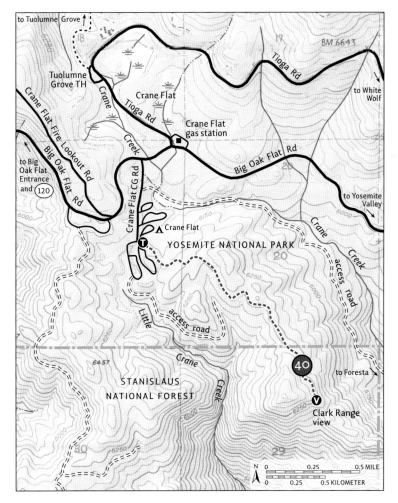

standards, this would be a multimillion-dollar view anywhere else. When coated with snow, the unfurling landscape assumes a magical quality.

Turn back when satisfied for an easy downhill walk back to your car.

41 Tuolumne Grove

RATING/ DIFFICULTY	ROUNDTRIP	ELEV GAIN/ HIGH POINT	SEASON
**/2	3 miles	600 feet/ 6229 feet	Year-round

Map: USGS 7.5-min Ackerson Mountain; **Contact:** Yosemite National Park, Big Oak Flat Information Station; **Notes:** Day-use only. Vault toilet at trailhead Food storage lockers; **GPS:** 37.7580, –119.8052

This small but picturesque sequoia grove was once a popular spot for travelers along Old Big Oak Flat Road. The old road doubles as today's route into the grove, which contains about twenty-five mature sequoias. Numerous curiosities, including a tunnel carved into the base of a long-dead giant, complement lush, lower montane forest with trickling streams and copious dogwood blossoms during the spring.

GETTING THERE

From the Big Oak Flat Entrance, drive south on Big Oak Flat Road/State Route 120 toward Yosemite Valley. After 7.7 miles, turn left onto Tioga Road/SR 120 toward Tioga Pass. After 0.6 mile, turn left into the parking area for the Tuolumne Grove Trailhead.

For winter hiking, park at the Crane Flat snow play area in Crane Flat Campground, which is 7.5 miles south from the Big Oak Flat Entrance and 0.5 mile south on the campground access road. From the Crane Flat parking area, walk along the access road back to Big Oak Flat Road and turn right toward Tioga Road. Turn left onto Tioga Road and walk for 0.6 mile to the trailhead. This adds a total of 2.6 miles of walking to the route.

ON THE TRAIL

Despite being the second road into the park—Coulterville Road was completed a month earlier—the Old Big Oak Flat Road connecting Groveland to El Capitan Meadow quickly became the preferred route into Yosemite Valley. Along the way, Old Big Oak Flat Road visited several highlights, including Carlon Falls, Hodgdon Meadow, Tamarack Flat, and Tuolumne Grove. Throughout the road's active history, the grove was a roadside stop until the new Big Oak Flat Road succeeded the old road. Today, much of the old road has reverted to discontinuous segments of trails through quiet, dense forests, including this segment down to the Grove Loop Trail exploring the heart of Tuolumne Grove.

To begin the hike, locate the trailhead at the northwest edge of the parking area; it's marked by a sign, several informative interpretive plaques, and a model of the base of a sequoia that illustrates the sheer size and age of the trees. Follow the paved road downhill through dense lower montane forest composed of sugar pines, white firs, and the occasional incense cedar—a

Opposite: Tuolumne Grove's signature sequoia, Big Red, towers above Old Big Oak Flat Road.

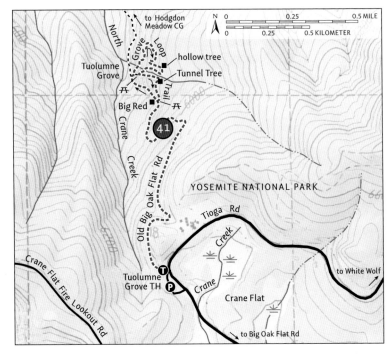

smaller, distant cousin to the giant sequoia. The road remains paved until it reaches the Grove Loop Trail at 1.3 miles. Although a long downhill walk on pavement will not do your knees many favors, the upshot is that the road is easy to follow when blanketed in snow, making this hike a great winter route.

Old Big Oak Flat Road enters Tuolumne Grove at 1.1 miles, marked by the grove's largest tree—Big Red. Adjacent to Big Red, look for a junction with the Grove Loop Trail on the right; you will return by this junction after completing the short loop that takes in the highlights in the heart of the grove. To reach the start of the Grove Loop, continue ahead for another 0.1 mile to a Y junction marked by a sign and several picnic tables.

Pick the right fork of this Y junction and follow it down to a bridge shaded by thickets of dogwood trees that produce showy white blossoms in late May and early June. The loop then passes through a sunny, open forest dotted with about a dozen medium-sized sequoia trees. Interpretive plaques placed at intervals describe some of the highlights of the grove. One such highlight is a massive, fallen tree that has partially shattered. This hollowed-out tree has enough room inside to allow curious children to explore—a wonderful novelty for both young and old.

The Grove Loop crosses the grove's creek one more time before returning to Old Big Oak Flat Road. Turn left here, but instead of following the road, keep far to the left to follow the final segment of the Grove Loop. This portion of the loop leads south to the Tunnel Tree, an enormous sequoia stump through which a tunnel was beveled into the base. Early visitors enjoyed the novelty of driving their stagecoaches through the tunnel, and you can walk through the tunnel to follow the Grove Loop Trail back to Big Red and Old Big Oak Flat Road. Note the presence of a handful of picnic tables, which offer an opportunity to rest for a bit before the uphill climb back to the parking area. From the picnic area, follow Old Big Oak Flat Road uphill back to the parking area.

42 El Capitan

RATING/ DIFFICULTY	ROUNDTRIP	ELEV GAIN/ HIGH POINT	SEASON
***/4	16.6 miles	3200 feet/ 7730 feet	May–Oct

Map: USGS 7.5-min El Capitan; **Contact:** Yosemite National Park, Big Oak Flat Information Station; **Notes:** Suitable for backpacking (Tamarack Creek). Vault toilets near trailhead. Food storage lockers near trailhead; **GPS:** 37.7522, –119.7371

Ever look up from the Yosemite Valley floor at the hulking form of El Capitan and wonder, "What's it like up there?" Maybe you've done so but then thought to yourself, "I'm no rock-climber. There's no way." Well, thankfully it is possible to walk up to the top of El Capitan without having to cling to the side of a sheer cliff like some of the legendary climbers of Yosemite lore. All it requires is a rather strenuous walk—with a lot of elevation gain—from Tamarack Flat Campground to reach the rounded summit graced with some remarkable views of the Yosemite high country.

GETTING THERE
From the Big Oak Flat Entrance, drive south on Big Oak Flat Road/State Route 120 toward Yosemite Valley. After 7.7 miles, turn left onto Tioga Road/SR 120 toward Tioga Pass. Follow Tioga Road for 3.8 miles to Old Big Oak Flat Road. After 2.8 miles, the road reaches Tamarack Flat Campground. Drive straight through the campground to a gate blocking continued access. Look for parking on the right just before the gate.

ON THE TRAIL
Be aware that this hike stretches the limits of what most day hikers are comfortable with. You will invariably get more out of this route if you can make it an overnight trip. However, if you get an early start and possess energy and determination to spare, you can complete the outing in a full, rather exhausting day.

The hike begins at the east end of the Tamarack Flat Campground. Step onto Old Big Oak Flat Road and follow it east through a sunny, spacious forest. Tamarack Creek, which rages early in the season and whispers later in the season, rumbles along to the south for the first mile until the trail crests a saddle and begins a long descent to Cascade Creek. At 1.75 miles, the road crosses Coyote Creek. Beyond this point look for spring-nourished thickets of wildflowers on both sides of the road, including ostentatious Western azaleas and graceful Sierra tiger lilies.

At 2 miles, continue straight past a signed junction on the right leading to Old Big Oak Flat Road (Hike 36). One-tenth of a mile later, the trail reaches a footbridge spanning

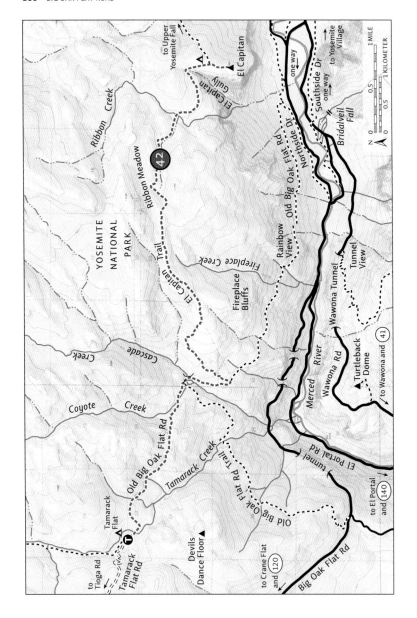

Cascade Creek, a rugged, often raging watercourse along whose banks Indian rhubarb and Western azaleas proliferate. After crossing the footbridge, the road continues descending through dense forest to a junction with the beginning of the El Capitan Trail at 2.7 miles. It is all uphill from here.

Turn left onto the El Capitan Trail and begin a prolonged climb along the western ramparts of Yosemite Valley to gain 2000 feet of elevation over the next 2.6 miles.

The climb can be broken down roughly into two phases. The first phase winds on a steep track through dense forest. The trail is occasionally rough, and it gets inconsistent maintenance, making it the most difficult part of the hike. The second, gentler phase begins at 4 miles when the incline eases. After a brief passage through forest, the trail reaches a sunny ridge dotted by pines and carpeted by manzanita. It continues dead ahead until cresting at the route's high

Half Dome and the Yosemite high country silhouetted by the early morning sun

point at 5.3 miles. This is a good spot to take an extended break now that you have the toughest part of the climb behind you.

From the crest, the trail begins a gentle descent into densely wooded valley laced through by lovely Ribbon Meadow. The shade and easy grade offer relief, but be prepared for an onslaught of mosquitos as you follow the trail along the meadow. After passing the meadow's eastern end, the trail follows the tributary creek that drains Ribbon Meadow down to a crossing of Ribbon Creek—the last water source before El Capitan's summit, for those who are backpacking. Cross Ribbon Creek at 6.7 miles to begin the final climb to the top of El Capitan.

At 7.5 miles, the trail wraps around the head of El Capitan Gully, a vertiginous gash separating the El Capitan massif from the valley wall. Beyond the gully, the trail climbs obliquely along the western flank of El Capitan, topping out at a rocky, open flat bewhiskered with pines at 7.8 miles. An unmarked spur trail leads south along the spine of El Capitan, which is surprisingly flat and easy to navigate, given how imposing the formation looks from below. Good campsites can be found along the spur trail, but be sure to remain at least 0.5 mile back from the rim of the valley when you select your site.

Views to the east reveal Half Dome and the Clark Range framed by pines. Directly across lies a handful of viewpoints along the south rim of the valley, including Dewey, Stanford, Crocker, and Old Inspiration Points. Look west to trace the sinuous thread of the Merced River as it moves toward El Portal and the rugged Merced River Gorge. Note that there is no one spot on El Capitan to get a full panorama, so you will have to wander around the top for a bit

to get every angle. Factor in an extra 0.5 mile to the route's overall distance to account for the walking if you are the sort who likes to squeeze out every last ounce of view from your summits.

You may be tempted to tiptoe to the edge to look straight down into the valley. The slope from the top becomes progressively steeper until it terminates at an abrupt cliff, so attempting to navigate this steep slope with little between you and the valley floor is a dangerous maneuver and not recommended. It *is* recommended that you content yourself with the spectacular views all around and take a pass on peering over a 3000-foot cliff.

The return route is not nearly as arduous as the approach, despite a steep descent on rocky slopes heading down to Old Big Oak Flat Road. The toughest part of the return trip is undoubtedly the 700 feet of elevation gain that occurs between the El Capitan Trail junction and Tamarack Flat. Consider taking a long break at Cascade Creek—a very pleasant spot in itself—before the long walk back to the campground.

43 Merced Grove

RATING/ DIFFICULTY	ROUNDTRIP	ELEV GAIN/ HIGH POINT	SEASON
**/2	3.3 miles	600 feet/ 5919 feet	Year-round

Maps: USGS 7.5-min Ackerson Mountain, El Portal; **Contact:** Big Oak Flat Information Station; **Notes:** Day-use only. Pit toilet at trailhead. Food storage lockers at trailhead; **GPS:** 37.7630, –119.8422

 *This peaceful stroll to a small grove of sequoias*

tucked into a quiet corner of the park brings you into close contact with the largest single-stemmed tree on the planet. Although the grove is small, this hike possesses the solitude lacking at Mariposa Grove, making it the better option for communing with sequoias in relative silence. Fragments of Yosemite's storied past add a bit of historical interest to the experience.

GETTING THERE

From Yosemite National Park's Big Oak Flat Entrance, head south on Big Oak Flat Road for 4 miles to the parking area and signed trailhead for Merced Grove on the right-hand (south) side of the road.

ON THE TRAIL

Follow the wide dirt road past the gate and past the toilets and begin a gentle stroll that

rises and falls imperceptibly. The forest on your right (west) burned during the 2013 Rim Fire, but the forest to your left (east) surrounding Moss Creek remains vibrant and green. Continue in this gentle fashion for 0.6 mile to a junction with a second gate. The right fork splits off toward Stanislaus National Forest territory, while the left fork begins a descent toward Merced Grove.

From the junction, the route now follows the Old Coulterville Road, which served, briefly, as the first road access to Yosemite Valley until the Old Wawona and Big Oak Flat Roads became the primary routes for accessing the park. The old road connected Coulterville to Foresta and then on to Yosemite Valley, but it now sees only foot traffic to Merced Grove and farther south from Foresta to Little Nellie Falls (Hike 38). Follow the road as it drops down toward

The old Merced Grove ranger station provokes log cabin envy.

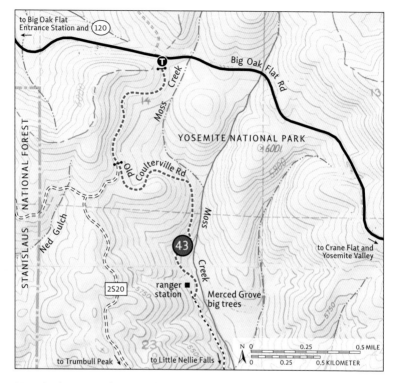

Moss Creek on a moderate grade before bending to the south toward Merced Grove.

At 1.5 miles, the trail reaches the boundaries of Merced Grove. The grove is relatively small by sequoia grove standards, containing perhaps two dozen trees. However, the trees here still dwarf the surrounding conifers, which are by no means small. An old ranger station constructed in 1935 still stands in place of what was originally a checking station along the old road. The park maintains the structure in its original form, and it adds a rustic historical echo to the grove.

The ranger station is the end of the line for this hike. In accordance with the hiking maxim that all things going down must come back up, you face an uphill climb on the hike back. This situation will make the return journey more strenuous than the approach, so be sure to fuel up with a snack and an extended break at the ranger station before beginning the long climb out.

Opposite: Lupines in the foreground with Hetch Hetchy Dome and Kolana Rock above Hetch Hetchy Reservoir (Hike 48)

hetch hetchy

Over 100 years ago, early visitors to the region northwest of Yosemite Valley marveled at another glacially carved valley laced with waterfalls feeding the mighty Tuolumne River. Although it lacked the overwhelming grandeur of Yosemite Valley, many, including John Muir, considered Hetch Hetchy Valley as a worthy counterpart to its sister valley to the south. But not all who considered Hetch Hetchy thought of it in terms of scenic value. Water managers looking to quench San Francisco's incessant thirst saw Hetch Hetchy as the perfect reservoir, and after a protracted legal battle, engineers constructed the O'Shaughnessy Dam, thus flooding Hetch Hetchy Valley.

To this day, Hetch Hetchy remains flooded despite decades of advocacy to tear down the dam and restore the valley. Controversy aside, the Hetch Hetchy region still contains worthwhile hikes that visit waterfalls, windswept peaks, lakes, and hidden valleys. Many of the trails here penetrate deep into Yosemite's northern backcountry, making Hetch Hetchy a good jumping off point for backpackers. Few services and no campgrounds exist within the park's Hetch Hetchy sector, but several lodges and campgrounds lie just outside the park boundary in Stanislaus National Forest.

Finally, be sure to note the times when the entrance gate opens and closes. Hikers who do not make it back to the Hetch Hetchy Entrance in time will be stuck on the wrong side of the gate with no way to get out.

Map: USGS 7.5-min Ackerson Mountain; **Contact:** Big Oak Flat Information Station; **Notes:** Day-use only. Vault toilets at the nearby Carlon Day Use Area; **GPS:** 37.8143, –119.8615

Not every waterfall in Yosemite is a towering, mist-churning spectacle that draws visitors by the thousands. In a few tucked-away spots, such as at Carlon Falls, you can find quiet waterfalls that feed pools that become inviting swimming holes in late summer when the South Fork Tuolumne River's flow dwindles. The gentle traverse through the forest to reach this pretty little waterfall is great for a late afternoon stroll.

GETTING THERE

From the Big Oak Flat Entrance Station, head north on Big Oak Flat Road for 1.1 miles to a junction with Evergreen Road. Turn right onto Evergreen Road and continue for 1 mile to the Carlon Day Use Area to park. The Carlon Falls Trail is on the right side of the road just beyond the bridge spanning the South Fork Tuolumne River. Note that the trailhead is on Stanislaus National Forest property, but the trail itself is primarily within Yosemite National Park.

ON THE TRAIL

For over twenty years, from 1916 to 1938, the Carlon Day Use Area across the road from the trailhead served as the site of the Carl Inn along the South Fork of the Tuolumne River. Formerly situated along the Old Big Oak Flat Road, the Carl Inn served visitors traveling to and from Yosemite Valley. The inn burned during a massive conflagration in 1920 but was rebuilt and remained successful until the park reconfigured Big Oak Flat Road in 1938

44 Carlon Falls

RATING/ DIFFICULTY	ROUNDTRIP	ELEV GAIN/ HIGH POINT	SEASON
**/1	2.8 miles	300 feet/ 4484 feet	Year-round

The Middle Fork Tuolumne River rumbles over rapids during the spring thaw.

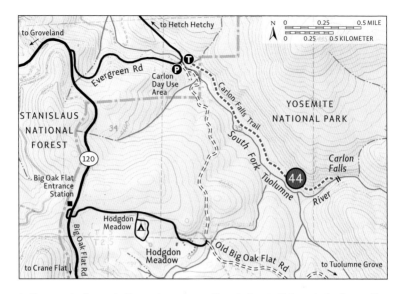

to its current alignment. The park service dismantled the inn, and Stanislaus National Forest converted the site into a campground before closing the campground down in 1995 due to streamside erosion issues. The day-use area features picnic tables and a peaceful ambiance, despite its proximity to the bustling Big Oak Flat Entrance Station.

One quick note of caution: The 2013 Rim Fire burned through the Carlon Falls area, and although the forest around the river mostly survived, you can count on having to navigate over or around blowdowns. The numerous downed trees along the way are not formidable obstacles, but they may require occasional gymnastics to navigate.

From the Carlon Falls Trailhead, follow the path southeast through mixed-conifer forest on a gently undulating track. The South Fork Tuolumne River rumbles or whispers, depending on the season, to the south, adding a pleasing musical note to

the relaxing stroll through the forest. After 1.1 miles of pleasant forest walking, the trail grade suddenly steepens. At this point, the trail bends to the northeast and picks up about 100 feet of quick elevation on the way to its terminus alongside Carlon Falls. Be sure to steer away from a user-created path that hugs the riverbank. This informal path will lead you close to the water, but it dead-ends at a spot where a scramble would become dangerous during high water.

The pools below the waterfall become popular for swimming in the late summer, but you will want to stay out of the water during spring and early summer. The South Fork does not drain as much terrain as the main stem of the Tuolumne, but it still carries a dangerous amount of icy runoff that can cause rapid hypothermia with a high likelihood of drowning. Additionally, the waterfall does not look as pretty during peak runoff, as the flow tends to overwhelm the falls. Unlike most other falls, summer's diminished flow brings out the character of Carlon Falls.

45 Lookout Point

RATING/ DIFFICULTY	ROUNDTRIP	ELEV GAIN/ HIGH POINT	SEASON
*/2	2.7 miles	700 feet/ 5309 feet	Year-Round

Hetch Hetchy Valley viewed from Lookout Point

Maps: USGS 7.5-min Lake Eleanor, Tom Harrison Maps Hetch Hetchy; **Contact:** Hetch Hetchy Information Station; **Notes:** Day-use only. No food storage lockers at trailhead. Restrooms adjacent to trailhead; **GPS:** 37.8931, –119.8413

 For sweeping views of the Tuolumne River Canyon, Hetch

Hetchy Reservoir, and the high country surrounding Hetch Hetchy, follow this short hike to the appropriately named Lookout Point. The views here are excellent, and like many hikes in the Hetch Hetchy area, the crowds are nonexistent. Although the Hetch Hetchy Entrance often closes before sunset, this is still a great hike to enjoy in the afternoon when the low angle of the sun casts the landscape into dramatic relief.

GETTING THERE

The trailhead lies about 50 yards beyond the Hetch Hetchy Entrance Station on the right-hand side of the road. The rangers will direct you to park your car on the opposite side of the road from the trailhead at a turnout that can hold about four or five cars.

ON THE TRAIL

After crossing the road to find the trailhead, follow the trail south along a small meadow. After only 0.15 mile, keep left at an unsigned junction with a trail that connects to the Evergreen Lodge's small network of footpaths. Beyond this left turn, the trail parallels Hetch Hetchy Road for 0.4 mile before peeling away from the road to ascend a rocky ravine rising to the northeast. Like most areas in Hetch Hetchy, the Rim Fire has left its mark on the landscape; expect charred trees and possible downed logs forming minor obstacles.

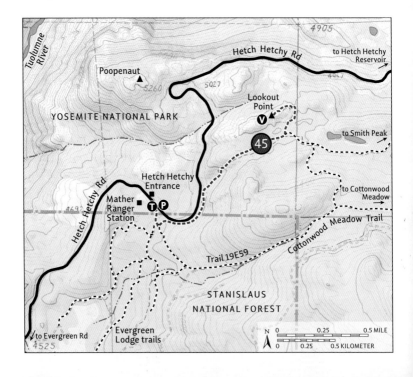

After a short, steep spurt of climbing, the trail emerges from the ravine into a small, marshy glade. Climbing ceases as you continue hiking east-northeast alongside an intermittent stream to a junction for the short spur trail to Lookout Point at 1.1 miles. Turn left here to begin a short climb heading north to a high point marked "5309" on topographic maps but marked as Lookout Point by the park service.

A short, rocky climb leads you to the summit of a boulder-studded peaklet surveying a landscape dominated by the Tuolumne River Canyon. Smith Peak (see Hike 47) rises from the burnt forest to the northeast, and the western end of Hetch Hetchy Reservoir glimmers like a sapphire set in rugged granite. This comfortable summit is a great spot for picnicking, and it will give kids—especially younger ones—a sense of accomplishment.

46 Poopenaut Valley

RATING/ DIFFICULTY	ROUNDTRIP	ELEV GAIN/ HIGH POINT	SEASON
**/3	2.4 miles	1250 feet/ 4593 feet	Nov–May

Maps: USGS 7.5-min Lake Eleanor, Tom Harrison Maps Hetch Hetchy; **Contact:** Hetch Hetchy Information Station; **Notes:** Suitable for backpacking (Poopenaut Valley). Food storage locker at trailhead; **GPS:** 37.9101, –119.8146

The exquisitely named Poopenaut Valley is the little hike that kicks some major behind, both in terms of its scenic value and what it does to your leg muscles. This surprisingly difficult hike pays big dividends by gifting you an entire valley all to yourself. Backpackers will enjoy a quick jaunt down to the valley where they can camp in solitude. Day hikers will enjoy a tranquil day on the banks of the Tuolumne spent with the pleasant company of rumbling water and pines whispering in the breeze.

GETTING THERE
From the Hetch Hetchy Entrance Station, drive north on Hetch Hetchy Road for 3.9 miles to the Poopenaut Valley Trailhead. The unobtrusive trailhead offers a handful of parking spots on the south side of the road.

ON THE TRAIL
After crossing the road to reach the trailhead, begin a deceptively innocent stroll through sparse woodland and scattered manzanita. The gentle grade soon becomes a startlingly steep descent down a wooded slope. The trail has little time to waste on such conveniences as switchbacks, and the result is a net elevation loss of 1250 feet over the next 0.9 mile. The trail itself receives little traffic, leaving it overgrown and occasionally difficult to follow. A lot of attention must be paid to prevent going astray, and in some places poison oak encroaches on the trail, compounding your need to keep a close eye on where you step.

The initial descent occurs primarily within a cool, dense forest of pines and cedars, but after 0.4 mile the conifers yield to an open woodland of black oaks. An intermittent stream gurgles along on the right during the spring, but it may run dry during the fall. A smattering of views to the northeast offers glimpses toward Hetch Hetchy Reservoir, but most of the scenic appeal comes from the black oaks themselves. These deciduous oaks put forth pink leaves in spring and flash gold in the fall, adding more color to the hike than you might expect.

At 0.9 mile, the descent comes to an end at the edge of a diamond-shaped valley bisected by the Tuolumne River. The trail briefly becomes hard to follow upon reaching a sign that warns backpackers against having a campfire—this is a good area to camp thanks to the shelter of the trees. If you lose the trail, keep close to the intermittent stream to your right, and resume the tread when you reach the edge of the meadow. The trail will lead you to a

The swollen Tuolumne River runs through the best-named valley in the Sierra Nevada.

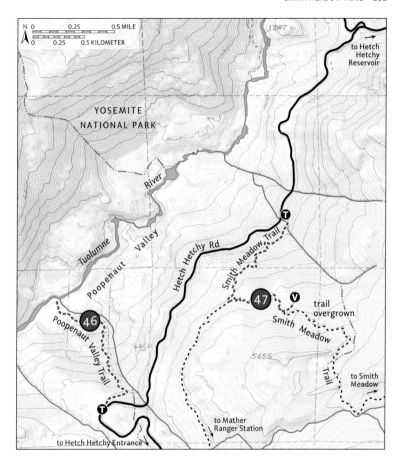

supremely peaceful spot on the banks of the Tuolumne River where you can lay down a picnic blanket and idle the day away.

Now comes the hard part: retracing your steps. The brutal climb out of the valley becomes excruciatingly hot during summer afternoons, and it's probably best to time your excursion to avoid hiking out during the afternoon in the late spring and summer.

47 Smith Meadow Trail

RATING/ DIFFICULTY	ROUNDTRIP	ELEV GAIN/ HIGH POINT	SEASON
**/3	3 miles	1050 feet/ 5141 feet	Apr–June; Oct–Nov

Maps: USGS 7.5-min Lake Eleanor, Hetch Hetchy Reservoir, Tom Harrison Maps Hetch

Hetchy; **Contact:** Hetch Hetchy Information Station; **Notes:** Day-use only. No toilets at trailhead. Food storage at trailhead; **GPS:** 37.9263, −119.7953

Once upon a time in Yosemite's history—perhaps when the park had more funding and more available trail crews—the Smith Meadow Trail provided a tough but ultimately rewarding summit ascent of Smith Peak, one of the highest points in the immediate vicinity of Hetch Hetchy. Wildfires and years of neglect have turned a tough hike into an ordeal marred by downed trees and wretched overgrowth. However, the first 1.5 miles of the trail feature some of the most glorious wildflower displays anywhere in the park, beginning in April and peaking in late May. Views from a set of granite outcrops provide a nice scenic reward for wildflower hounds looking to enjoy vibrant colors and beautiful blooms.

GETTING THERE

From the Hetch Hetchy Entrance Station, drive north on Hetch Hetchy Road for 5.5 miles to the Smith Peak Trailhead on the right (east) side of the road. A few parking spots are available in front of the trailhead.

ON THE TRAIL

From the parking area, step onto the steep trail and follow it away from Hetch Hetchy Road. The trail's deteriorating condition becomes apparent immediately, as grasses and brush occasionally obscure the trail tread only a few hundred yards in. Cross a seasonal creek with a small but pretty waterfall and continue the steep climb through a forest of pine, cedar, live oak, and black oak. The deciduous black oak's leaves turn beautiful shades of yellow and gold during

October and early November, and thus this hike may also make for an enjoyable excursion during the fall season.

The principal highlight of the hike is springtime wildflowers, however, and those wildflowers blossom in a way that this author has not experienced anywhere else on the Yosemite trail system. Displays of miniature lupine, owl's clover, and Fort Miller clarkias carpet the grassy, exposed areas along the trail. Crimson heartleaf milkweed offers a standing invitation to migrating monarch butterflies, while harlequin lupines intermingle with owl's clover and spur lupines. Red columbines nod sleepily along intermittent streams.

This dazzling floral display offers plenty of excuses to stop and catch your breath on what is a steep and rugged climb. At 1 mile, shortly before a junction with a trail leading west toward the Hetch Hetchy Entrance Station, look for an outcrop on the right that offers a nice view across Poopenaut Valley and the west end of Hetch Hetchy Reservoir. You might feel tempted to turn back here, but push ahead a little farther after keeping left to remain on the Smith Meadow Trail at the aforementioned junction. The trail begins a flat traverse through a delightful, narrow meadow fed by a seasonal creek. Isolated ponderosa pines rise from grassy flats, juxtaposing nicely against the carpets of wildflowers that grace the meadows. At the 1.5-mile mark, scramble your way up to the bouldery ridge to your left to find some enjoyable views north across Poopenaut Valley. This is a nice place to rest and enjoy a snack before turning back toward the trailhead. The trail continues, but downed trees and overgrown shrubs make forward progress something of a nightmare.

Wildflowers abound on the Smith Meadow Trail.

EXTENDING YOUR TRIP

Determined hikers with good navigational skills can push ahead through the blowdowns and fire damage left behind by the 2013 Rim Fire for another 3.5 miles of steep climbing to Smith Meadow. From there, turn left onto a badly overgrown, difficult-to-follow path that climbs over 1000 feet in 1.5 miles to the summit of Smith Peak. Campsites can be found at Smith Meadow and at Smith Peak itself. The park may one day clean up the Smith Meadow Trail, so inquire ahead of your visit if you have ambitions to climb Smith Peak.

48 | Wapama Falls

RATING/ DIFFICULTY	ROUNDTRIP	ELEV GAIN/ HIGH POINT	SEASON
****/3	5.3 miles	600 feet/ 4170 feet	Year-Round

Maps: USGS 7.5-min Lake Eleanor, Hetch Hetch Reservoir, Tom Harrison Maps Hetch Hetchy; **Contact:** Hetch Hetchy Information Station; **Notes:** Restroom adjacent to trailhead. No food storage lockers at trailhead. Wapama Falls bridges may be impassable at high water; **GPS:** 37.9465, –119.7875

Hetch Hetchy's signature hike leads you across the O'Shaughnessy Dam and along the northern shore of Hetch Hetchy Reservoir to a spectacular waterfall that rivals the Yosemite Valley showstoppers. Gorgeous views of Hetch Hetchy Valley complement an appealing mixture of grassy flats, aromatic woodlands composed of bay laurel and live oak, and several sunny spots that are perfect for relaxing at the base of ephemeral waterfalls.

GETTING THERE
From the Hetch Hetchy Entrance Station, drive north on Hetch Hetchy Road for 7.1 miles to a split in the road. Keep right here to follow the one-lane road in a circle to the parking area just past the southern end of the O'Shaughnessy Dam for the Rancheria Falls Trailhead at 7.8 miles. Park your car and backtrack to the trailhead at the beginning of the walkway across the dam.

ON THE TRAIL
Begin your hike by walking across the O'Shaughnessy Dam, from which the first full glimpses into Hetch Hetchy Valley emerge. This controversial engineering feat transformed Hetch Hetchy into San Francisco's water supply, much to the consternation of conservationists spearheaded by John Muir, who fought a losing battle to preserve the valley against water interests. Controversy aside, the large body of water is beautiful in its own way, as are notable landmarks such as Kolana Rock on the south side of the valley and Hetch Hetchy Dome on the north side of the valley.

On the opposite side of the dam, follow the trail through a dimly lit tunnel before emerging onto a wide path shaded here and there by fragrant California bay laurels and stately canyon live oaks. The occasional ponderosa pine or incense cedar interrupts the broadleaf tree canopy, but the woods here have an open character that provides consistent views of the reservoir and surrounding landmarks from start to finish. The trail remains mostly flat for the first 0.8 mile until beginning a short climb that leads to a junction with the Laurel Lake Trail at 1.2 miles. Keep right here to follow the trail due east through an attractive mixture of oak woodland punctuated by pines alternating with grassy, granite shelves yielding fine views.

From the Laurel Lake junction, the trail undulates through occasional wooded sections where you will need to keep your eyes peeled for poison oak encroaching onto the path. At 1.9 miles, take a quick break to enjoy the pools below seasonal (and barely pronounceable) Tueeulala Falls. Please note that the park asks visitors not to enter the water, which drains into the reservoir. The good people of San Francisco do not want any extra additives in their drinking water, after all.

As you continue hiking east, you pass through an endlessly pleasing assortment of tiny meadows and leafy woodlands. At 2.4 miles, the rumble of Wapama Falls becomes evident just as the trail begins a sharp descent, concluding at the first of several footbridges that span the numerous forks where Wapama Falls splits before rushing into the reservoir. The footbridges give a startling up-close look at the falls, and you can expect a prodigious amount of mist early in the season. Each footbridge offers a slightly different look at the waterfall, but the trail may become impassable during peak snowmelt when the falls are so swollen that they overtake the bridge. Do not attempt to cross if water is splashing over the first bridge. For a moderate day hike, the bridges serve as the turnaround spot.

EXTENDING YOUR TRIP

The route to Wapama Falls doubles as a backcountry portal that reaches, among other destinations, Rancheria Falls, Tiltill Valley, and Lake Vernon. Hikers can reach Rancheria Falls by continuing beyond the bridges on an occasionally rough incline until they reach a backpacker's camp and spur trail leading to cascading Rancheria Falls. For a three-day backpacking trip,

The nearly flooded footbridges across Wapama Falls

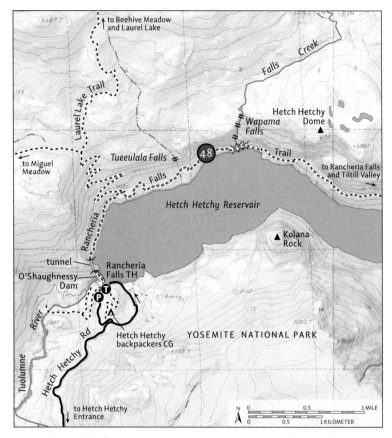

continue beyond the falls, then turn north at 6.4 miles toward Tiltill Valley (8.9 miles) and Lake Vernon (15.5 miles). Follow the trail to Laurel Lake westward, turning south at Beehive Meadow (18.6 miles). From there, it's an 8-mile descent back to the dam. The full loop spans 24.5 miles with 6000 feet of elevation gain.

Opposite: The translucent waters of Tenaya Lake (Hike 56)

white wolf to tenaya lake

At Crane Flat, State Route 120 splits away from Big Oak Flat Road, becoming the legendary Tioga Road, which traverses the park from Crane Flat to Tioga Pass. Tioga Pass is both the highest road-accessible mountain pass in the Sierra Nevada and the only road-accessible entry point on the east side of the park. The segment of Tioga Road stretching from White Wolf to Tenaya Lake features outstanding hiking routes that visit sparkling lakes, soaring peaks, and rounded domes blessed with some great views of Yosemite Valley.

Several hubs of activities and services dot Tioga Road, beginning with the tent cabins, campground, store, and café at White Wolf. Three small, seasonal, first-come, first-served campgrounds (White Wolf, Yosemite Creek, and Porcupine Flat) lie at intervals along Tioga Road. Another cluster of roadside

destinations can be found between Olmsted Point and Tenaya Lake, including the viewpoint at Olmsted Point and several picnic areas along Tenaya Lake, the latter of which boasts fine beaches on either end of the lake that are popular with families and sunbathers.

49 Harden Lake

RATING/ DIFFICULTY	ROUNDTRIP	ELEV GAIN/ HIGH POINT	SEASON
*/2	5.8 miles	400 feet/ 7843 feet	June–Oct

Maps: USGS 7.5-min Tamarack Flat, Hetch Hetchy Reservoir, Tom Harrison Maps Yosemite High Country; **Contact:** Tuolumne Meadows Visitor Center; **Notes:** Day-use only. Vault toilets near trailhead.

Morning reflections on Harden Lake

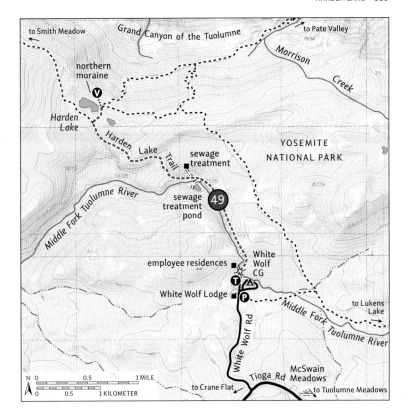

Food storage at trailhead; **GPS:** 37.8726, –119.6494

This mellow hike leads to a small lake perched atop the rim of the Grand Canyon of the Tuolumne. Unlike the typical Sierran lake that lies nestled into a sculpted glacial basin, seasonal Harden Lake occupies a grassy depression between two rocky moraines. Early season visitors may also experience colorful gardens of wildflowers along the gently descending trail to the lake.

GETTING THERE

From the Big Oak Flat Entrance Station, drive south on Big Oak Flat Road/State Route 120 for 7.7 miles to a junction with Tioga Road/SR 120 and turn left. Follow Tioga Road/SR 120 for 14.5 miles to a junction with White Wolf Road and turn left. Follow White Wolf Road for 1.1 miles to a parking area for hikers. The unmarked trailhead is due north from the parking area just before a bridge spanning the fledgling Middle Fork Tuolumne River.

ON THE TRAIL

From the parking area across from the White Wolf Lodge, follow the unpaved access road north past the campground and the employee residences. You may notice a signed trailhead near the parking area with trails leading to Lukens Lake and Harden Lake. However, the full roundtrip hike to Harden Lake from this trailhead is 11.4 miles, which is a bit too long for a hike that, while pleasant, isn't going to blow any minds. Follow the road, instead, which leads north to a sewage treatment pond about 1.2 miles ahead. Before you get too excited at the prospect of an intimate encounter with White Wolf's human waste, know that the treatment areas lie far off the main road. Instead, expect a pleasant downhill stroll through dense upper montane forest. The fledgling Middle Fork Tuolumne River, which you cross just beyond the employee residences, proves a pleasant companion along the way.

At 1.2 miles, keep right where an access road turns left toward a sewage treatment pond. In another 0.3 mile, keep right at a second junction where an ominous sign warns against drinking any water near the sewage treatment area. Shortly beyond the second junction, the road devolves into a single-track path; a recent Yosemite Conservancy project reverted the road back to wilderness, adding another 4 acres to Yosemite's sprawling backcountry.

The single-track trail leaves the river behind as it traverses a densely wooded slope. At 1.7 miles, another set of signs indicating 0.9 mile to Harden Lake signals both the final approach and the impending entry into the 2009 Harden Fire burn zone. Lush gardens of wildflowers proliferate around the charred corpses of lodgepole pines as

Mountain shooting stars grace the banks of Lukens Lake.

the trail concludes a final, flat traverse at a junction with a trail leading northwest to Smith Meadow at 2.8 miles. The Harden Fire and the 2013 Rim Fire caused considerable damage to the trail leading to Smith Meadow, and anybody considering extending their hike to Smith Peak will need expert navigation skills to find the way.

Continue northeast through the junction and walk up and over a low, rocky moraine. After crossing over the moraine, look to the left to find Harden Lake. This small, marshy body of water sits between the first moraine and a second moraine on the rim of the Grand Canyon of the Tuolumne. The lake's inconsistent inflow leaves it mostly dependent on snowmelt, and the water level can vary or even disappear altogether in dry years. If you visit on the early side of the summer season following a wet year, you may find the lake full to the brim with shimmering water—not so much during fall of a dry year.

For a peek into the Grand Canyon of the Tuolumne, continue beyond the lake, and head cross-country on the lake's northern moraine. Through gaps in the trees, you can enjoy a partial glimpse into the western reaches of the canyon before it reaches Hetch Hetchy Reservoir. Whether it's along the northern moraine or along the edge of the lake, find a pleasant spot to sit down and pass an hour or two before returning the way you came to White Wolf.

50 Lukens Lake

RATING/ DIFFICULTY	ROUNDTRIP	ELEV GAIN/ HIGH POINT	SEASON
**/1	2.6 miles	300 feet/ 8350 feet	June–Oct

Maps: USGS 7.5-min Yosemite Falls, Tom Harrison Maps Yosemite High Country; **Contact:** Tuolumne Meadows Visitor Center; **Notes:** Day-use only. Food storage lockers at trailhead; **GPS:** 37.8503, –119.6152

Although Lukens Lake cannot compete on a scenic level with Yosemite's high-alpine aquatic destinations, this easy-to-reach body of water boasts more than its share of sylvan charm. The easy

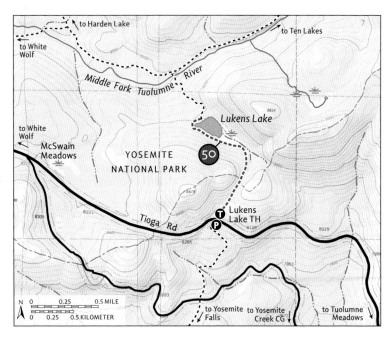

approach to the lake and its surrounding meadow make this route easy enough for hikers of all ages and skill levels.

GETTING THERE

From the Big Oak Flat Entrance Station, drive south on Big Oak Flat Road/State Route 120 for 7.7 miles to a junction with Tioga Road/SR 120, and turn left. Follow Tioga Road/SR 120 for 16.4 miles to the Lukens Lake Trailhead on the left (north) side of the road. The parking lot is on the right (south) side of the road just past the trailhead.

ON THE TRAIL

Step onto the signed trail and begin a gentle incline through dense upper montane forest dominated by red firs and lodgepole pines. The trail crests at 0.4 mile, at which point it begins an equally mellow descent along a bubbling creek toward a large meadow on Lukens Lake's eastern shore. Mountain shooting stars add vivid splashes of pink and purple to the meadow's lush, green expanse during early summer. Keep to the left upon reaching the meadow to avoid following an older trail that once passed directly through the meadow to the north side of the lake; this trail has been abandoned in order to allow meadow vegetation to recover. The new trail skirts the southern edge of the meadow and, starting at 0.75 mile, the southern shore of Lukens Lake.

Follow the new trail as it hugs the southern shore of the lake toward its outlet. The trail wraps around the outlet, crossing a small creek at 1.1 miles. The trail doubles back to the east to reach the northern shore of the lake at 1.3 miles, where a trail signed for White Wolf leads away to the west. This is a good place to find a shady spot to sit and enjoy the scenery. Dragonflies of multiple

colors flit about the lake's shore, and brilliant sunlight shimmers on the rippling surface of the water. Enjoy the views from this spot before retracing your steps back to the parking area.

51 Ten Lakes

RATING/ DIFFICULTY	ROUNDTRIP	ELEV GAIN/ HIGH POINT	SEASON
***/4	12.6 miles	2900 feet/ 9670 feet	June–Oct

Maps: USGS 7.5-min Yosemite Falls, Ten Lakes, Tom Harrison Maps Yosemite High Country; **Contact:** Yosemite National Park, Tuolumne Meadows Visitor Center; **Notes:** Suitable for backpacking (Ten Lakes). Food storage lockers at trailhead. Vault toilets across Tioga Road at the Yosemite Creek Trail parking area; **GPS:** 37.8522, –119.5761

This stunning route has a little something for everybody: a chain of lakes, incredible views of the Grand Canyon of the Tuolumne, vast meadows, wildflowers, dense upper montane forests, and miles of glaciated granite wonderlands. Although only backpackers can fully appreciate all that Ten Lakes has to offer, day hikers can enjoy the views and one or two of the lakes on a strenuous, full-day adventure.

GETTING THERE

From the Big Oak Flat Entrance Station, drive south on Big Oak Flat Road/State Route 120 for 7.7 miles to a junction with Tioga Road/ SR 120 and turn left. Follow Tioga Road/SR 120 for 19.7 miles to the Ten Lakes Trailhead on the left (north) side of the road. Parking is available at the Ten Lakes Trailhead, but if there's no space, park in the lot across

Views from Ten Lakes Pass take in the Sierra Crest crowned by Mount Conness.

the road that services the Yosemite Creek Trailhead.

ON THE TRAIL

From the signed trailhead just beyond the food storage lockers, hike northeast through dense forest on an initially flat grade. At 0.2 mile, keep right at a junction with the Yosemite Creek Trail. Climbing begins at 0.4 mile on a mellow grade that becomes steeper at 0.9 mile, where the trail begins ascending along the rocky slopes of Yosemite Creek's broad canyon. This section of trail meanders through numerous granite slabs bewhiskered with Jeffrey pines and Western junipers. The trail is occasionally rocky and tricky to follow, but the views across the granite wonderland and into a tributary canyon crowned by

Mount Hoffmann to the east showcase some great scenery as you progress.

The grade of the ascent eases at 1.6 miles as the trail returns to the forest. Continue straight through a junction with a trail leading west to White Wolf at 2.1 miles; a handful of good campsites lie just to the east of this junction. After passing through the junction and crossing an unnamed creek shortly afterward, the trail begins a moderate ascent through dense forest with another unnamed creek to navigate at 3.2 miles. Enjoy a short pause in the uphill work after crossing over a moraine at 3.8 miles; from here, the trail drops down to the edge of Half Moon Meadow. This vast, beautiful meadow, nourished by the headwaters of Yosemite Creek, unfurls within a granite amphitheater gouged out by ancient glaciers that originated from Ten Lakes Pass directly to the northeast. Just past the meadow (4.2 miles), look for a spur trail leading to another set of campsites in a small clearing shaded by red firs.

After passing the meadow, the toughest part of the climb begins, as the Ten Lakes Trail gains 700 feet of elevation over the next 0.6 mile. The initial ascent passes through forest that eventually yields to a beautiful, stream-nourished meadow at 4.5

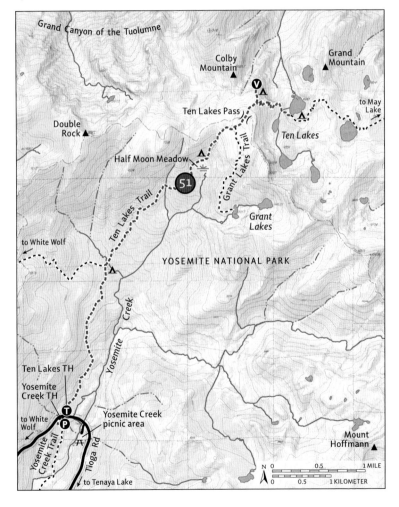

Grand Canyon of the Tuolumne

Colby Mountain

Grand Mountain

to May Lake

Ten Lakes Pass

Ten Lakes

Double Rock

Half Moon Meadow

51

Grant Lakes Trail

to White Wolf

Ten Lakes Trail

Grant Lakes

YOSEMITE NATIONAL PARK

Yosemite Creek

Ten Lakes TH

Yosemite Creek TH

to White Wolf

Yosemite Creek picnic area

Yosemite Creek Trail

Tioga Rd

Mount Hoffmann

to Tenaya Lake

N 0   0.5   1 MILE
0   0.5   1 KILOMETER

miles. The trail veers away from the meadow into an open forest of lodgepole pines before reaching a junction with a trail that travels southeast toward the Grant Lakes at 4.8 miles. The Grant Lakes lie 1.3 miles southeast from this spot. This optional side trip may be too much of an add-on for day hikers, but the lakes are a suitable side trip or a quiet camping destination for overnight hikes.

To continue to Ten Lakes Pass, continue straight through the junction for a last burst of climbing along a spacious, dry meadow that reveals glorious views north and northeast to Yosemite's wild high country, dominated by the vaguely pyramidal form of Mount Conness crowning the Sierra Crest. The trail crosses over Ten Lakes Pass at 5 miles, and from that point it begins its descent into the Ten Lakes basin. As the trail begins to descend, look for an informal trail that climbs along the east slope of a wooded knoll just north of the pass. This can't-miss side trip reveals a spectacular view into the depths of the Grand Canyon of the Tuolumne over 4000 feet below. Good but dry campsites can be found atop the knoll.

Day hikers are now faced with a decision. They can either continue downhill on a 700-foot descent over the next 0.9 mile to the largest of the Ten Lakes, or they can remain atop the knoll to enjoy the incredible views. This route is called "Ten Lakes" for a reason, and if you want to see the lakes, by all means, do so. However, be prepared for a grueling return ascent back up to the pass. The lakes themselves—at least the ones accessible from the trail—are quite nice, but the views are nothing compared to what you see at the pass. Furthermore, the most interesting lakes lie south and east from the largest lake by way of an informal

trail that adds a considerable amount of distance to the overall hike. For most day hikers, it will be more than enough to visit the first and the largest of the lakes before the trail begins climbing again on its way to May Lake. Some hikers may find it preferable to skip the lakes and hang out near Ten Lakes Pass for the great views. There is no right or wrong choice to make, as you spend your time either around a Sierran lake or surveying splendid alpine vistas. Win-win.

Whatever choice you make, the largest lake will be your turnaround point unless you are backpacking. If you camp overnight, or preferably for two nights, you will have abundant time to explore all Ten Lakes and the Grant Lakes.

EXTENDING YOUR TRIP

For a three-day, one-way backpacking trip, continue beyond the Ten Lakes along the South Fork of Cathedral Creek and then around the northern base of Tuolumne Peak. At 16.6 miles, turn right onto the trail leading to May Lake and the May Lake High Sierra Camp. The route ends after 20 miles at the May Lake Trailhead, where you would need to leave a second car. Note that there is a lot of climbing into and out of basins along this route, making the travel fairly strenuous.

52 North Dome

RATING/ DIFFICULTY	ROUNDTRIP	ELEV GAIN/ HIGH POINT	SEASON
***/4	9.5 miles	2200 feet/ 8371 feet	June–Oct

Maps: USGS 7.5-min Half Dome, Tom Harrison Maps Yosemite High Country; **Contact:** Tuolumne Meadows Visitor Center; **Notes:** Suitable for backpacking (Porcupine Creek).

Food storage at trailhead. Vault toilets at trailhead; **GPS:** 37.8067, –119.5462

Half Dome is an omnipresent and dominant landform from virtually every viewpoint along the rim of Yosemite Valley. But the absolutely best view of Half Dome is from North Dome, which lies directly across from Half Dome separated by the void of Tenaya Canyon. This full-day hike visits the summit of North Dome, from which you can survey Half Dome and many other Yosemite landmarks in their full glory. A side trip to a rare granite rock arch and a possible overnight stay at one of the park's most spectacular backcountry campsites round out this glorious adventure.

GETTING THERE

From the Big Oak Flat Entrance Station, drive south on Big Oak Flat Road/State Route 120 for 7.7 miles to a junction with Tioga Road/SR 120, and turn left. Follow Tioga Road/SR 120 eastbound for 24.9 miles to the Porcupine Creek Trailhead and parking on the right (south) side of the road.

ON THE TRAIL

Start by following the Porcupine Creek Trail downhill along an old roadbed into upper montane forest dominated by red fir. The route continues on the roadbed for 0.7 mile, at which point it reverts to single-track trail shortly after crossing Porcupine Creek. The trail continues in a south-southwest direction, crossing a tributary creek at 1.2 miles before reaching a junction with a connecting trail leading east to the Snow Creek Trail at 1.7 miles. Continue straight through this junction, then keep left at a second junction

with the Lehamite Creek Trail to follow the North Dome Trail south to North Dome.

The North Dome Trail begins a moderately steep climb up to Indian Ridge and a junction with a trail leading to Indian Rock at 2.8 miles. Take a left turn here to follow the spur as it leads north to the rock arch 0.3 mile uphill—a 0.6-mile roundtrip diversion. Arch formations are unusual in granite since it does not erode in the same way as sandstone, the more common rock type that forms rock arches. The 15-foot-tall arch—the only such formation in the park—also offers some nice teaser views of what you will see on the descent along Indian Ridge toward North Dome.

Return to the North Dome Trail and turn left to descend Indian Ridge, traveling southbound to North Dome. You will catch your first glimpses of Half Dome at 3.6 miles, but the full reveal does not come until 3.8 miles at a spur trail leading south to a set of campsites. These campsites have views of Half Dome and many of the high landmarks around Yosemite Valley, including Clouds Rest, the Clark Range, Sentinel Dome, and Glacier Point. If you take this as an overnight route, absolutely make plans to camp here, but be prepared to share the area with others. The campsites are hardly a secret, but the strict quota limits prevent overcrowding and overuse.

From the camping area, the trail makes a left turn back into the forest before course-correcting south to continue its descent along Indian Ridge. At 4.5 miles, the trail reaches the edge of a cliff with North Dome clearly in view. It will feel logical to keep going straight, but doing so would require a difficult and dangerous scramble

Opposite: *Half Dome, top-to-bottom, seen from North Dome*

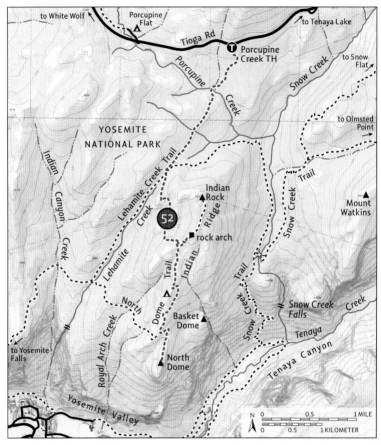

down the cliff. Instead, follow the trail as it peels away to the left to descend on a rough, dilapidated tread along the base of the cliff. The trail again turns to the south as it drops into a saddle separating North Dome from the main body of Indian Ridge. Continue due south up the spine of North Dome to reach the summit (5.1 miles), then continue a short distance beyond to find an appealing spot to sit and take in the views.

Even though you have had looks at Half Dome for the last mile, the eyeful from the dome takes the cake. From here, you can see the full height of Half Dome from Tenaya Canyon's floor to the summit. The views east up Tenaya Canyon, crowned by Clouds Rest, Basket Dome, and Mount Watkins, are equally impressive, as are the views west down Yosemite Valley toward El Capitan. There is no one "perfect spot" to see all of this, so you will have to move around the dome a bit to get a clean look at every highlight.

The hike back up involves a substantial amount of climbing from North Dome to the Indian Rock junction. Be sure to take your time on North Dome, not only to enjoy the views but also to shore up your energy for the uphill trek back to the trailhead. Note that you do not have to hike up to the rock arch again on the return trip, which saves you 0.6 mile on the return journey.

EXTENDING YOUR TRIP
Porcupine Creek is a fine trailhead for the North Rim Route, which traverses the northern rim of Yosemite Valley from North Dome to El Capitan. Leave a car parked at the Tamarack Flat Trailhead for the El Capitan Trail (see Hike 42), and take a second vehicle to Porcupine Creek Trailhead. Follow the route to North Dome (4.5 miles), and continue west toward Yosemite Point (8.3 miles) and Yosemite Falls (9.2 miles). Turn north on the Yosemite Creek Trail and then take a left turn on the trail to Eagle Peak (9.7 miles). After stopping to admire the views from Eagle Peak (11.9 miles), continue west toward Tamarack Flat, stopping at El Capitan (14.3 miles), and finish by hiking downhill to Tamarack Flat Campground. The entire route spans 22.6 miles, with 4800 feet of elevation gain, and 6600 feet of elevation loss.

53 May Lake

RATING/ DIFFICULTY	ROUNDTRIP	ELEV GAIN/ HIGH POINT	SEASON
***/2	3.5 miles	600 feet/ 9401 feet	June–Oct

Maps: USGS 7.5-min Tenaya Lake, Yosemite Falls, Tom Harrison Maps Yosemite High Country; **Contact:** Tuolumne Meadows Visitor Center; **Notes:** Suitable for backpacking (May Lake). Vault toilets at trailhead. Food storage at trailhead; **GPS:** 37.8326, –119.4910

Ease of access, the presence of a High Sierra Camp, and serene beauty make May Lake a popular destination for hikers of all abilities. This picturesque subalpine lake nestles into a basin at the foot of Mount Hoffmann, which sets a memorable backdrop. Those with a taste for vistas can continue a short distance past the camp for a stellar view toward the Cathedral Range, accentuated by the iconic form of Cathedral Peak.

GETTING THERE
From Yosemite's Arch Rock Entrance east of El Portal, head east for 4.6 miles to a junction with Big Oak Flat Road and turn left. Follow Big Oak Flat Road for 9.5 miles to a junction with State Route 120/Tioga Road, and drive east for 27 miles to May Lake Road. Turn left to follow May Lake Road north for 1.8 miles until it ends at a parking area for the May Lake Trailhead. The trailhead parking fills up quickly, and additional parking can be found along the road.

ON THE TRAIL
Start by locating the trailhead, which lies between the vault toilets and a small but pretty pond. The trail wraps around the pond before traveling north on a moderately ascending slope. After passing through a short section of shady forest, you spend much of the next mile climbing through rocky, open tree cover that yields partially obstructed views to the south and east. At 0.75 mile, those views improve somewhat

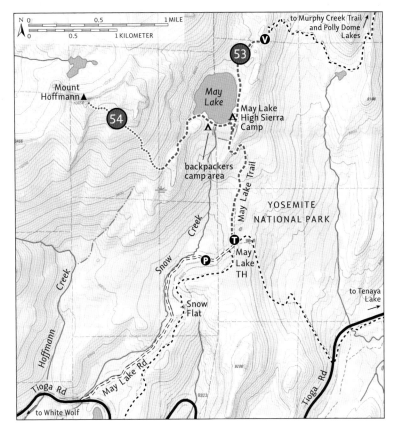

as the trail reaches a few spots with unobscured views south toward the Clark Range.

After dipping back into thick tree cover at 1 mile, the trail reaches a fork next to a set of hitching posts at 1.1 miles. Keep right here to follow the trail along the east shore of May Lake toward the High Sierra Camp. Side paths lead left to the lake, but the best views, which include Mount Hoffmann's granite massif, lie beyond the camps.

Continue hiking for 0.2 mile past the camp to a handful of spots close to the shore where you can plop down and enjoy sparkling waters capped by Mount Hoffmann's distinctive form.

You could stop here if inertia settles in, or you can proceed northbound for one final highlight. Hike north, passing the lake's north shore, and pass through a handful of meadows enlivened by early summer

Opposite: Mount Hoffman rises above the peaceful waters of May Lake.

wildflowers. Just beyond the meadows, the trail makes a short descent that ends at the rim of a spacious, unnamed valley at 1.75 miles from the trailhead. Climb up a low rise at the rim to enjoy a gorgeous view of the Cathedral Range, with Cathedral Peak providing the focal point. Scan the horizon from north to south to spot Mount Conness, Polly Dome, Mount Dana, Mount Gibbs, Medlicott Dome, Cathedral Peak, Sunrise Mountain, and Clouds Rest. This is a great spot to enjoy a leisurely lunch before the easy downhill hike back to the trailhead.

EXTENDING YOUR TRIP

For an extended overnight hike that spans some rugged high country, leave a car at the Ten Lakes Trailhead (see Hike 51) and park a second car at the May Lake Trailhead. Hike to and continue past May Lake and turn left on a connector with the Murphy Creek Trail toward Ten Lakes. Arrive at the Ten Lakes at 14.6 miles, and from there follow the Ten Lakes Trail back to the trailhead to retrieve your car. This route adds up to 20.4 miles, with 4200 feet of elevation gain and 5600 feet of elevation loss.

54 Mount Hoffmann

RATING/ DIFFICULTY	ROUNDTRIP	ELEV GAIN/ HIGH POINT	SEASON
****/4	6 miles	2000 feet/ 10,850 feet	June–Oct

Maps: USGS 7.5-min Tenaya Lake, Yosemite Falls, Tom Harrison Maps Yosemite High Country; **Contact:** Tuolumne Meadows Visitor Center; **Notes:** Suitable for backpacking (May Lake). Navigation required. Pit toilet at

trailhead. Food storage at trailhead; **GPS:** 37.8326, –119.4910

 Scraping the sky at 10,850 feet near the geographic center of Yosemite National Park, Mount Hoffmann offers some of the best views in the park, as well as a great introduction to cross-country mountain travel. This informal route is easy enough to follow provided you have some basic navigation skills and a good fitness level. Bring along a comprehensive map of the park to acquaint yourself with the pantheon of landmarks that grace the landscape in every direction.

GETTING THERE

From Yosemite's Arch Rock Entrance east of El Portal, head east for 4.6 miles to a junction with Big Oak Flat Road and turn left. Follow Big Oak Flat Road for 9.5 miles to a junction with State Route 120/Tioga Road and drive east for 27 miles to May Lake Road. Turn left to follow May Lake Road north for 1.8 miles to the May Lake Trailhead. The road ends in a parking lot, which can fill quickly. Parking along the road is an option.

ON THE TRAIL

The initial segment of this route follows the trail to May Lake (Hike 53) for the first 1.1 miles. At the 1.1-mile mark, keep left at a fork in the trail adjacent to a pair of hitching posts. Follow this informal trail as it bends to the west to skirt the south shore of May Lake. Backpackers are allowed to camp along this stretch of trail, so pitch your tent here if this is an overnight hike. If you booked a stay at the High Sierra Camp, find the camp by following the right fork

Opposite: *Mount Hoffman's summit block exhibits intriguing geologic formations.*

from the hitching posts along the lake's east shore.

At 1.4 miles, near the lake's southwest shore, the trail turns to the south to ascend a granite ledge. As you climb through a narrow, stream-fed meadow, be sure to turn around to admire the view northeast across May Lake toward Mount Conness. Once you reach the top of the ledge, views east toward the Cathedral Range and south toward the Clark Range emerge. After a brief, flat stretch on this ledge, the trail enters forest cover and begins a short descent. Look off to the left to see a meadow occupying a steep ravine, which is your cue that the ascent of Mount Hoffmann is about to begin.

At 2 miles, the trail turns to the northwest to begin a prolonged ascent on an informal path toward the summit. Fallen trees and diverging paths have confused the navigation at this point, necessitating close attention to find the spot where the trail turns northwest. It doesn't help that previous hikers have set up cairns (stacked rocks intended to serve as navigational markers) at each of these diverging trails; you might encounter some misdirection if you rely too much on the markers.

Once you find the correct path, follow it out of the forest cover and up a rocky slope through thickets of whitebark pines. The divergent path/unnecessary cairn problem persists for another 0.25 mile, but with some effort you can discern the proper route, which is more well-worn than the divergent paths. This path leads you steeply uphill, and with every step you take, the views across the south half of the park, including the upper elevations of Yosemite Valley, become more remarkable. Over the next 0.4 mile, the trail gains 700 feet, and the views will give

you plenty of excuses to stop and catch your breath.

At 2.4 miles, the grade eases somewhat as the trail passes one of Mount Hoffmann's false eastern summits. The trail continues an oblique ascent across the mountain's open, south face, aiming for a rock pile on the west end of the mountain crowned by an RF transmitter. Hike to the base of this rock pile for the final stretch—a mostly Class 2 scramble, with a bit of Class 3 mixed in for seasoning. Aim for the left (south) side of the summit block; the right side is exposed, and the scrambling starts impinging on Class 4 territory.

Once atop the summit block, turn north for a brief stroll along the ridge toward the RF antennae. The benchmark is located nearby, and the flat, spacious summit has room to spare for a long, leisurely lunch. If you brought a map, you'll be able to identify famous landmarks such as Mount Conness, Matterhorn Peak, Mount Dana, Cathedral Peak, Echo Peaks, Mount Lyell, Mount Clark, Clouds Rest, Half Dome, Glacier Point, North Dome, Eagle Peak, and even the top of El Capitan.

55 Mount Watkins

RATING/ DIFFICULTY	ROUNDTRIP	ELEV GAIN/ HIGH POINT	SEASON
***/3	9.2 miles	1800 feet/ 8500 feet	June–Oct

Maps: USGS 7.5-min Tenaya Lake, Yosemite Falls, Tom Harrison Maps Yosemite High Country; **Contact:** Tuolumne Meadows Visitor Center; **Notes:** Day-use only. No restroom or food storage at trailhead. Navigation required; **GPS:** 37.8107, –119.4854

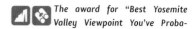 *The award for "Best Yosemite Valley Viewpoint You've Proba-*

bly Never Heard Of" goes to . . . (drumroll, please!), Mount Watkins! This rounded ridge of granite extrudes into the airy expanses of Tenaya Canyon, across which stand the imposing forms of Half Dome and Clouds Rest. The journey to reach Mount Watkins also satisfies the adventurous hiker with a mélange of habitats and geologic features that showcase the best of Yosemite's middle elevations.

GETTING THERE

Driving: From Yosemite's Arch Rock Entrance east of El Portal, head east for 4.6 miles to a junction with Big Oak Flat Road, and turn left. Follow Big Oak Flat Road for 9.5 miles to a junction with State Route 120/ Tioga Road, and drive east for 29.3 miles to the turnout parking area for Olmsted Point on the south side of Tioga Road.

Half Dome playing peek-a-boo from the summit of Mount Watkins

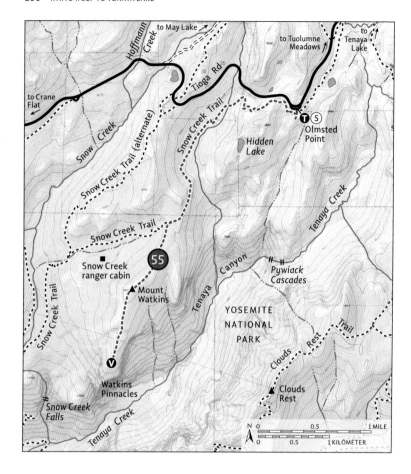

Transit: The Yosemite Valley–Tuolumne Meadows Hikers Bus travels from Yosemite Valley to the west end of Tuolumne Meadows. Exit at Olmsted Point.

ON THE TRAIL

This route begins at Olmsted Point, a popular roadside destination that teems with tourists. Most people content themselves with views of Half Dome and some casual exploration of fractured granite formations peppered with glacial erratics. Stop and enjoy these features, but know that the views here, famous though they are, pale in comparison to what you'll see on Mount Watkins.

To begin your adventure, find the stone staircase descending from the east end of the Olmsted Point parking area and drop into a wooded swale. To visit the true Olmsted Point, keep left at the junction 0.1 mile from the parking area, and continue up to the top of the point for some fine views. Backtrack to the same junction and turn left toward Yosemite Valley on the Snow Creek Trail. This initial section weaves, wends, winds, and bobs through a boulder garden choked with chaparral and isolated conifers before finally ejecting you onto an open, rocky trail paralleling Tioga Road at 0.5 mile.

From here, make a short climb up and over a ridge, which the trail briefly traverses toward a small pond at 0.9 mile. Beyond the pond, the trail begins a sharp, switchbacking descent into a densely wooded valley nurtured by a handful of Snow Creek tributaries. The open forest that has dominated the first 1.3 miles of the route gives way to a lush forest of lodgepole, red fir, and mountain hemlock where the cool shade caresses your skin and provides a welcome reprieve on a warm day. The descent finally ceases at 1.8 miles. Enjoy a section of flat walking through sheltering forest until the climbing resumes—which it will do all too soon.

A significant amount of uphill work—about 750 feet worth—awaits over the next 2.2 miles to the summit of Mount Watkins. The trail leaves the shelter of dense forest, which reveals imposing views of Clouds Rest's pyramidal form looming high above the deep crease of Tenaya Canyon. The views improve as you climb obliquely along Mount Watkins's ridge, expanding to include Tenaya Lake, Tenaya Peak, and beyond to Medlicott Dome and Mount Conness. At 2.9 miles, the trail bends to the west and levels out as it reaches the crest of the Mount Watkins ridge. Keep a sharp lookout for an unmarked, informal trail at 3 miles

that heads south toward the summit of Mount Watkins.

This informal trail continues south through open forest with sandy, granite surfaces toward the summit of Mount Watkins, which is this route's high point. You'll reach the summit at 3.7 miles, but aside from a partial view of Half Dome and Clouds Rest, the views here are unremarkable. The real scenery occurs at the end of the Mount Watkins ridge just above the nearly sheer cliff that rises straight up from Tenaya Canyon. It's another 0.8 mile of mostly downhill walking along the gradually narrowing ridge until you reach a point where it becomes blindingly obvious that you can go no farther without sprouting a set of wings.

Here at the end of the ridge, you can perch upon one of the granite boulders and soak in a spectacular vista dominated by Half Dome and Clouds Rest. The view extends west across Yosemite Valley toward El Capitan. You'll also be able to spot Glacier Point, North Dome, Basket Dome, Mirror Lake (when there's water), Mount Starr King, Sentinel Rock, Sentinel Dome, and parts of the Clark Range. Save plenty of time for this viewpoint, then retrace your steps back to Olmsted Point to wrap up the hike.

56 Tenaya Lake

RATING/ DIFFICULTY	ROUNDTRIP	ELEV GAIN/ HIGH POINT	SEASON
****/2	3.3 miles	250 feet/ 8186 feet	June–Oct

Maps: USGS 7.5-min Tenaya Lake, Tom Harrison Maps Yosemite High Country; **Contact:** Tuolumne Meadows Visitor Center; **Notes:** Day-use only. Vault toilets at trailheads. Food storage at both trailheads;

GPS: 37.8256, -119.4701 (West Trailhead), 37.8376, –119.4518 (East Trailhead)

One of Yosemite's most beautiful and celebrated high country features, Tenaya Lake sparkles within a stunning granite amphitheater. Because it is the only road-accessible subalpine lake in the park, Tenaya Lake gets a lot of attention from tourists, sunbathers, and beachgoers (yes, there's a beach), but many of those visitors ignore a scenic, gentle hiking trail on the lake's south shore. Follow this mellow there-and-back route to get a good look at the lake and the surrounding formations from an ever-evolving perspective.

GETTING THERE

Driving: From Yosemite's Arch Rock Entrance east of El Portal, head east for 4.6 miles to a junction with Big Oak Flat Road and turn left. Follow Big Oak Flat Road for 9.5 miles to a junction with State Route 120/ Tioga Road, then drive east for 30.7 miles to the parking lot at the Tenaya Lake/Clouds Rest Trailhead on the south side of the road. This busy trailhead services three separate routes (Clouds Rest, Sunrise Lakes, and Tenaya Lake), so expect to see a lot of traffic here. An early or late start will help you avoid the worst of the midday crowds. Alternatively, you can park in the quieter parking lot at the east end of the lake to hike this route in reverse.

    Transit: The Tuolumne Meadows Shuttle Bus departs from the Tuolumne Meadows Lodge and stops at both the east trailhead for Tenaya Lake and the Sunrise Lakes Trailhead on the west side of the lake. The Yosemite Valley–Tuolumne Meadows Hikers Bus travels from Yosemite Valley to the Sunrise Lakes Trailhead.

Tenaya Lake acts as a mirror for Mount Hoffman on a calm fall day

ON THE TRAIL

From the west trailhead, head due east on the well-beaten path and remain straight at a junction marking the Tenaya Lake Overlook. Skip the overlook; the trail to the overlook quickly becomes hard to follow, and the views at the lake are better. After crossing or rock-hopping over Tenaya Creek, which can cover the trail early in the season, keep left at a junction with a connector trail leading south to the Clouds Rest Trail at 0.1 mile. After the turn, the trail leads to the west shore, where you can enjoy famous views across the lake toward Polly, Pywiack, and Medlicott Domes. At 0.3 mile, take another left turn at a second junction with the Clouds Rest Trail to follow the Tenaya Lake Trail northeast toward the east shore.

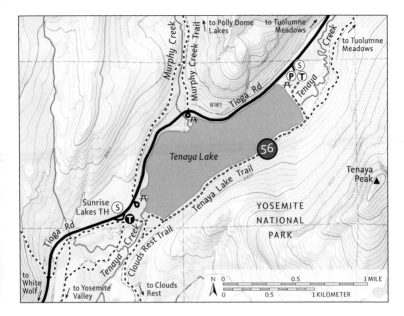

For the next mile, the trail passes through a dense forest of lodgepole, red fir, and mountain hemlock. Wherever the forest thins enough to allow views across the lake, keep an eye out for landmarks like Polly Dome, Mount Hoffmann, Tuolumne Peak, and then later Olmsted Point and Tenaya Peak. On mornings where little to no breeze blows, the lake holds reflections of the surrounding granite domes and peaks, creating perfect mirror images.

At 1.3 miles, the trail reaches the east shore, which harbors the nicest beach anywhere in Yosemite. If Tenaya Creek's flow is too heavy at the lake's inlet, turn around here to avoid the difficult crossing. If the creek is fordable, continue north along the beach until you find a spot you like. At that point, you can plop down and enjoy a bit of beach time—a rare experience in the Sierra.

The beach makes a fitting turnaround spot. The trail does continue through the forest along a boardwalk with a few interpretive panels, but most people don't need to follow this section unless they are hiking this route in reverse from the east trailhead.

57 Sunrise Lakes

RATING/ DIFFICULTY	ROUNDTRIP	ELEV GAIN/ HIGH POINT	SEASON
**/3	6.5 miles	1600 feet/ 9437 feet	June– Oct

Maps: USGS 7.5-min Tenaya Lake, Tom Harrison Maps Yosemite High Country; **Contact:** Tuolumne Meadows Visitor Center; **Notes:** Suitable for backpacking (Sunrise Lakes). Vault toilets at trailhead. Food storage at trailhead; **GPS:** 37.8257, –119.4701

The first of the Sunrise Lakes reflecting Sunrise Mountain

Sandwiched between the glorious views at Clouds Rest and the family-friendly pleasures of Tenaya Lake, a day hike to the Sunrise Lakes often gets overlooked. While most day hikers head elsewhere, the route does receive a fair amount of traffic from backpackers and High Sierra Camp hikers. Whichever way you choose to tackle this route, the three lakes at the heart of the route will reward you with sylvan peace pervading an afternoon bathed in Sierra sunlight.

GETTING THERE

Driving: From Yosemite's Arch Rock Entrance east of El Portal, head east for 4.6 miles to a junction with Big Oak Flat Road and turn left. Follow Big Oak Flat Road for 9.5 miles to a junction with State Route 120/ Tioga Road and drive east for 30.7 miles to the parking lot at Sunrise Lakes Trailhead on the south side of the road.

Transit: The Tuolumne Meadows Shuttle Bus departs from the Tuolumne Meadows Lodge and stops at the Sunrise Lakes Trailhead on the west side of the lake. The Yosemite Valley–Tuolumne Meadows Hikers Bus travels from Yosemite Valley to the Sunrise Lakes Trailhead.

ON THE TRAIL

From the Sunrise Lakes Trailhead, head east on the wide trail, then continue straight through a junction signed for the Tenaya Lake Overlook. At 0.1 mile, continue across Tenaya Creek (overflowing in spring, nonexistent in fall), and make an immediate right turn onto a connector trail leading to the Clouds Rest Trail. Turn right onto the Clouds Rest Trail at 0.2 mile, leaving Tenaya Lake behind you.

For the next 0.3 mile, follow a gently undulating passage along Tenaya Creek through mixed coniferous forest featuring lodgepole, mountain hemlock, and Western white pine. The trail turns southeast at 0.5 mile, crossing over granite outcrops before darting back into the forest. The mellow passage through cool forest comes to a jarring end at 1.4 miles when the trail begins a prolonged, grueling climb to the rim of upper Tenaya Canyon. As the trail switchbacks up the canyon slope, it picks up 1000 feet of elevation in the span of 0.9 mile, leaving you huffing, puffing, and possibly uttering the occasional expletive.

The tough climb mercifully ends at 2.3 miles where the Clouds Rest Trail and Sunrise Lakes Trails diverge. Turn left onto the Sunrise Lakes Trail and begin a gentle eastbound traverse along an open, sunny ridge from which Sunrise Mountain's forested heights are easily discernible. The

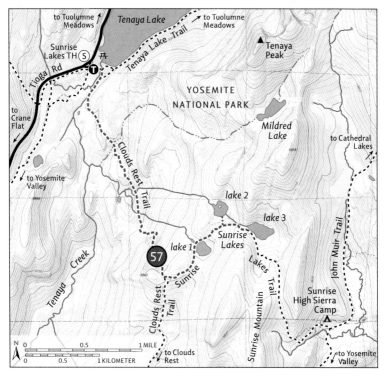

mountain's sheer slopes and forested crown set the distinctive backdrop for each of the lakes, which lie ahead.

At 2.6 miles, the trail dips into the first lake's basin, passing a handful of good campsites at 2.7 miles. After crossing the first lake's outlet, the trail resumes climbing toward the second and third lakes. You won't find a formal trail leading to the second lake, so you'll have to cut cross-country due north for 0.2 mile from the 3-mile mark to reach it. The second lake is the smallest of the three, but it also receives the least amount of traffic. If you take this diversion, return to the main trail after enjoying lake 2, and continue east to the third and largest lake. You can find nice views across the lake at 3.25 miles where the trail approaches the lake's outlet.

For a day hike, the third lake's outlet is a good turnaround spot since the only destination beyond the third lake is the Sunrise High Sierra Camp, which is only worth the extra effort if you're staying at the tent cabins there. If you are staying or camping at the high camp, continue hiking 1.6 miles southeast from the third lake to the other side of the north ridge of Sunrise Mountain.

58 Clouds Rest

RATING/ DIFFICULTY	ROUNDTRIP	ELEV GAIN/ HIGH POINT	SEASON
*****/4	11.6 miles	2800 feet/ 9926 feet	July–Oct

Maps: USGS 7.5-min Tenaya Lake, Tom Harrison Maps Yosemite High Country; **Contact:** Tuolumne Meadows Visitor Center; **Notes:** Suitable for backpacking (Sunrise Lakes). Pit toilet at trailhead. Food storage at trailhead; **GPS:** 37.8257, –119.4700

 Are you craving incredible scenery from a granite high point seasoned with a dash of vertiginous heights and precipitous drop-offs? Are you also reluctant to navigate the Half Dome permit system or the long lines on the cables? If so, this outstanding full-day hike to the fin-shaped summit ridge of Clouds Rest is what you need. A short visit to Tenaya Lake and miles of beautiful forest walking round out this memorable odyssey.

GETTING THERE

Driving: From Yosemite's Arch Rock Entrance east of El Portal, drive east for 4.6 miles to a junction with Big Oak Flat Road then turn left. Follow Big Oak Flat Road for 9.5 miles to a junction with State Route 120/Tioga Road. Turn right and continue east for 30.7 miles to the parking lot at the Sunrise Lakes Trailhead on the south side of the road.

Transit: The Tuolumne Meadows Shuttle Bus departs from the Tuolumne Meadows Lodge and stops at the Sunrise Lakes Trailhead on the west side of the lake. The Yosemite Valley–Tuolumne Meadows Hikers Bus travels from Yosemite Valley to the Sunrise Lakes Trailhead.

ON THE TRAIL

Follow the combined Sunrise Lakes, Tenaya Lake, and Clouds Rest Trailhead southeast from the parking area for 0.1 mile to the western shore of Tenaya Lake. Take some time to enjoy the views across the water toward Pywiack Dome. Cross Tenaya Creek, which may be a challenging ford early in the season, then turn right onto a connector trail that leads to the Clouds Rest Trail on the opposite side of the creek. Turn right upon reaching the Clouds Rest Trail.

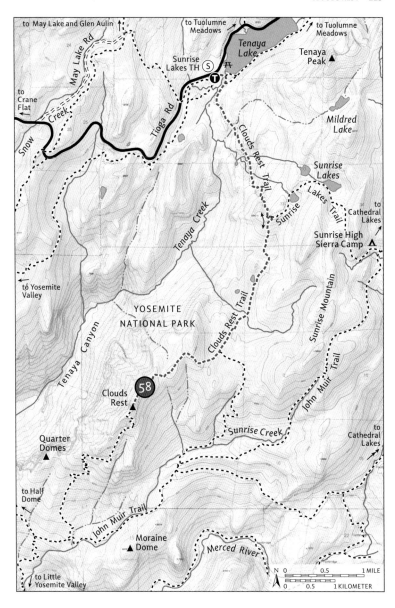

to May Lake and Glen Aulin

to Tuolumne Meadows

to Tuolumne Meadows

Tenaya Lake

Tenaya Peak ▲

Sunrise Lakes TH Ⓢ ⊼

🅣

May Lake Rd

to Crane Flat

Snow Creek

Tioga Rd

Mildred Lake

Clouds Rest Trail

Sunrise Lakes

Sunrise Lakes Trail

to Cathedral Lakes

Sunrise

Sunrise High Sierra Camp ⛺

Tenaya Creek

to Yosemite Valley

Tenaya Canyon

YOSEMITE NATIONAL PARK

Clouds Rest Trail

Sunrise Mountain

John Muir Trail

58

Clouds Rest ▲

Quarter Domes ▲

Sunrise Creek

to Cathedral Lakes

to Half Dome

John Muir Trail

Moraine Dome ▲

Merced River

to Little Yosemite Valley

N 0   0.5   1 MILE
0   0.5   1 KILOMETER

There are few views in Yosemite as impressive as those from the top of Clouds Rest.

The Clouds Rest Trail turns south for a gentle ascent through cool, shady forest above the south banks of Tenaya Creek. Easy walking ends at 1.4 miles as the trail gets a significant amount of climbing out of the way with a grueling 1000-foot climb to a junction with the Sunrise Lakes Trail at 2.3 miles. Make a right turn at the junction with the Sunrise Lakes Trail to remain on the Clouds Rest Trail, which now begins descending to lose a disheartening 400 feet of elevation that you will have to regain on the return trip.

After the trail bottoms out, commence a delightful stretch of mostly flat hiking through mixed-conifer forest composed of Western white pine, red fir, lodgepole pine, and mountain hemlock. A small lake at 3.2 miles presents an appealing opportunity to stop and rest, provided the mosquitos are not lining up for the blood buffet. Climbing resumes, albeit gently, at 3.7 miles as the trail leads to the lip of Tenaya Canyon; keep right at a junction at 4.2 miles with a trail leading south to the John Muir Trail. Upon reaching a delightful scenic reveal on the lip of the canyon at 4.8 miles, look across the canyon through gaps in the forest for an impressive view of Yosemite's high country dominated by Mount Hoffmann to the north of your position.

From the lip of the canyon, the trail ascends through sparse forest until the tree cover ends abruptly at 5.4 miles. The tree line signals the beginning of the final approach to Clouds Rest, which follows the narrow summit fin. A jaw-dropping escarpment into glacier-carved Tenaya Canyon on the right and a slightly less precipitous drop-off to Sunrise Creek on the left may send waves of anxiety through those with a fear of heights. However, the width of the fin and the easily negotiated granite slab terrain make the final climb easier than it appears at first.

After carefully working over granite slabs, find yourself standing nearly 6000 feet above Yosemite Valley. Half Dome, which protrudes from the southern rim of Tenaya Canyon 3 miles to the southwest, looks almost quaint from this high vantage point. Your eyes can follow the length of Yosemite Valley as it stretches west toward El Portal. Consider bringing a good regional map along with you to help you pick out other notable high points, including Mount Hoffmann, Tenaya Peak, Tuolumne Peak, Mount Dana, Mount Conness, Mount Gibbs, Mount Starr King, Vogelsang Peak, and the Clark Range.

EXTENDING YOUR TRIP

Not epic enough for you? Secure yourself a Half Dome permit and arrange a shuttle so that you can hike up to Clouds Rest and then descend to the Half Dome Trail. Ascend Half Dome, and then follow the Half Dome route (Hike 29) downhill toward Happy Isles. You'll

probably need to camp unless you're a real speed demon with knees of steel. Several flat areas below Clouds Rest and the camping area at Little Yosemite Valley are good options for tent pitching—just be aware that camping is not allowed on the summit.

59 Polly Dome Lakes

RATING/ DIFFICULTY	ROUNDTRIP	ELEV GAIN/ HIGH POINT	SEASON
**/2	5.8 miles	700 feet/ 8714 feet	June–Oct

Maps: USGS 7.5-min Tenaya Lake; Tom Harrison Maps Yosemite High Country; **Contact:** Tuolumne Meadows Visitor Center; **Notes:** Suitable for backpacking (Murphy Creek). Food storage and vault toilets adjacent to trailhead. Navigation required; **GPS:** 37.8342, –119.4631

A secluded set of lakes pairs well with fascinating geologic features on this moderate foray into the wildlands north of Tenaya Lake. Along with the lakes, hikers will find a generous amount of peace and quiet thanks to this route's off-the-beaten-path nature.

GETTING THERE

From Yosemite's Arch Rock Entrance east of El Portal, drive east for 4.6 miles to a junction with Big Oak Flat Road then turn left. Continue north on Big Oak Flat Road for 9.5 miles to a junction with State Route 120/ Tioga Road. Turn right, then drive east for 31.4 miles to the Murphy Creek Trailhead. Park either at the turnout just in front of the trailhead on the north side of Tioga Road or in the picnic area on the south side of the road.

Quiet waters and solitude at Polly Dome Lake

ON THE TRAIL

The Murphy Creek Trail quickly abandons the hustle and bustle surrounding Tenaya Lake as it proceeds north on a moderate incline through dense forest shading the eastern banks of rumbling Murphy Creek. A mellow, relatively uneventful walk along the creek follows for the next 0.9 mile until the trail emerges into a spacious valley polished to a high sheen by past glacial activity. Geology nerds will find plenty of inspiration and fascination, including glacial polish and copious glacial erratics—boulders carried by glaciers that were left behind when the glaciers melted.

For the next 0.5 mile, the trail progresses north through this valley before returning to the forest. At 1.75 miles, the trail crosses

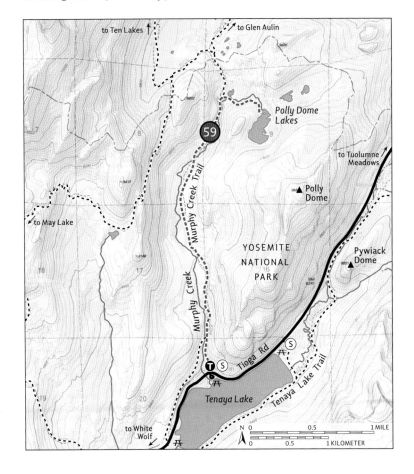

Murphy Creek (a possible ford early in the season) before resuming a second round of climbing through more dense forest. At 2.3 miles, keep a careful lookout for a meadow on your right (east) side. Continue past the meadow to find an informal trail that may or may not be marked by cairns.

Turn right onto this trail and head east on a vague, meandering path that ultimately leads to the largest of the Polly Dome Lakes. Abundant water within the Polly Dome Lakes basin nurtures mosquito swarms, which can be a nightmare during July and August. The trail crosses the outlet of a small, grassy lake before beginning a rough, occasionally hard-to-follow climb over a moraine ridge bounding the largest Polly Dome Lake. After cresting this ridge, a brief descent brings you to the banks of the lake. The lake itself is not large or particularly remarkable, at least by Tenaya Lake standards. However, the dense forest and rounded form of Polly Dome bless the lake with its own unique, intimate charm. Polly Dome Lake is a fine place to spend a quiet hour contemplating the numerous boulders punctuating the lake's surface or a whisper of wind rustling the pine trees above you.

60 Medlicott Dome

RATING/ DIFFICULTY	ROUNDTRIP	ELEV GAIN/ HIGH POINT	SEASON
**/3	4.4 miles	1200 feet/ 9638 feet	June–Oct

Maps: USGS 7.5-min Tenaya Lake, Tom Harrison Yosemite High Country; **Contact:** Tuolumne Meadows Visitor Center; **Notes:** Day-use only. No restrooms or food storage at trailhead; **GPS:** 37.8608, –119.4348

This unusual hike takes a wilder approach to lower Cathedral Lake by way of a climbers route accessing the west wall of Medlicott Dome. While technical climbing at Medlicott Dome lies outside the domain of day hikers, you can still reach the top of the dome by way of a fun and easy cross-country ramble that takes you past a small, sheltered lake before revealing some memorable views west across Tenaya Lake.

GETTING THERE

From Yosemite's Arch Rock Entrance east of El Portal, drive east for 4.6 miles to a junction with Big Oak Flat Road, then turn left. Follow Big Oak Flat Road north for 9.5 miles to a junction with State Route 120/Tioga Road. Turn right onto 120/Tioga Road to drive east for 34 miles to an unmarked parking area on the south side of Tioga Road. The unmarked climbers route begins from the south side of the parking area.

ON THE TRAIL

Head southeast from the parking area through a lush forest nurtured by Tenaya Creek (a possible ford early in the season). Once across the creek, the rough, sometimes hard-to-follow climbers trail begins a steep, no-nonsense climb, gaining 500 feet in the space of 0.4 mile. The trail reaches the base of Medlicott Dome at 0.6 mile, at which point it turns south along the base of the dome. A short distance ahead (at 0.7 mile), look for a granite outcrop on your right. You can walk out onto the outcrop for a teaser glimpse of Tenaya Lake and the surrounding landmarks, including Tenaya Peak, Polly Dome, and Olmsted Point.

After crossing an intermittent stream flowing down a granite slab at 0.8 mile, climbing resumes as the trail cuts straight up the slab. After finding the continuation of the trail, keep following along until you crest a wooded flat. Look to the left to note a slanting ramp of granite that leads north toward Medlicott Dome. You will follow that slab eventually, but for the time being, continue south until you reach a junction with a fisherman's trail tracing the banks of lower Cathedral Lake at 1.2 mile. While you're here, you might as well stop and enjoy the lake; usually a much longer approach on the dusty John Muir Trail is required for you to have this relaxing opportunity.

After enjoying Cathedral Lake, continue east a short distance along the lakeshore and then turn north to follow a sloping granite slab as it swells toward Medlicott Dome. Stay on the western side of this slab to avoid going off course. At 1.8 miles, keep to the left to avoid climbing a ridge that leads to a dome-like formation that can cause some confusion—this "false dome" is not the true Medlicott Dome, although the views from the top aren't bad. The true Medlicott Dome is the granite shelf due west from the misleading formation directly ahead. Keep this deceiving fact in mind since following the

Medlicott Dome offers some great views across Tenaya Lake.

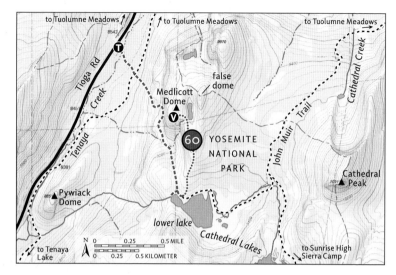

promising-looking ridgeline due north will lead you astray.

Instead, turn to the northwest to head toward a depression that contains a beautiful little lake nestled into the surrounding granite. Cross the lake's outlet and continue due west toward the edge of Medlicott Dome. From here, a fantastic view unfurls toward some of central Yosemite's high-country highlights: Tenaya Lake, Tenaya Peak, Tresidder Peak, Clouds Rest, Olmsted Point, Mount Hoffmann, Tuolumne Peak, and Polly Dome. You can even spot Half Dome in the distance beyond Olmsted Point. This destination makes a great picnic spot, and if you hang around long enough, you might spot a peregrine falcon drifting on the breeze as it watches for prey below.

Opposite: *The Tuolumne River and the Cathedral Range*

tuolumne meadows

Second only to Yosemite Valley in fame and scenic grandeur, the high country surrounding Tuolumne Meadows, the largest subalpine meadow in the Sierra, showcases some of the best hiking in Yosemite National Park. Backcountry portals throughout Tuolumne Meadows provide access to shimmering alpine lake basins, towering peaks, popular backpacking destinations, tumbling waterfalls, and the legendary High Sierra Camps. Many remarkable hiking destinations with famous names mix with remote, lesser known trips, guaranteeing a range of memorable experiences.

Tuolumne Meadows features a wealth of visitor services, including the Tuolumne Meadows Visitor Center for general information and interpretive programs, the Tuolumne Meadows Wilderness Center for permits, sprawling Tuolumne Meadows Campground, the Tuolumne Meadows Lodge, a restaurant, and a store. Half a dozen trailheads lead to the Yosemite backcountry.

61 Pothole Dome

RATING/ DIFFICULTY	ROUNDTRIP	ELEV GAIN/ HIGH POINT	SEASON
***/2	1.2 miles	225 feet/ 8783 feet	June–Oct

Maps: USGS 7.5-min Falls Ridge, Tom Harrison Maps Tuolumne Meadows; **Contact:** Tuolumne Meadows Visitor Center; **Notes:** Day-use only. Navigation required; **GPS:** 37.8770, –119.3947

Pick an evening to summit Pothole Dome for excellent views across Tuolumne Meadows.

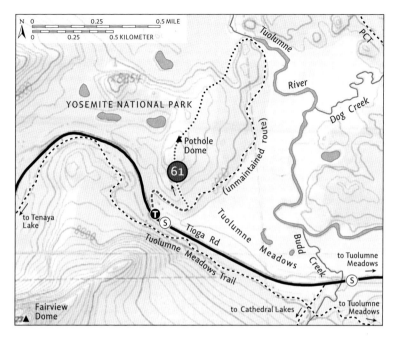

This short, free-form exploration of a gently swelling
granite dome on the western edge of Tuolumne
Meadows delivers spectacular views across
the Yosemite high country. Although most
cross-country adventures are too complex and
challenging for inexperienced and younger
hikers, Pothole Dome is a great place to get
your feet wet with off-trail exploration. Late
evening and early morning golden hour light
draw out the color and character of the surrounding scenery.

GETTING THERE

From Lee Vining at the junction of State
Route 120 (Tioga Road) and US Highway 395,
drive west for 21.4 miles, passing through
the Tioga Pass Entrance, to a parking area on
the right shoulder of the road. The trailhead
is adjacent to the parking area.

ON THE TRAIL

Locate the beginning of the trail and follow the narrow path as it wraps around
the extreme western edge of Tuolumne
Meadows. Be sure to remain on the path
and avoid cutting across the meadow;
recent work has restored the meadow to a
healthy state but walking across the sensitive habitat quickly causes new damage.
Loop around the meadow for 0.3 mile until
you reach the base of the dome. Turn north,
stepping onto bare granite, to follow the
slope straight to the top. Look for a prominent crack in the granite that leads almost
all the way to the top. Stick to this crack

nearly all the way as you gain 225 feet over the next 0.3 mile.

Upon reaching the top and catching your breath, scan the 360-degree view, which encompasses the twin red peaks dominating the Tioga Pass area, Mount Dana and Mount Gibbs. Clearly visible on the Sierra Crest are White Mountain, Mount Conness, and North Peak to the east. Closer afoot, Cathedral Peak, Unicorn Peak, the Echo Peaks, and the Cockscomb are the standouts in the Cathedral Range to the southeast and south. Look west to find Fairview Dome, Polly Dome, and Mount Hoffmann rising from a complex system of granite ridges blanketed in forest. Looking north, see if you can pick out Matterhorn Peak and the distinctive form of the Finger Peaks rising out of the park's remote northern backcountry.

In addition to admiring the views, you can poke around the top of the dome to your heart's content. A continuation of the opening stretch of trail wraps around the eastern and northern base of the dome, so if you head east or north, you will be able to pick up that trail to return back to the trailhead by looping around the east base of the dome. But if you prefer an easier out-and-back, follow the crack down to the trail and retrace your steps to your car.

62 Cathedral Lakes

RATING/ DIFFICULTY	ROUNDTRIP	ELEV GAIN/ HIGH POINT	SEASON
***/3	9.4 miles	1600 feet/ 9610 feet	July–Oct

Maps: USGS 7.5-min Tenaya Lake, Tom Harrison Maps Tuolumne Meadows; **Contact:** Tuolumne Meadows Visitor Center; **Notes:** Suitable for backpacking (Cathedral Lakes).

Portable toilets and food storage at trailhead; **GPS:** 37.8733, –119.3827

This lake basin shelters a pair of subalpine lakes in the shadow of one of Yosemite's iconic formations, Cathedral Peak. By taking a trip on the Sierra Superhighway (better known as the John Muir Trail), you can reach both Cathedral Lakes to revel in their subalpine splendor either as a day hike or an overnight camping trip. Lovely meadows and seasonal wildflowers round off one of the more popular hiking experiences in the Tuolumne Meadows region.

GETTING THERE

From Lee Vining at the junction of State Route 120 (Tioga Road) and US Highway 395, drive west for 20.7 miles, passing through the Tioga Pass Entrance, to the Cathedral Lakes Trailhead, which is on the south side of the road. Park on the shoulder of either side of the road.

ON THE TRAIL

From the Cathedral Lakes Trailhead, follow a short connector trail south to a junction with the John Muir Trail (JMT). Continue straight to remain on the westbound segment of the JMT, and quickly begin a stiff 500-foot climb through densely wooded forest on the JMT's wide, dusty, and heavily used tread. After 0.8 mile, the climb levels out for an extended flat section that meanders through a rich forest of lodgepole pine, mountain hemlock, red fir, and Western white pine. At 1.25 miles, the forest canopy opens so that you can get a nice look at the northern buttress of the Cathedral Peak massif.

Flat hiking comes to an end at the banks of Cathedral Creek; carefully hop over the creek to find the extension of the trail.

Climbing resumes under dense forest cover toward a curious bubbling spring on the trailside at 1.9 miles. The grade of the climb eases shortly thereafter before cresting an almost imperceptible saddle at 2.5 miles. The trail then begins a mellow descent to a junction with a spur trail to the lower Cathedral Lake at 3 miles. Turn right on this spur trail.

The Cathedral Lake spur continues downhill along a creek draining upper Cathedral Lake to the south. At 3.2 miles, the trail emerges from the forest cover at the edge of a sprawling meadow that unfurls toward the eastern bank of lower Cathedral Lake. At 3.4

miles, the trail splinters with a shorter spur reaching the lake's eastern bank, which is hemmed in by a granite ledge. If you keep to the main trail, it devolves into a fisherman's trail that traces the lake's northern shore. Several open spots on the western side of the lake afford memorable views of the lake with Cathedral Peak beyond.

To reach the upper lake, follow the spur trail back to the JMT and turn right, heading south. The JMT climbs gently to the upper Cathedral Lake at 4.7 miles. Look for a spur trail leading to the water and be sure to follow the correct one—in a restoration effort, the park closed an older trail that traveled

Cathedral Peak towers over the scene at the lower Cathedral Lake.

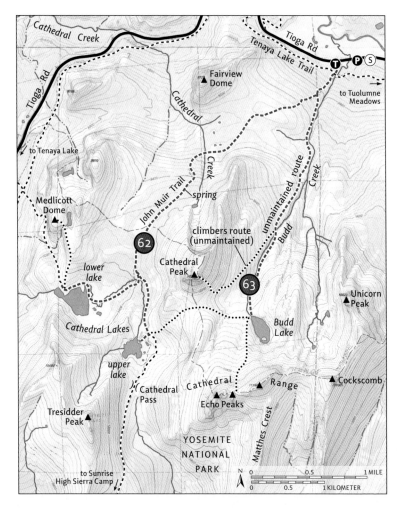

through a meadow. The correct path lies just past the meadow, and it travels over granite slabs to the northeast corner of the lake. The upper lake is your turnaround point unless you fancy some extended exploration in the area.

EXTENDING YOUR TRIP

From the lower Cathedral Lake, you can follow the cross-country section of the Medlicott Dome route (see Hike 60) by following granite slabs north and then northwest to Medlicott Dome for some great views toward Tenaya Lake. If you've got some cross-country chops, you can work your way from the upper Cathedral Lake up to a saddle just south of Cathedral Peak for some amazing views of the peak before continuing east cross-country toward Budd Lake (see Hike 63). From there, follow the Budd Lake route back to the Cathedral Lake Trailhead.

63 Budd Lake

RATING/ DIFFICULTY	ROUNDTRIP	ELEV GAIN/ HIGH POINT	SEASON
***/3	5 miles	1500 feet/ 10,001feet	July–Oct

Maps: USGS 7.5-min Tenaya Lake, Tom Harrison Maps Tuolumne Meadows; **Contact:** Tuolumne Meadows Visitor Center; **Notes:** Day-use only. Portable toilets and food storage at trailhead. Navigation required; **GPS:** 37.8733, –119.3827

While hundreds of hikers teem the shores of Elizabeth Lake and the Cathedral Lakes, the sublime waters of Budd Lake sparkle in near obscurity. This phenomenon is all the more shocking once you see Budd Lake and realize that it's one of the most beautiful high-country lakes accessible by a day hike in the entire park. The lake sits within a picture-perfect basin capped by the distinctive forms of the Cockscomb, Unicorn Peak, and Cathedral Peak, and this scenery can be all yours for the relatively low price of a moderately strenuous climb on an obscure, informal footpath.

Silvery lupine on the shore of Budd Lake

GETTING THERE

From Lee Vining at the junction of State Route 120 (Tioga Road) and US Highway 395, drive west for 20.7 miles, passing through the Tioga Pass Entrance, to the Cathedral Lakes Trailhead, which is on the south side of the road. Park on the shoulder of either side of the road.

ON THE TRAIL

From the bustling Cathedral Lakes Trailhead, join the connector trail heading south to the John Muir Trail (JMT), and continue south on the JMT as it begins a moderately steep climb through dense forest. The trickiest bit of navigation occurs at precisely 0.45 mile. An unmarked side path diverges from the JMT at this point, and to make sure the heavier flow of traffic on the JMT doesn't go astray, rangers have laid out branches and debris to discourage hikers from turning left here. However, this is the beginning of the informal trail to Budd Lake, so turn left here and leave the JMT behind.

The Budd Lake Trail is narrower, rougher, and occasionally less defined than the wide boulevard of the JMT. The trail climbs at a consistently moderate pace, occasionally requiring some small-scale routefinding through a series of fractured granite slabs along the banks of Budd Creek. This slightly confusing section occurs shortly after the split and continues until the 1.6-mile mark. The trail becomes better defined before crossing Budd Creek at 1.7 miles. Just a few dozen yards before this crossing, you may notice a second path branching off on the right. This is the climbers trail leading to Cathedral Peak. Keep left to continue toward Budd Lake.

Once upon the east bank of Budd Creek, continue through a ribbon-like meadow sprinkled with bright blue bursts of silvery lupine that blossom in early summer. The scene developing behind you is glorious; take a moment to sample the view north toward Mount Conness and numerous high points along the Sierra Crest—you will be feasting on this view on the hike back. Continue chugging along on a consistent uphill grind along the banks of Budd Creek for another 0.8 mile. Views west through open forest toward Cathedral Peak at the 2.4-mile mark herald the proximity of your destination. Shortly after the views of the peak emerge, the trail reaches Budd Lake's outlet, revealing the gorgeous lake and its beautiful surroundings.

A fisherman's path continues along the west bank of the lake for another 0.5 mile before eventually petering out. You can pick any point along the way to soak in the scenery before you make your way back. The return route is even more enjoyable than the ascent, thanks to the beautiful high-country views toward the Sierra Crest that you can savor on the way back.

EXTENDING YOUR TRIP

There are several popular mountaineering destinations on the ridges enclosing Budd Lake's basin, including the Cockscomb, Unicorn Peak, Cathedral Peak, and the Echo Peaks. You can tack on the climbers route to Cathedral Peak, which brings you to the top of the summit block. You won't be able to summit without mountaineering gear and skills, but you can get about 98 percent of the way. You can also follow a cross-country climbers route south toward the Echo Peaks, which also requires some tricky mountaineering work to conquer. If mountaineering is not your thing, you can approach the base of the Echo Peaks and then veer to the right (west) across large granite slabs. Head due south along a well-defined ridge to a spot overlooking the Echo Lake basin and beyond toward the Merced River drainage and the Clark Range—an inspiring view. This is prime country for cross-country exploration, but you will need to know how to use a map and compass to explore safely.

64 Soda Springs and Parsons Memorial Lodge

RATING/ DIFFICULTY	ROUNDTRIP	ELEV GAIN/ HIGH POINT	SEASON
**/1	1.3 miles	50 feet/ 8604 feet	June–Oct

Maps: USGS 7.5-min Tioga Pass, Tom Harrison Maps Tuolumne Meadows; **Contact:** Tuolumne Meadows Visitor Center; **Notes:** Day-use only. Restrooms at nearby Tuolumne Meadows Visitor Center; **GPS:** 37.8788, –119.3582

For a dose of Yosemite history coupled with some lovely meadow scenery, consider taking this family-friendly stroll to Soda Springs and Parsons Memorial Lodge. Built in 1915 by the Sierra Club to honor the memory of Edward Parsons, a fierce advocate for Hetch Hetchy's protection and a pioneering adventurer, the lodge has long served as a meeting place and reading room. Today, the lodge also acts as the backdrop for ranger-led interpretive programs and other special events. Nearby Soda Springs consists of several springs of mysterious origin that pump out carbonated water that, before it became contaminated through human use, was described as the most delicious water ever tasted.

GETTING THERE

Driving: From Lee Vining at the junction of State Route 120 (Tioga Road) and US Highway 395, drive west for 20 miles, passing through the Tioga Pass Entrance, to a parking area on the right shoulder of the road. The trailhead, which doesn't have a formal name but does have a sign indicating distance to Soda Springs, lies on the northern shoulder of the road.

Transit: Several shuttles, including YARTS, the Tuolumne Meadows Shuttle, and the Yosemite Valley–Tuolumne Meadows Shuttle stop at the nearby Tuolumne Meadows Visitor Center. From the center, it's

The wooden shack encasing Soda Springs with the Cathedral Range beyond

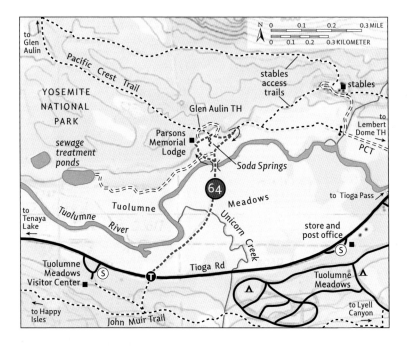

a short walk east along Tioga Road to reach the trailhead.

ON THE TRAIL

Set out north on the wide crushed-gravel path as it cuts directly across Tuolumne Meadows. Views east toward Mount Dana and Lembert Dome combine with views west and south toward Cathedral Peak and Pothole Dome to compose beautiful scenery that is at its best when illuminated by golden light near sunrise and sunset. Early morning and late afternoon are also great times for wildlife spotting when the area's larger mammals (deer and bears) are most active.

At 0.5 mile, the trail reaches and then crosses a bridge over the Tuolumne River. Just beyond the bridge, look for a single-track trail that leads away from the bridge heading northwest toward Parsons Memorial Lodge, which is clearly visible from this point. If you are staying at the Tuolumne Meadows area, consider joining one of the interpretive programs hosted here by rangers several times per day to learn about the myriad historical and natural wonders of the Tuolumne Meadows area.

From Parsons Lodge, continue north a short way to a junction with the Pacific Crest Trail. Turn right here on a trail that leads to a wooden shack constructed on red, barren, and wet soil. The shack protects Soda Springs, a mysterious carbonated water source that baffles geologists to this day. The water supply is contaminated now, but prior to this area receiving heavy foot traffic, visitors used to enjoy the flavorful, carbonated water. Although the springs are more fascinating than beautiful, this spot also affords nice views south toward the Cathedral Range.

Continue east past the springs to reach an old roadbed that turns to the south. Follow this roadbed and it will lead you back to the bridge over the Tuolumne River. Head south for 0.5 mile back to the trailhead.

EXTENDING YOUR TRIP

The trail connecting the Tuolumne Meadows Visitor Center and Soda Springs makes a nice alternative starting point to the Glen Aulin and Waterwheel Falls route (Hike 70). Simply follow this route to the Pacific Crest Trail and turn left to follow the route to Glen Aulin. The overall distance and elevation gain are roughly the same.

65 Tuolumne Meadows Loop

RATING/ DIFFICULTY	ROUNDTRIP	ELEV GAIN/ HIGH POINT	SEASON
**/3	6.3 miles	450 feet/ 8751 feet	June–Oct

Maps: USGS 7.5-min Tioga Pass, Tom Harrison Maps Tuolumne Meadows; **Contact:** Tuolumne Meadows Visitor Center; **Notes:** Day-use only; **GPS:** 37.8788, –119.3582

Originating from the snowpacks blanketing high points along the Sierra Crest and the Cathedral Range, numerous watercourses flow downhill to collect in the broad Tuolumne River basin. Within this basin lies Tuolumne Meadows, one of the largest high-elevation meadows in the Sierra. The meadows exist thanks to subsurface water collecting within glacial sediment that has accumulated over thousands of years. These natural wonders combine with numerous visitor services to make this area one of the most accessible destinations in the Yosemite high country. By following a pair of world-famous paths and a handful of connector trails, hikers can enjoy the full array of scenic features in and around Tuolumne Meadows.

GETTING THERE

Driving: From Lee Vining at the junction of State Route 120 (Tioga Road) and US Highway 395, drive west for 20 miles, passing through the Tioga Pass Entrance, to a parking area on the right shoulder of the road. An unmarked trailhead accessing two connecting trails lies along the shoulder of the road. The north trailhead leads to Soda Springs, while the southern trailhead connects to the John Muir Trail.

Transit: Several shuttles, including YARTS, the Tuolumne Meadows Shuttle, and the Yosemite Valley–Tuolumne Meadows Shuttle stop at the nearby Tuolumne Meadows Visitor Center. From the center, it's a short walk east along Tioga Road to reach the trailhead.

ON THE TRAIL

Starting from the Soda Springs Trail parking area, carefully cross Tioga Road to walk south on a connecting trail. After about 150 yards, merge left onto another connecting trail, which soon connects with the John Muir Trail (JMT). Turn left to begin a short stint on the famous hiking trail, which runs from Happy Isles in Yosemite Valley to the summit of Mount Whitney, which lies nearly 175 trail miles to the south in Sequoia National Park. Even a brief taste of walking on the JMT is enough to fill most hikers with visions of a month-long trip through the most beautiful

corners of the High Sierra. After crossing Unicorn Creek at 0.5 mile, the JMT makes a short climb onto a slope above Tuolumne Meadows Campground. This short segment skirts the south end of the campground through a cool forest of lodgepole pines with occasional mountain hemlocks and Western white pines.

After crossing the Elizabeth Lake Trail at 1 mile, the trail leaves the bustle of the campground behind as it descends toward the banks of the Lyell Fork Tuolumne River. From 1.6 miles to 2.3 miles, the JMT traces the banks of the river on a peaceful passage accompanied by the deep bass sounds of the rumbling water. This passage concludes at a junction with the Sierra's other world-famous trail, the Pacific Crest Trail (PCT). Turn left on the PCT, then continue a short distance to a pair of bridges spanning the Lyell Fork Tuolumne River. During the early part of the season, the Lyell Fork will be swollen with snowmelt coursing down from passes on the Sierra Crest. During late summer and early fall, the river's flow recedes enough to reveal several inviting swimming holes. Do not attempt to swim here if the water is high, as the icy-cold river can and will sweep swimmers away.

After crossing the Lyell Fork, the trail climbs over a low, broad ridge dividing the Lyell Fork from the Dana Fork of the Tuolumne River. Less than a mile to the west, the two rivers combine at their confluence, forming the main stem of the Tuolumne River that courses through its grand canyon en route to Hetch Hetchy Reservoir. At 2.9 miles, cross a bridge spanning the Dana Fork, then keep left again immediately after to avoid following a connector trail to the

Rafferty Creek Trailhead. Continue hiking west on the PCT along the Dana Fork toward Tuolumne Meadows Lodge Road at 3.25 miles. From here, the PCT parallels the road, passing the Tuolumne Meadows Wilderness Center at 3.6 miles. Shortly beyond the wilderness center, the trail crosses a meadow with views west toward Unicorn Peak before reaching Tioga Road at 4 miles.

Cross over Tioga Road to reach the Lembert Dome parking area. The PCT crosses through the parking area and continues along the road leading to the Glen Aulin Trailhead, which features several interpretive signs describing the meadow's history and habitats. Pass through the gate at 4.3 miles, then continue heading west toward Soda Springs on the PCT at a junction where a trail connecting Soda Springs and the Tuolumne Meadows Visitor Center splits off to lead south to the trailhead. To reach this curiously carbonated water source, keep right at this junction, and keep right again on the PCT as it passes by the historical cabin sheltering the springs. Just beyond the cabin, turn left to follow a path toward Parsons Memorial Lodge. This historic stone structure, built in 1915 by the Sierra Club, is the location for ranger-led interpretive talks and events as well as other special functions.

After visiting the springs and the lodge, return to the junction of the PCT and the Soda Springs Trail. Continue south for a short distance to one last junction at 4.8 miles with an access road leading to the most beautiful sewage treatment pond on the planet. If you are intrigued at the thought of a beautiful sewage treatment pond, follow the access road west along the northern rim of Tuolumne Meadows for 0.5 mile. From

Opposite: *Lembert Dome at dawn*

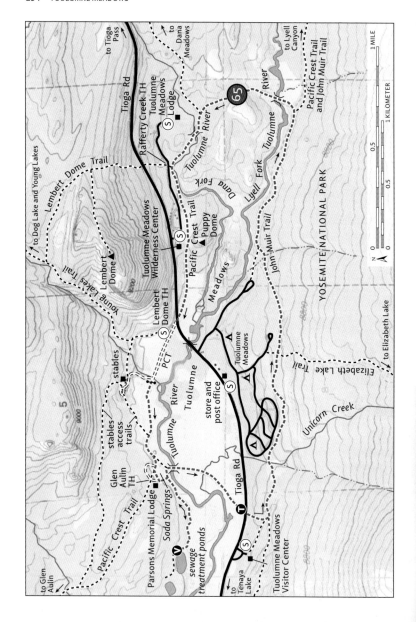

a spot on the east side of the pond, you can peer across the tranquil water (just don't think too much about what's in it) toward Cathedral Peak beyond the grassy expanse of meadows.

To wrap up the hike, return to the connecting trail that leads south to the visitor center (5.8 miles). Turn right to hike south for 0.5 mile to the parking area along Tioga Road.

66 Elizabeth Lake

RATING/ DIFFICULTY	ROUNDTRIP	ELEV GAIN/ HIGH POINT	SEASON
**/3	4.6 miles	850 feet/ 9505 feet	July–Oct

Maps: USGS 7.5-min Tioga Pass, Vogelsang Peak, Tom Harrison Maps Yosemite High

Country; **Contact:** Tuolumne Meadows Visitor Center; **Notes:** Day-use only. Restroom and food storage at trailhead; **GPS:** 37.8707, –119.3559

Tucked into a basin overlooked by Unicorn Peak, Elizabeth Lake's tranquil environs showcase the pleasures of a subalpine lake basin. From its starting point within Tuolumne Meadows Campground, this moderate jaunt through cool forest shading a wildflower garden of mariposa lilies and lupines offers one of the quickest and easiest hikes into Yosemite's high country.

GETTING THERE
From Lee Vining at the junction of State Route 120 (Tioga Road) and US Highway 395, drive west for 19.1 miles through the Tioga Pass Entrance toward Tuolumne

Unicorn Peak from the southeast shore of Elizabeth Lake

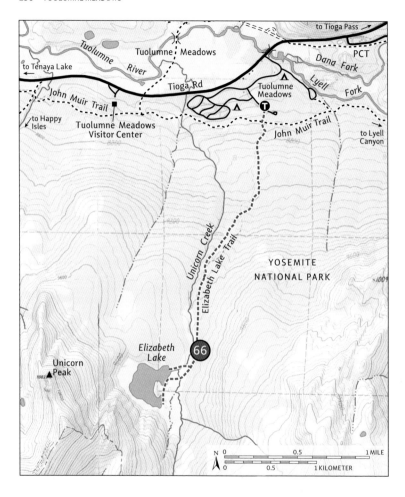

Meadows Campground. Turn left into the campground, pass through the entrance to the campground, and keep right after the entrance kiosk. After 0.3 mile from the right turn, turn left toward the Elizabeth Lake Trailhead. Reach a day-use parking area just before the equestrian camping area.

ON THE TRAIL

After locating the trailhead, follow the trail south and uphill through a dense forest of lodgepole pines. During July and August, look for a pleasing variety of wildflowers, including asters, lupines, paintbrushes, and the standout Leichtlin's mariposa lily. Continue straight through a junction with the John Muir Trail at 0.1 mile and dig in for a moderately strenuous climb that picks up 600 feet of elevation over the next mile.

At 1.1 miles, the grade eases into a more gradual ascent. At 1.4 miles, the forest cover opens up when the trail reaches Unicorn Creek. Continue south along the creek and the ribbon-like meadow through which it runs. Granite peaks and ridges visible from the trail signal your proximity to Elizabeth Lake. At 1.7 miles, you'll get your first clear look at Unicorn Peak.

Just before reaching the lake, the trail splits. If you keep right, you will arrive at the eastern shore of the lake. If you turn left at the split, your route continues south along a wooded peninsula jutting out into the east side of the lake. About 0.3 mile past the peninsula, you'll reach the southeast shore, which also offers pleasing views toward Unicorn Peak. This is your turnaround spot—from here retrace your steps back to the campground.

67 Lembert Dome

RATING/ DIFFICULTY	ROUNDTRIP	ELEV GAIN/ HIGH POINT	SEASON
***/2	3.8 miles	850 feet/ 9439 feet	July–Oct

Maps: USGS 7.5-min Tioga Pass, Tom Harrison Maps Tuolumne Meadows; **Contact:** Tuolumne Meadows Visitor Center; **Notes:** Day-use only. Vault toilets and food storage at trailhead; **GPS:** 37.8775, –119.3536

Several granite domes polished by eons of glacial scouring rise above the otherwise gentle landscape surrounding Tuolumne Meadows. Of *these domes, Lembert Dome is the most renowned, and its summit offers splendid panoramic views. Hikers can reach this summit via a pleasant looping hike that includes a short stretch on the Pacific Crest Trail.*

GETTING THERE
From the junction of US Highway 395 and State Route 120/Tioga Road, drive west for 12.7 miles to the Tioga Pass Entrance. From the Tioga Pass Entrance, continue west for 6.7 miles to the Lembert Dome parking area and the trailhead.

ON THE TRAIL
From the north side of the parking area, find and follow a wide, sandy trail marked for Dog Lake and the Young Lakes into dense lodgepole forest and then across a granite outcrop. Beyond the outcrop, continue north through a meadow with views west across Tuolumne Meadows. Leaving the meadow behind, the trail begins a 400-foot climb over 0.5 mile through dense forest alongside a bubbling creek that drains Dog Lake to the north.

When the climb ends at 1 mile, turn right onto the Lembert Dome Trail, which traverses the northern base of Lembert Dome. As the trail bends to the south, look for an unmarked informal trail at 1.5 miles that traces the dome's spine to its summit. Turn right on this informal trail to follow it west on a moderate climb through increasingly sparse forest that soon yields to bare granite. Continue along the sloping shoulder of Lembert Dome to the summit 100 yards to the west. At first, the going is easy, but a steep pitch just below the summit requires some careful hand and foot work. In addition to the summit, you can wander over to the western edge of the dome, from which point you get the best views of the Tuolumne River as it snakes its way through its namesake meadow.

The return route descends along the spine of the dome back to the main trail. Turn right to hike south toward a crossing of Tioga Road at 2.7 miles. Cross the road and walk a short distance until the trail reaches a parking area at 2.8 miles. Continue through the parking area and then across Tuolumne Meadows Lodge Road to reach a connector trail that continues south to a junction with the Pacific Crest Trail.

Turn right onto the Pacific Crest Trail and follow it west as it parallels the Dana Fork of the Tuolumne River, which rumbles along through a corridor of trees on your left. The trail peels away from the river at 3.1 miles and heads due west, passing Puppy Dome before entering another meadow that reveals good views west toward Unicorn Peak. At 3.7 miles, the trail reaches Tioga Road once again. Cross the road to return to the Lembert Dome parking area.

The summit of Lembert Dome showcases some of the best views around Tuolumne Meadows.

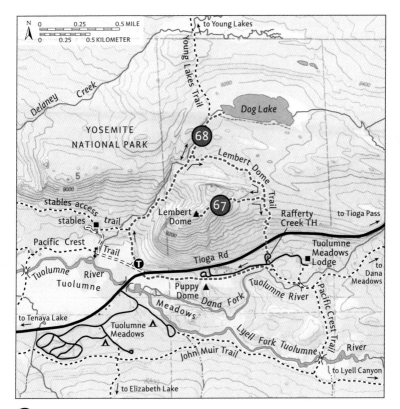

68 Dog Lake

RATING/ DIFFICULTY	ROUNDTRIP	ELEV GAIN/ HIGH POINT	SEASON
**/2	2.5 miles	600 feet/ 9183 feet	June–Oct

Maps: USGS 7.5-min Tioga Pass; Tom Harrison Maps Tuolumne Meadows; **Contact:** Tuolumne Meadows Visitor Center; **Notes:** Day-use only. Vault toilets and food storage at trailhead; **GPS:** 37.8775, –119.3536

Visiting a Sierran lake usually requires the sort of time and effort that excludes a considerable fraction of hikers. The Tuolumne Meadows area features a notable exception to this general rule—Dog Lake. For a relatively modest amount of effort, hikers can traverse a quiet lodgepole forest to reach a lake where forest and distant peaks reflect in a perfect mirror image in tranquil waters. Consider timing your visit for sunrise so you can watch the sun appear over the Sierra Crest across the lake's tranquil waters.

GETTING THERE

From the junction of US Highway 395 and State Route 120/Tioga Road, drive west for 12.7 miles to the Tioga Pass Entrance. From the Tioga Pass Entrance, continue west for 6.7 miles to the Lembert Dome parking area and the trailhead.

ON THE TRAIL

From the north side of the parking area, follow the wide, sandy trail north through dense lodgepole pine forest before crossing a granite outcrop. Beyond the outcrop, the trail enters a meadow revealing views west across Tuolumne Meadows toward Unicorn and Cathedral Peaks. At 0.4 mile, the trail begins a short but tough ascent through a densely wooded ravine, gaining 400 feet over the next 0.5 mile.

With the hard work out of the way, pass straight through a junction with the Lembert Dome Trail at 1 mile, then turn right at the next junction at 1.1 miles where the Young Lakes Trail continues north. After 0.15 mile of flat walking through dense forest, you reach the western shore of Dog Lake. The placid lakeshore ringed by lodgepole pines offers plenty of peace, shade, and tranquility. If you're an early bird, be sure to check out the pre-dawn views east across the lake

Dawn reflections of Mount Dana and Mount Gibbs at Dog Lake

toward Mount Dana and Mount Gibbs. On a calm morning, the reflection of forest and mountains creates a perfect mirror image of sylvan serenity. Retrace your steps to return to your vehicle at the trailhead.

EXTENDING YOUR TRIP
You can add the loop to Lembert Dome (Hike 67) for a 4.6-mile roundtrip hike with 900 feet of elevation gain.

69 Young Lakes

RATING/ DIFFICULTY	ROUNDTRIP	ELEV GAIN/ HIGH POINT	SEASON
****/4	14.4 miles	2200 feet/ 10,231 feet	July–Oct

Maps: USGS 7.5-min Tioga Pass, Falls Ridge, Tom Harrison Maps Yosemite High Country; **Contact:** Tuolumne Meadows Visitor Center; **Notes:** Suitable for backpacking (Young Lakes via Dog Lake; Young Lakes via Glen Aulin Trail). Restroom and food storage at trailhead; **GPS:** 37.8774, –119.3536

This trio of subalpine lakes backdropped by the craggy form of Ragged Peak lies at the heart of a long, looping route that starts from the Lembert Dome parking area. Highlights along the way include meadows, dense forests, sweeping views of the Cathedral Range, and an optional side trip to Soda Springs and Parsons Memorial Lodge. This route works well both as an ambitious one-day trip or as an overnight or two-night backpacking trip.

GETTING THERE
From the junction of US Highway 395 and State Route 120/Tioga Road, drive west for 12.7 miles to the Tioga Pass Entrance. From the Tioga Pass Entrance, continue west for 6.7 miles to the Lembert Dome parking area and the trailhead.

ON THE TRAIL
From the Dog Lake/Lembert Dome Trailhead, head north on a wide, sandy trail that first passes through a dense grove of lodgepole pines and then a granite outcrop at 0.1 mile and a meadow at 0.2 mile. Beyond the meadow, the trail darts into the forest again to climb through a steep ravine alongside Dog Lake's outlet creek. At 1 mile, keep left at a Y-junction with the Lembert Dome Trail. At 1.1 miles, keep left again to join the Young Lakes Trail, unless you wish to follow the 0.15-mile spur trail to Dog Lake for a quick breather.

After a brief, gentle passage through a grassy meadow, the trail resumes climbing through dry lodgepole forest before descending to a long meadow nourished by Delaney Creek. Hop over Delaney Creek (or ford it early in the season) and cross the meadow to resume climbing up and over a ridge dividing Delaney Creek from Dingley Creek, which the trail crosses at 3.3 miles.

After crossing Dingley Creek, begin a traverse across a vast, sloping meadow dotted with whitebark and lodgepole pines. Turn around to look south for a fantastic view spanning the Cathedral Range. This view improves while you climb toward yet another ridge at 3.8 miles, but then the views vanish as the trail begins a prolonged, 300-foot descent to a junction with the western leg of the Young Lakes Trail (your return route) at 4.3 miles. Keep right at this junction to continue north and northeast to wrap around Ragged Peak. The initial portion of the arc

Infinity pool effect at the third Young Lake

around Ragged Peak is mostly flat, and a few grassy meadows allow good views of the heavily fractured high point that later provides a picturesque backdrop at each of the Young Lakes.

After one more spurt of climbing, arrive at the first Young Lake at 5.8 miles. You'll find good campsites near the wooded western and northern shores along with good views of the granitic wall bounding the south side of the lake. The first lake makes for a fine spot to stop, but the second and third lakes are each beautiful in their own unique ways. To reach them, continue along the northern shore of the first lake to cross over its outlet creek. The continuation of the trail is a little hard to spot owing to misdirection caused by adjacent informal trails. The correct trail travels east, uphill, and 100 yards north of a creek draining the second lake.

The second lake (6.4 miles) is smaller, with grassy meadows surrounding it on three sides and the same massive granite wall to the south. More campsites can be found on the second lake's north side adjacent to the increasingly rugged trail to the third lake. At 6.5 miles, the trail devolves into a brushy, rocky scramble leading up and over the third lake's moraine. After gaining 200 feet over 0.2 mile, this messy section of trail tops out and then vanishes within a vast meadow that surrounds the final lake. While the first two lakes were heavily wooded, here there are only stunted whitebark pines in isolated clusters—possible campsites may be found there. A handful of boulders situated along the lakeshore allow you to bask in glorious alpine sunshine while admiring the infinity pool effect created by the lake's western moraine.

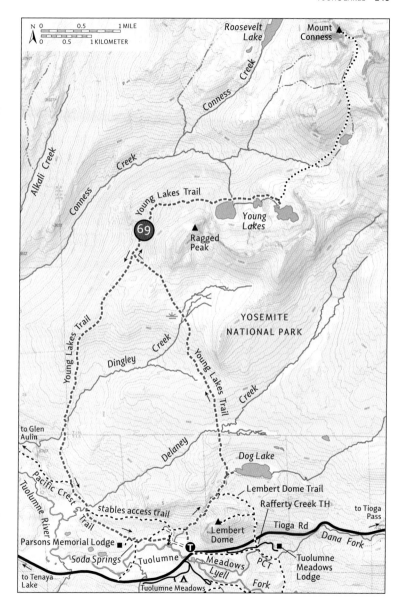

N 0   0.5   1 MILE
0   0.5   1 KILOMETER

Roosevelt Lake

Mount Conness

Conness Creek

Alkali Creek

Conness Creek

Young Lakes Trail

Young Lakes

69

Ragged Peak

Young Lakes Trail

YOSEMITE NATIONAL PARK

Dingley Creek

Young Lakes Creek

to Glen Aulin

Delaney

Pacific Crest Trail

Dog Lake

Lembert Dome Trail

Rafferty Creek TH

to Tioga Pass

Tioga Rd

Dana Fork

stables access trail

Tuolumne River

Parsons Memorial Lodge

Lembert Dome

PCT

Tuolumne Meadows Lodge

Soda Springs

Tuolumne

T

Meadows Lyell Fork

to Tenaya Lake

Tuolumne Meadows

The return route follows the trail back along the first two lakes to the Y junction with the eastern and western legs of the Young Lakes Trail at 9.4 miles. Turn right onto the western leg of the trail, which will minimize the ups and downs you endure on the long walk back. After a short climb, the trail settles into an extended and uneventful descent through dense forest. Hop several branches of Dingley Creek at 11.6 miles, then breathe a sigh of relief as the descent ends at an open, rocky outcrop at 12.1 miles. The views south toward the Cathedral Range are a nice reward following the long descent through omnipresent forest cover.

At 12.5 miles, turn left to join the Pacific Crest Trail and follow it east on a wide, sandy track toward Parsons Memorial Lodge and Soda Springs. Keep right at a trail accessing the Tuolumne Meadows stables (13 miles) and continue straight across a dirt road at 13.6 miles. Soda Springs lies directly across the dirt road, and it is worth a quick side trip if you have any energy left. Just past the springs, the trail merges with a dirt road, which you will follow all the way back to the Dog Lake/Lembert Dome parking area at 14.4 miles.

EXTENDING YOUR TRIP

The Young Lakes Trail doubles as one of the more popular ascent routes to Mount Conness, one of Yosemite's signature high-country peaks. Although there are shorter and more direct routes to the top, many of them verge on technical climbing. The Young Lakes route eschews the mountaineering in favor of a long, steep approach from the third lake. Find and follow an informal route running west to east north of the lake. This route turns northeast through a deep valley dividing the Conness massif from the White Mountain massif to the south. Beyond the banks of an ephemeral lake (8.75 miles), the route turns north and begins its steepest section of climbing toward the Sierra Crest. Upon reaching the crest (10 miles), the route turns to the west toward the summit. The summit lies 0.2 mile to the west. This cross-country segment adds 5.5 miles of hiking with another 2500 feet of elevation gain.

70 Glen Aulin and Waterwheel Falls

RATING/ DIFFICULTY	ROUNDTRIP	ELEV GAIN/ HIGH POINT	SEASON
*****/4	17.4 miles	2000 feet/ 8655 feet	Jun–Oct

Maps: USGS 7.5-min Tioga Pass, Falls Ridge, Tom Harrison Maps Yosemite High Country; **Contact:** Tuolumne Meadows Visitor Center; **Notes:** Suitable for backpacking (Glen Aulin). Vault toilets at Lembert Dome Trailhead. Food storage lockers at Lembert Dome trailhead; **GPS:** 37.8788, –119.3582

 Rejoice, oh lovers of waterfalls! This outstanding odyssey follows the Tuolumne River from Tuolumne Meadows as it descends to Glen Aulin and the Grand Canyon of the Tuolumne. Along the way, the route passes four major named waterfalls and countless smaller waterfalls en route to Waterwheel Falls, which produces a dramatic aqueous display during peak runoff. Backpackers can stop overnight at Glen Aulin High Sierra Camp,

Opposite: *One of the many cascades along the Tuolumne River*

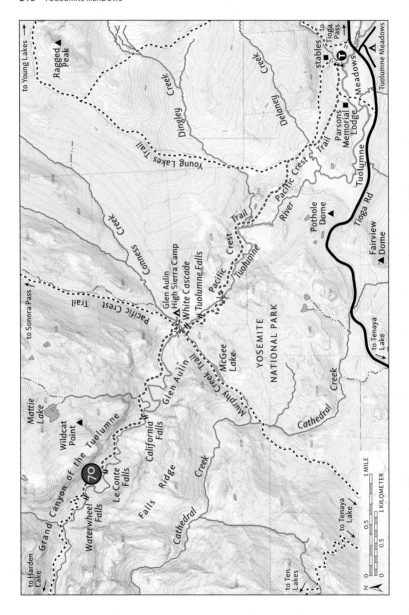

which may make the out-and-back to Water-wheel Falls more palatable for less determined hikers.

GETTING THERE

From the junction of US Highway 395 and State Route 120/Tioga Road in Lee Vining, drive west for 12.7 miles to the Tioga Pass Entrance. From the Tioga Pass Entrance, continue west for 6.7 miles to the Lembert Dome parking area, and turn right. Continue past the Lembert Dome parking area on a dirt road for 0.3 mile to a gate that doubles as the official start of this route. It's unlikely that there will be parking available in front of the gate, but you can park along the road between the Lembert Dome parking area and the gate.

ON THE TRAIL

From the gate west of the parking area, hike west along the dirt road, which doubles as the fabled Pacific Crest Trail (PCT), along the north edge of Tuolumne Meadows. Interpretive panels along the way tell you about the indigenous people who inhabited the area, along with the region's myriad natural features. Continue straight on the PCT where an access trail from the horse stables joins the PCT, then stay straight again where a trail splits off on the left toward the Tuolumne Meadows Visitor Center. Shortly beyond this split, the route continues straight through a jumble of junctions accessing Soda Springs and Parsons Memorial Lodge (see Hike 64). At 0.8 mile, you arrive at the signed trailhead for the route to Glen Aulin. Once more, continue hiking straight ahead.

The next two miles on the PCT are somewhat uneventful, with only a crossing of Delaney Creek (1.6 miles) and a junction with the western branch of the Young Lakes Trail at 2 miles. At 2.8 miles, the PCT reaches the banks of the Tuolumne River. The open forest along the river reveals beautiful views south toward high points of the Cathedral Range with the wide, placid waters of the Tuolumne in the foreground. The PCT continues along the river, sometimes across spacious granite outcrops and occasionally through forest until 4.1 miles, where the first glimpses toward Glen Aulin come into view at a granite outcrop. This spot also marks the beginning of the descent into the Grand Canyon of the Tuolumne, and shortly beyond lies the first of countless cascades and waterfalls.

At 4.4 miles, cross a footbridge to the south side of the Tuolumne to descend toward several picturesque cascades. Informal side paths lead closer to the riverbank, from which you can get a closer look at the various cascades. At 5.1 miles, the PCT dips into a small basin dominated by thundering Tuolumne Falls, which spills in several torrents over a 50-foot ledge. To get a good look from the base, you will need to step off trail; exercise caution if you approach the rocky base of the falls, especially during high water.

Continuing past Tuolumne Falls, keep right at a junction with the Murphy Creek Trail (5.4 miles). From the Murphy Creek Trail, the descent continues through dense forest as the trail bends north toward White Cascade, which spills into a broad pool fed by the Tuolumne River. White Cascade also heralds your arrival to the Glen Aulin High Sierra Camp and backpacking area at 5.6 miles. Expect to cross paths with PCT through-hikers during the summer, as this junction is a popular stopping point before the PCT diverges north from Glen Aulin.

The name Glen Aulin is a Gaelic phrase meaning "beautiful valley," which is exactly what you'll find as you continue west from the high camp. After a brief, rocky descent along a thundering cascade, the trail reaches a flat, glacially carved valley dominated by granite cliffs that evoke Yosemite Valley. Even if you don't plan to continue to Waterwheel Falls, you owe it to yourself to stop at a sandy beach along the Tuolumne River where you can enjoy the view west into Glen Aulin. This is a worthy turnaround spot at the 5.6-mile mark for those uninterested in the full iteration of this route.

If you do have the will and the stamina, or if you're camping at the high camp, continue west for an extended flat traverse through Glen Aulin, where you'll be treated to quiet walking along the banks of the river and through groves of quaking aspens. This flat section comes to an end, at 7 miles, at the top of California Falls—a multi-tiered cascade that also signals the resumption of moderate descending farther into the Grand Canyon of the Tuolumne. An informal path on the left leads to the base of these cascades—a nice opportunity for an extended break.

The descent is now more pronounced as you continue, and, yes, this will be a challenge on the return journey. But for now, enjoy the views down the U-shaped Grand Canyon of the Tuolumne as the trail approaches and then passes LeConte Falls (8.2 miles). LeConte Falls is the only major waterfall that's difficult to access, and you may wish to skip it in favor of the final destination, Waterwheel Falls, which lies a mere 0.5 mile farther down-canyon.

At Waterwheel Falls during peak runoff (usually early June) during a wet year, the waters of the Tuolumne River hit numerous ledges submerged along the cascading

waterfall. When the water hits these ledges, it shoots up into the sky, which reminded early explorers of an old-fashioned waterwheel. The view from the granite slab also impresses with views down the U-shaped Grand Canyon of the Tuolumne. Plan to spend at least an hour or more at this fantastic lunch spot to enjoy the waterfall and outstanding scenery. Moreover, a long break may be necessary before you begin the uphill return journey, which is more demanding than the approach.

EXTENDING YOUR TRIP

Backpackers can continue down the Grand Canyon of the Tuolumne as it descends toward Hetch Hetchy Reservoir. Just beyond Pate Valley and above the reservoir, the trail climbs out of the canyon up to Harden Lake (see Hike 49). From there, the trail leads south to White Wolf. A shuttle is required to complete this multi-day, 28.5-mile hike.

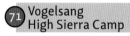

71 Vogelsang High Sierra Camp

RATING/ DIFFICULTY	ROUNDTRIP	ELEV GAIN/ HIGH POINT	SEASON
***/4	14.4 miles	1600 feet/ 10,148 feet	July–Oct

Maps: USGS Tioga Pass, Vogelsang Peak, Tom Harrison Maps Yosemite High Country; **Contact:** Tuolumne Meadows Visitor Center; **Notes:** Suitable for backpacking (Rafferty Creek to Vogelsang). Food storage at trailhead; **GPS:** 37.8777, –119.3386

 This challenging excursion on the Rafferty Creek Trail leads you to

Opposite: Vogelsang Peak looms large beyond Tuolumne Pass.

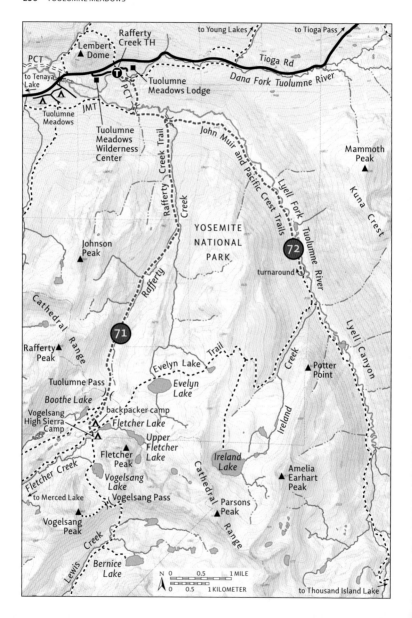

PCT

to Young Lakes

to Tioga Pass

Rafferty
Creek TH

Lembert
Dome

Tioga Rd

Dana Fork Tuolumne River

to Tenaya
Lake

T

PCT

Tuolumne
Meadows Lodge

Tuolumne
Meadows

JMT

Tuolumne
Meadows
Wilderness
Center

Rafferty Creek Trail

Creek

John Muir and Pacific Crest Trails

Mammoth
Peak

Lyell Fork

Tuolumne River

Kuna Crest

Johnson
Peak

YOSEMITE
NATIONAL
PARK

72

turnaround

Rafferty

71

Cathedral Range

Lyell Canyon

Creek

Rafferty
Peak

Trail

Evelyn Lake

Potter
Point

Tuolumne Pass

Evelyn
Lake

Ireland

Boothe Lake

backpacker camp

Vogelsang
High Sierra
Camp

Fletcher Lake

Fletcher
Peak

Upper
Fletcher
Lake

Ireland
Lake

Amelia
Earhart
Peak

Fletcher Creek

Vogelsang
Lake

Vogelsang Pass

Cathedral Range

Parsons
Peak

to Merced Lake

Vogelsang
Peak

Creek

Lewis

Bernice
Lake

N   0   0.5   1 MILE
     0   0.5   1 KILOMETER

to Thousand Island Lake

Yosemite's highest elevation High Sierra Camp, which serves as a fitting jump-off point for numerous high-country excursions. Although a backpacking trip is really the best way to enjoy everything the Vogelsang area has to offer, day hikers can still get a taste of what makes this area so special by way of a full-day hike to the camp and just slightly beyond to the banks of Fletcher Lake.

GETTING THERE

From the junction of US Highway 395 and State Route 120/Tioga Road, drive west for 12.7 miles to the Tioga Pass Entrance. From the Tioga Pass Entrance, continue west for 6.5 miles to a junction with Tuolumne Meadows Lodge Road on the left. Turn left, noting the wilderness center on the right just after the turn, then follow the road for another 0.5 mile to a parking area on the left (north) side of the road for the Rafferty Creek Trailhead. If you are backpacking, park at the wilderness center and walk an additional 0.4 mile east on the Pacific Crest Trail.

ON THE TRAIL

From the parking area, follow the signed connector trail due south to the Pacific Crest Trail (PCT). Turn left to continue south on the PCT paralleling the Dana Fork Tuolumne River on a pleasant, level grade through lodgepole forest. Cross the Dana Fork footbridge at 0.25 mile, then continue for another 0.6 mile to a second bridge spanning the Lyell Fork Tuolumne River. At this bridge, take in the first appreciable views of the hike with a vista looking east toward Mount Gibbs. During late summer and early fall, a handful of pools make for good swimming and relaxing. Just beyond the bridge, turn left at the junction where the John Muir Trail (JMT) meets the PCT at 0.9 mile. From

here, continue east for the next 0.6 mile on the combined JMT/PCT to a junction with the Rafferty Creek Trail at 1.5 miles.

Turn right onto the Rafferty Creek Trail and begin a short but steep climb away from the Tuolumne River plain. The ascending trail reaches a more level grade at 2 miles, and here begins a long but gentle ascent along Rafferty Creek toward Tuolumne Pass. Open sections of the forest reveal views toward the Kuna Crest to the east, but otherwise this section of the route is unremarkable. Settle into cruise control mode for the next 3 miles until you reach a spot where the forest recedes at the edge of a linear meadow revealing impressive views north and south. To the north (behind you) stand Mount Conness and high points along the Sierra Crest. The dramatic formations of Fletcher Peak and Vogelsang Peak loom in intimidating fashion beyond forested Tuolumne Pass directly ahead. These splendid views highlight the hike, so be sure to stop often to enjoy them fully.

At 6.3 miles, the trail arrives at Tuolumne Pass, which divides the Tuolumne River and Merced River watersheds. Look for a junction leading right toward Boothe Lake, which is worth a quick 1-mile diversion if you have time and energy to spare. Otherwise, keep left to follow the trail uphill from the pass as it traverses the north face of Emeric Creek's canyon. The trail tops out at 7 miles at a 4-way junction just north of the High Sierra Camp. The camp itself—a handful of tent cabins and stone buildings—is not much of a scenic destination. To find a suitable turnaround spot, turn left on the trail signed for Evelyn Lake and the backpacker camp and continue east for 0.2 mile to the banks of petite but scenic Fletcher Lake. A spur trail also leads north to the backpacker camp, which provides a great base camp for some of the explorations described in the Extending Your Trip section. Otherwise, Fletcher Lake is your turnaround spot. Follow your approach route back to Tuolumne Meadows to conclude your journey.

EXTENDING YOUR TRIP

If camping at Vogelsang, consider the following options. Continue south from the Vogelsang Camp junction for 0.5 mile and 220 feet of climbing to reach Vogelsang Lake. If you want to bag Vogelsang Peak, continue beyond the lake another 0.75 mile to a spot just shy of Vogelsang Pass. From there, you can work your way west cross-country and then north to the summit of Vogelsang Peak. From Fletcher Lake, you can continue east, up and over a ridge to a broad, 1.3-mile basin containing a vast meadow and Evelyn Lake. Finally, you can turn this into a 20-mile overnight loop if you continue beyond Evelyn Lake past the Ireland Lake junction (add a 5-mile out-and-back diversion to Ireland Lake) and down a steep descent into Lyell Canyon. From there, you can follow the PCT/JMT back to your starting point.

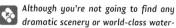

Although you're not going to find any dramatic scenery or world-class waterfalls on the pleasant hike into Lyell Canyon, you will find a number of lovely scenes that, when paired with easy walking on one of the most famous footpaths in the United States, makes for an enjoyable excursion. Backpackers can use the route described here as a jumping-off point to bigger and more dramatic overnight excursions leading to stunning destinations south of Yosemite's border within the Ansel Adams Wilderness.

GETTING THERE

From the junction of US Highway 395 and State Route 120/Tioga Road in Lee Vining, drive west for 12.7 miles to the Tioga Pass Entrance. From the Tioga Pass Entrance, continue west for 6.5 miles to a junction with Tuolumne Meadows Lodge Road on the left. Turn left, noting the wilderness center on the right just after the turn, then follow the road for another 0.5 mile to a parking area on the left (north) side of the road for the Rafferty Creek Trailhead. If you are backpacking, park at the wilderness center and walk an additional 0.4 mile east on the Pacific Crest Trail.

72 Lyell Canyon

RATING/ DIFFICULTY	ROUNDTRIP	ELEV GAIN/ HIGH POINT	SEASON
**/3	9.2 miles	500 feet/ 8886 feet	Jun–Oct

Maps: USGS 7.5-min Tioga Pass, Vogelsang Peak, Tom Harrison Maps Yosemite High Country; **Contact:** Tuolumne Meadows Visitor Center; **Notes:** Suitable for backpacking (Lyell Canyon). Food storage at trailhead; **GPS:** 37.8777, –119.3386

ON THE TRAIL

From the parking area, set out due south on a connector trail that quickly reaches the Pacific Crest Trail (PCT). Keep to the left to head south on the PCT paralleling the Dana Fork Tuolumne River on a level grade through lodgepole forest. Cross the Dana Fork footbridge at 0.25 mile then continue for another 0.6 mile to a second bridge spanning the Lyell Fork Tuolumne River. This two-span bridge passes a picturesque section of the river that has some nice swimming holes that usually become safe for swimming in September. This open section also reveals views east toward Mount Dana and Mount Gibbs, making this a nice spot for casual hikers to turn around.

Just beyond the bridge, keep left at the junction where the John Muir Trail (JMT) meets the PCT at 0.9 mile. From here, the JMT and the PCT run parallel for over 200 miles south to Mount Whitney. Follow the PCT/JMT east on a pleasant traverse through pine forest and along grassy meadows; take care to continue straight at 1.5 miles at a junction with the Rafferty Creek Trail. At 2.5 miles, the trail begins a gradual arc to the south as it enters the mouth of Lyell Canyon. The PCT/JMT undulates gently as it continues along the gradually inclining canyon through patches of forest alternating with open meadow bounding the Lyell Fork Tuolumne River.

At several spots along the trail, views emerge up-canyon toward high points along the Mammoth Crest. Be sure to stick to the trail and avoid trampling meadow habitat. The temptation to stray will be considerable since views up-canyon are best from the open meadow areas, but restrain yourself. Besides, if you continue to the 4.6-mile

Sunrise crowns Mount Gibbs from the Lyell Fork Tuolumne River.

mark, the trail approaches the river, and you can rock-hop over granite slabs to the banks of the river to gain a beautiful view up-canyon that includes a deep, clear stretch of river populated with trout.

EXTENDING YOUR TRIP

Backpackers looking to take in part, or even most, of the John Muir Trail can continue south through Lyell Canyon to the park boundary at Donahue Pass—12.3 miles from the trailhead—where the JMT/PCT enters the Inyo National Forest's Ansel Adams Wilderness. Follow the JMT/PCT south for another 6.6 miles to a spur trail leading to campsites on the north shore of Thousand Island Lake. This vast, spectacular lake overlooked by Mount Ritter is one of the most iconic locations in the Sierra high country. For a one-way, 26-mile multi-day hike, leave a car at the Rush Creek Trailhead near June Lake, follow the PCT to Thousand Island Lake, then head east on the Rush Creek Trail down to the June Lake area.

Opposite: *Exploring the Sierra Crest below Mount Lewis (Hike 76)*

tioga pass

Tioga Pass boasts the distinction of being both the southernmost and the highest road-accessible mountain pass on the Sierra Crest, which opens up a wealth of options for hikers seeking high-altitude adventures without the burdens of backpacking. The gentle landscape, at least as compared to the more severe topography of the Sierra Crest in the Southern Sierra, has made the Tioga Pass area a crucial artery for visitor traffic as well as the only eastern road entrance to Yosemite Park. Thanks to the pass's high elevation, massive winter snowpacks can accumulate and then linger as late as early July. Snowfall closes the pass from mid-fall to late spring, closing off access to the park from Lee Vining. Check the park website for road conditions to determine if Tioga Pass is accessible. If the pass is closed, you can count on the trails in this section being closed as well.

There are no visitor services within the Tioga Pass area inside the park boundaries aside from the entrance station itself. A handful of formal trailheads and a few informal trailheads allow access to the gorgeous high country north and south of Tioga Road. However, there are several campgrounds, one lodge, and many services east of Tioga Pass between the pass and the town of Lee Vining.

73 Lower Gaylor Lake

RATING/ DIFFICULTY	ROUNDTRIP	ELEV GAIN/ HIGH POINT	SEASON
**/3	4.4 miles	800 feet/ 10,072 feet	July–Oct

Upper Granite Lake is nestled within a stadium-sized basin.

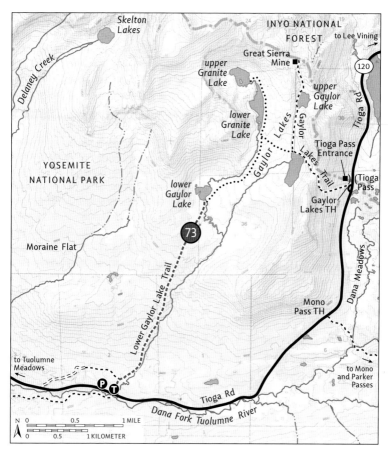

Maps: USGS 7.5-min Tioga Pass, Tom Harrison Maps Yosemite High Country; **Contact**: Tuolumne Meadows Visitor Center; **Notes**: Day-use only. No restroom or food storage at trailhead; **GPS**: 37.8797, –119.3030

This simple, quiet hike leads you to the lowest of the three Gaylor Lakes. Although not quite as scenic as its higher-elevation brothers, the lower lake has

a peaceful ambiance offering quite a bit of solitude, thanks in part to the difficult-to-locate trailhead. This is a great hike for Yosemite visitors who simply want to relax at a pretty spot while soaking in the alpine scenery in solitude.

GETTING THERE

From the junction of US Highway 395 and State Route 120/Tioga Road, drive west for

12.7 miles to the Tioga Pass Entrance. From the Tioga Pass Entrance, continue west for 4 miles to the obscure trailhead on the right (north) side of Tioga Road. Park at one of a handful of spots along the road; some of those parking spots may require a 50- to 100-yard walk along the shoulder of Tioga Road.

ON THE TRAIL

After doing the work of finding the trailhead (the most difficult navigational challenge on this hike), follow the lightly traveled single-track trail northeast on a moderate incline. At 0.15 mile, keep right at a junction with an abandoned roadbed, then continue northeast along a meadow that yields views south toward Mammoth Peak. Beyond this spot, settle in for a moderate climb through lodgepole forest as the trail travels northeast to the lower reaches of the Gaylor Lakes basin.

At 1.6 miles, the trail reaches the basin, heralded by an open meadow with nice views toward a handful of named and unnamed peaks along and around the Sierra Crest. The trail leads directly toward a conical, unnamed peak dominating the scene at the lower Gaylor Lake, which lies 0.8 mile ahead. The grade flattens as the path progresses through the meadow, making it easy to enjoy the scenery gracing the approach to the lake.

At 2 miles, the trail begins a modest descent and now the best views of the lake and the Sierra Crest begin to emerge. After another 0.4 mile, the trail terminates at the lake's southern shoreline. Lower Gaylor Lake is unlikely to crack many "top 10 most beautiful lakes in the Sierra Nevada" lists, but the quiet ambiance and solitude add to its appeal. And anyway, is there such a thing

as an "ugly" Sierra lake? (Spoiler alert: No, there is no such thing.)

EXTENDING YOUR TRIP

If you came armed with a topo map and don't mind doing a bit of routefinding, hop over the lake's outlet creek, and continue north along the eastern lakeshore to the lake's inlet creek. Work your way northeast, then due north along this creek—taking care to avoid dense thickets of willows—until you reach the Granite Lakes. A fisherman's trail follows the bank of the lower Granite Lake to the second lake, which is found within a beautiful granite amphitheater. This excursion adds an additional 2 miles of hiking and another 300 feet of elevation gain.

74 Spillway Lake

RATING/ DIFFICULTY	ROUNDTRIP	ELEV GAIN/ HIGH POINT	SEASON
***/3	8.5 miles	1000 feet/ 10,486 feet	July–Oct

Maps: USGS 7.5-min Tioga Pass, Mt. Dana, Koip Peak, Tom Harrison Maps Yosemite High Country; **Contact:** Tuolumne Meadows Visitor Center; **Notes:** Day-use only. Pit toilet and food storage at trailhead; **GPS:** 37.8909, –119.2625

This alpine destination's uninspiring name does little to impress upon hikers the beauty of its shimmering sapphire centerpiece set in a vast meadow bound by the multicolored Kuna Crest. It may be too late to rename Spillway Lake, but you're sure to come up with more worthy adjectives following the completion of this 8.5-mile trek through forest, meadow, and glade.

The blue waters of Spillway Lake are worth a visit.

GETTING THERE

From the junction of State Route 120/Tioga Road and US Highway 395 just south of Lee Vining, drive west on SR 120/Tioga Road through the Tioga Pass Entrance. At 13.5 miles, turn left into the Mono Pass Trailhead parking area.

ON THE TRAIL

The route to Spillway Lake follows a segment of the Mono Pass Trail that also serves as the beginning of the Parker Pass and Mount Lewis route (Hike 76) and the Mono Pass route (Hike 75). You can combine these routes together into one route if you don't mind a little backtracking, or if you have some cross-country navigation skills. The initial segment of the Mono Pass Trail dips toward the fledgling Dana Fork Tuolumne River, crossing two separate forks at 0.45 and 0.5 mile. Beyond the river, the trail passes through a pleasant but viewless lodgepole forest with an understory of lush grasses and wildflowers. Views emerge at a meadow lined by Parker Pass Creek at 1.4 miles, revealing Mammoth Peak and the Kuna Crest to the west.

Continue southeast for another 0.9 mile to a junction where the Mono Pass Trail and the Spillway Lake Trail part ways. Keep right to follow the Spillway Lake Trail due south through a beautiful meadow on a mellow incline. The incline becomes steeper as the trail enters a wooded ravine through which Parker Pass Creek flows melodiously. At 3.8 miles, the trail arrives at a vast meadow encompassing Spillway Lake, which lies in a shallow depression to the south.

The trail comes to an end at 4 miles, but you can work your way across the grassy

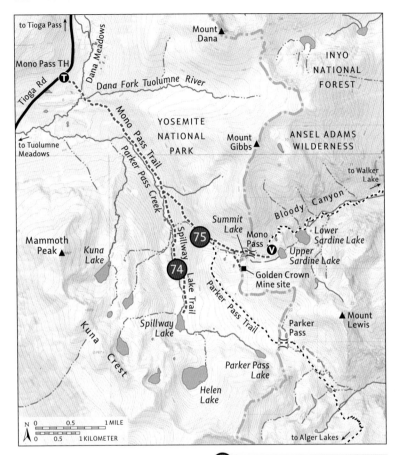

meadow toward a handful of rock outcrops along the shores of the lake. As you do so, be sure to look back across Spillway Lake's outlet to see the high points of the Sierra Crest north of Tioga Pass looming in the distance, including Gaylor Peak, White Mountain, and Mount Conness. The lake is your turnaround spot; from here reverse course to return to the trailhead.

75 Mono Pass

RATING/ DIFFICULTY	ROUNDTRIP	ELEV GAIN/ HIGH POINT	SEASON
***/3	9.1 miles	1200 feet/ 10,642 feet	July–Oct

Maps: USGS 7.5-min Tioga Pass, Mt. Dana, Koip Peak; **Contact:** Tuolumne Meadows

Visitor Center; **Notes:** Suitable for backpacking (Mono Pass/Parker Pass; set up east of Mono Pass on Inyo National Forest land). Vault toilets and food storage at trailhead; **GPS:** 37.8909, –119.2625

For thousands of years, Mono Pass served as a migratory route for the Paiute people as they traveled the Central Sierra to trade with their Miwok cousins in the west. Prior to the establishment of Yosemite National Park, miners trickled into the Mono Pass and Tioga Pass area in search of veins of silver, displacing the Paiute and establishing the ultimately unprofitable Golden Crown Mine. The Mono Pass Trail leads you to this historical and scenic place, from which you can admire views into the Mono Basin all while regarding historical relics and the distant echoes of the Mono people passing through.

GETTING THERE
From the junction of State Route 120 (Tioga Road) and US Highway 395 just south of Lee Vining, head west on SR 120/Tioga Road through the Tioga Pass Entrance to Yosemite National Park. At 13.5 miles, turn left into the Mono Pass Trailhead parking area.

ON THE TRAIL
The route to Mono Pass follows a segment of trail that also serves as the beginning of the Parker Pass and Mount Lewis route (Hike 76) and the Spillway Lake route (Hike 74). You can combine these routes together

Climb a short way past the Golden Crown Mine for a great view of Mono Lake.

into one route with a little backtracking or through cross-country navigation. The initial segment of the Mono Pass Trail dips down toward the fledgling Dana Fork Tuolumne River, crossing two separate forks at 0.45 and 0.5 mile. Beyond that, the trail passes through a pleasant but viewless lodgepole forest with an understory of lush grasses and wildflowers. Views emerge at a meadow nurtured by Parker Pass Creek at 1.4 miles, revealing the towering forms of Mammoth Peak and the Kuna Crest to the west.

Continue southeast for another 0.9 mile to a junction where the Mono Pass Trail and Spillway Lake Trail part ways. Keep left here to continue your moderate incline as the Mono Pass Trail wraps around the southern and then eastern flank of Mount Gibbs. Views are unremarkable until you reach a junction with the Parker Pass Trail at 3.4 miles (keep left), at which point views toward the high points of the Kuna Crest and Sierra Crest to the south and west unfurl beyond a spacious meadow.

At 3.6 miles, look for an unmarked spur trail leading south from the Mono Pass Trail. This path crosses a streambed feeding a grassy tarn before climbing through whitebark pines to five preserved cabin structures that commemorate the ruins of the Golden Crown Mine. Take a short climb up the slope behind these log cabins to gain a great view north toward Mount Gibbs's towering massif and east down Bloody Canyon toward Mono Lake.

After completing this diversion and returning to the Mono Pass Trail, turn right to continue east to Mono Pass and the park boundary. Summit Lake lies just beyond the park boundary sign, which indicates the location of Mono Pass itself. Backpackers can pitch their tents east of Mono Pass on Inyo National Forest property. For one final scenic reward, continue a short distance down into Bloody Canyon just beyond the pass. As the Bloody Canyon Trail wraps around a prominent ridge, it emerges at a viewpoint peering down Bloody Canyon toward Walker Lake and beyond to the Mono Craters and the south shore of Mono Lake.

EXTENDING YOUR TRIP

If you arrange a car shuttle with one car at the Bloody Canyon Trailhead and one car at Mono Pass Trailhead, you can continue down Bloody Canyon from Mono Pass, past the Sardine Lakes, and then out to the trailhead just south of Walker Lake. This route replicates a famous Mono migratory route in reverse for a total of 8.5 miles with 1500 feet of elevation gain and 3000 feet of elevation loss. The road to Bloody Canyon Trailhead can be rough, and low-clearance vehicles are not recommended. Details on the location of the Bloody Canyon Trailhead are in Appendix I.

76 Parker Pass and Mount Lewis

RATING/ DIFFICULTY	ROUNDTRIP	ELEV GAIN/ HIGH POINT	SEASON
***/4	13 miles	3000 feet/ 12,350 feet	July–Oct

Maps: USGS 7.5-min Tioga Pass, Mt. Dana, Koip Peak; **Contact:** Tuolumne Meadows Visitor Center; **Notes:** Suitable for backpacking beyond Parker Pass (Mono Pass/Parker Pass). Vault toilet and food storage at trailhead; **GPS:** 37.8909, –119.2625

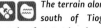 *The terrain along the Sierra Crest south of Tioga Pass consists largely of rust-colored metamorphic moun-*

The multi-colored rocks of the Kuna Crest

tain peaks that survey spectacular panoramas spanning the entirety of the park to beyond the Mono Basin. Accessing most of these peaks usually requires a grueling hike where you'll spend more time looking at your feet than the surrounding scenery. However, this lengthy approach to Mount Lewis by way of Parker Pass allows you to enjoy a much more relaxing approach with only a little bit of steep routefinding to the top of Mount Lewis, a 12,500-foot peak with stellar panoramic views often overlooked in favor of more famous destinations like Mount Dana.

GETTING THERE

From the junction of State Route 120 (Tioga Road) and US Highway 395 just south of Lee Vining, drive west on SR 120/Tioga Road through the Tioga Pass Entrance to Yosemite National Park. At 13.5 miles, turn left into the Mono Pass Trailhead parking area.

ON THE TRAIL

The beginning of this route shares the same 2.3-mile trail segment as the Mono Pass route (Hike 75) and the Spillway Lake route (Hike 74). This easy stretch passes mostly through lodgepole forest as it threads its way south between Parker Pass Creek and the base of Mount Gibbs. Keep left at the junction where the Spillway Lake Trail splits off at 2.3 miles to continue on the Mono Pass Trail on a moderate incline through more lodgepole forest with only sporadic views until a second junction with the Parker Pass Trail at 3.4 miles. Turn right here.

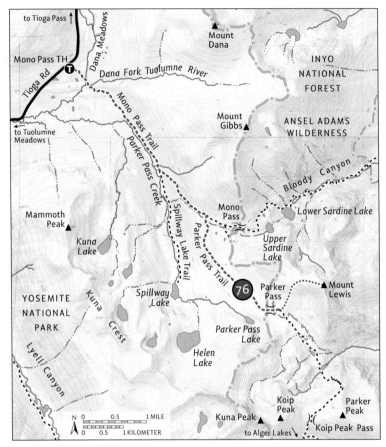

As the Parker Pass Trail leads away from the Mono Pass Trail, it crosses a grassy meadow nourished by a Parker Pass Creek tributary before ascending a broad ridge bewhiskered with whitebark pines. The sparse forest enables views east across Mono Pass and beyond toward Mono Lake and west toward the colorful blend of granite and metamorphic rock composing the Kuna Crest. Spillway Lake shimmers as a sapphire gem set within an emerald field encompassed by the crest. A memorable traverse across a vast meadow just above the tree line begins at 4.3 miles. This meadow erupts in wildflowers, including little elephant heads, owl's clovers, buckwheats, lupines, and penstemons during midsummer, and the views of the surrounding metamorphic peaks leave an indelible imprint on your memory.

At the 5.2-mile mark, the trail reaches the park's boundary with the Inyo National Forest Ansel Adams Wilderness area at Parker Pass. Unlike most mountain passes, Parker Pass doesn't offer a grand scenic reveal; you'll have to walk another 0.3 mile to a ledge overlooking a handful of alpine tarns to get any sort of view. From this spot, turn to the northeast to face the summit ridge of Mount Lewis. Climb cross-country on steep scree to begin the summit approach.

After gaining a quick 700 feet over 0.5 mile, attain the apex of the rounded ridge and then turn due east toward Mount Lewis. Mount Lewis is not visible until you're nearly on it; make sure you continue east to reach the top and avoid descending the steep slopes to the north and south. The summit itself (6.5 miles) is an easy walkup with no scrambling involved. There are three distinct peaklets, each of which reveals a different perspective on the spectacular scene unfolding before you.

Look east to scan the entirety of the Mono Basin along with the pumice slopes of the Mono Craters. From the easternmost peaklet, you can peer down into Parker Lake's canyon and beyond toward June Lake and the peaks surrounding Mammoth Lakes. From the westernmost peaklet, you get a great view of Mount Gibbs and the deep crease of Bloody Canyon (see Appendix I) below. Look west to see the Sierra Crest north of Tioga Road, crowned by Mount Conness, along with a broad, forested expanse of the Tuolumne River basin containing Tuolumne Meadows.

You can turn around and retrace your steps for an out-and-back hike. Or, if you've got the cross-country navigation chops, why not follow Mount Lewis's ridge west along a sheer escarpment overlooking Bloody Canyon? This enjoyable traverse ends with an unpleasant but short descent on jagged scree that reaches the ruins of the Golden Crown Mine south of Mono Pass. From there, you can return to the trailhead by way of the Mono Pass Trail (Hike 75), which allows you to weave two hikes into one.

77 Upper Gaylor Lakes

RATING/ DIFFICULTY	ROUNDTRIP	ELEV GAIN/ HIGH POINT	SEASON
***/3	5.8 miles	1400 feet/ 10,794 feet	July– mid-Oct

Maps: USGS 7.5-min Tioga Pass, Tom Harrison Maps Yosemite High Country; **Contact:** Tuolumne Meadows Wilderness Center; **Notes:** Day hiking only. Food storage lockers at trailhead. No restroom at trailhead; **GPS:** 37.9101, –119.2582

From the highest trailhead in the park adjacent to Tioga Pass, you can follow a surprisingly tough trail up to the Gaylor Lakes basin. These alpine lakes shimmer within a primeval landscape rich with beautiful flora and pre-park mining history. The first lake's western shore creates a memorable "infinity pool" illusion, with high points of the Cathedral Range on the horizon.

GETTING THERE

From the junction of US Highway 395 and State Route 120/Tioga Road in Lee Vining, drive west for 12.7 miles to the Tioga Pass Entrance. From the entrance, drive west for

Splashes of mountain huckleberry brighten the view above Gaylor Lake.

50 yards to the Gaylor Lakes Trailhead on the right (west) side of the road.

ON THE TRAIL

Not one for preambles or pleasantries, the Gaylor Lakes Trail commences an immediate steep climb away from Tioga Road through sparse forests graced with plentiful viewpoints from which you can scan the Dana Meadows and beyond toward Mammoth Peak. Take full advantage of the vistas for frequent breaks to cope with the thin atmosphere and steep grade, especially if you have not had a few days to acclimate to the higher elevations.

After 0.5 mile of hard climbing, the trail tops out at a saddle between an unnamed peak to the south and Gaylor Peak to the north. If you have energy to spare, consider climbing Gaylor Peak due north from the saddle, which adds 1 mile and 500 feet of

elevation gain. The trail descends 200 feet from this saddle to the eastern shore of the first of the two upper Gaylor Lakes. Keep right to follow the trail along the lake, making sure to look west to enjoy the illusion of an infinity pool yielding to a horizon spiked by Johnson, Unicorn, and Cathedral Peaks to the southwest.

At 0.9 mile, the trail turns away from the first lake to travel due north on a moderate, grassy incline toward the second lake. The trail sidles along the creek that drains the second lake, with running water adding a melodious note early in the season. At 1.3 miles, the trail reaches the rocky outlet of the second Gaylor Lake, which lies nestled within a basin north of Gaylor Peak. Colorful metamorphic rock rings the lake basin, rising to the Sierra Crest. The Great Sierra Mine lies to the north of the second lake by way of an easy-to-follow old roadbed that climbs for 0.5 mile. Mining companies established the mine around the same time as mining operations in nearby Bennettville, Mono Pass, Bodie, and Lundy. There's quite a bit of old mining detritus lying about, and the views are pretty stellar as well.

Backtrack to the first lake, then look to the west from the lake's inlet to identify a conical-shaped peak about 0.75 mile to the west-northwest. If you fancy a cross-country exploration to another lake basin, head west-northwest toward the peak across the spacious meadow in front of you. After about

0.4 mile, turn right at a creek draining the Granite Lakes. Find a fisherman's trail that runs along the east bank of the lower Granite Lake for 0.5 mile before cutting to the west toward the upper Granite Lake, which sparkles within a stunning, stadium-sized amphitheater. Note that if you skip this segment, you can subtract 1.8 miles from this hike's overall distance.

Retrace your steps back to the first Gaylor Lake to reconnect with the trail. Follow it back up and over the saddle and then drop back down to the trailhead.

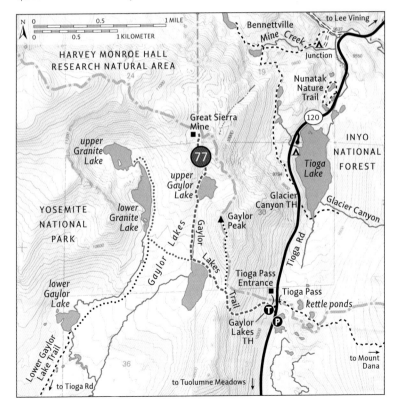

78 Mount Dana

RATING/ DIFFICULTY	ROUNDTRIP	ELEV GAIN/ HIGH POINT	SEASON
*****/4	5.2 miles	3100 feet/ 13,057 feet	July–Oct

Map: USGS 7.5-min Tioga Pass; **Contact:** Yosemite National Park, Tioga Pass; **Notes:** Day-use only. Unmaintained route; **GPS:** 37.9108, –119.2577

Towering 3000 feet above Tioga Pass, the rust-red summit of Yosemite's second-highest point, Mount Dana, affords some of the most magnificent views anywhere in the park. Peak-bagging afficio-nados and anybody with an appreciation for views spanning a hundred-mile radius across the Sierra and the Mono Basin must not miss this breathtaking (both literally and figura-tively) hike.

GETTING THERE

From the junction of US Highway 395 and State Route 120/Tioga Road, drive west for 12.7 miles to the Tioga Pass Entrance. From the Tioga Pass Entrance, continue for 100 yards to a pullout on the right (west) side of the road that allows parking for day-use. From here, backtrack to the park entrance to find the unsigned start of the route to Mount Dana leaving from a staff parking lot east of the park entrance kiosk.

ON THE TRAIL

This difficult route begins innocently enough on a semi-formal trail departing from an employee parking area across from the Tioga Pass Entrance Station. The trail travels south across Tioga Pass, threading its way through a series of kettle ponds. As glaciers

retreated through the ages, they gouged out small depressions that fill with snowmelt through spring, summer, and occasionally into fall. A variety of Tioga Pass–area peaks poke their heads above each respective pond, creating a series of picture-perfect lakeside scenes. Even if you have no appe-tite for the challenging climb ahead, consider following the mostly flat trail for 0.35 mile to the last pond as a short excursion on its own before the climb starts.

The pretty stroll turns into a steep climb at 0.4 mile. Be aware that if you have not had a chance to acclimate for a few nights at high elevation before attempting this hike, you may encounter altitude sickness issues. As the climb progresses, you will undoubtedly find that you cannot hike at your usual pace due to the steep grade (over 1000 feet per mile) and the high elevation (10,000 feet to 13,000 feet). The best strategy is to pick a speed that allows you to climb without being winded. This may mean you end up moving more slowly than a 1-mile-per-hour pace, but I encourage you to remember that your speed does not matter here. What matters is that you do not starve yourself of oxygen at an elevation where the oxygen level is about 80 percent of what it is at sea level. Tortoises do better than hares on Mount Dana.

The initial ascent climbs through a spa-cious forest of lodgepole and whitebark pines. Occasional gaps in the tree cover reveal views to the west across Dana Mead-ows toward Mammoth Peak, providing a tantalizing taste of the views that await. The tree cover disappears abruptly, and from here all that stands between you and the relentless Sierra sun is a thin atmosphere, a wide-brimmed hat, and a layer of sunscreen. At 1 mile, the trail enters a beautiful hillside meadow laced with countless spring-fed

From the summit of Mount Dana, Mono Lake looks like a bright-blue donut.

streams. These streams produce vivid wildflower displays in July and August as the resident plants take advantage of the alpine environment's short growing season.

At 1.2 miles, the trail leaves the meadow behind, and the only flora ahead is lichens, small flowers, and, near the summit, the brilliant sky pilot. Despite the mountain's rocky surface, a well-defined path leads uphill on a steep, winding incline that ascends 600 feet over the next 0.3 mile. A wind shelter constructed at 1.5 miles offers a welcome spot to take a break and soak in the views across Tuolumne Meadows and the Cathedral Range. Shortly beyond the wind shelter, the trail traverses a gently sloping plateau where the grade temporarily eases into something far more reasonable than the 2000-feet-per-mile incline you enjoyed up to this point. Continue across this plateau with the massive, steep, conical form of Mount Dana's summit taunting you with the

inevitability of a final relentless push to the top.

That climb begins at 1.8 miles with 1200 feet of elevation left to gain over the next 0.75 mile to the summit. To make matters more interesting, the next quarter mile passes through jagged scree where it is next to impossible to maintain a well-defined path. Huge cairns up to five feet tall placed at 100-yard intervals show hikers the way, and each cairn makes a convenient stopping point to catch up with the breathing that has been threatening to run away throughout the climb. The steepest part of the ascent occurs over the last 0.4 mile just as you are reaching the elevation at which most people start struggling with altitude sickness. Again, hike very slowly and rest often. The slow forward progress may be frustrating, but if you continue uphill at a turtle's pace, you eventually crest the summit where an astonishing panorama awaits.

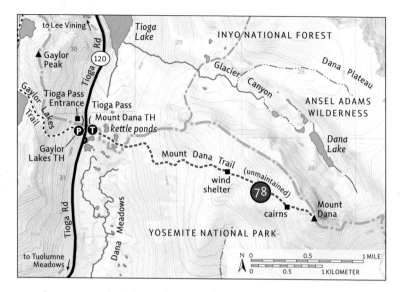

Look east to see the entirety of Mono Lake, looking no bigger than a blue donut from this vantage. The rust-colored peaks of the Lee Vining Canyon and Lundy Canyon drainages loom to the north, and you can pick out Saddlebag Lake shimmering in a basin beyond a ribbon of green around Lee Vining Creek. The Gaylor Lakes basin lies to the northwest, and that basin yields to a vast, dark-green forest descending to the green fields of Tuolumne Meadows. The rugged high country of Mount Hoffmann and Ten Lakes Pass lies beyond the meadows to the west, and to the southwest, the iconic peaks of the Cathedral Range—Cathedral, Unicorn, the Cockscomb, the Echo Peaks, Mount Lyell, and Vogelsang—rise above this complex granitic mountain block. To the southwest, the Kuna Crest blends into the highest reaches of the Cathedral Range before merging with the rust-colored peaks above Parker Pass to the south. In other words, the view is amazing—perhaps more amazing than any other day hike–accessible high point in the park.

With gravity on your side again, the descent will be easier on your cardiovascular system. However, the trade-off is that gravity assaults your knees with vindictive glee. Trekking poles can help take pressure off your knees, and a slow and easy pace will also help avoid too much pain in your feet from stepping on jagged scree. Slowly and surely, make your way back to the Tioga Pass Entrance with a phenomenal experience to treasure.

Opposite: Sunrise and tufa at the banks of Mono Lake.

lee vining canyon
and mono basin

As you pass east over the Yosemite National Park boundary into the Inyo National Forest on the east side of Tioga Pass, you enter the "Eastern Sierra," a general term referring to the Sierra Nevada on the eastern side of the Sierra Crest. Although the destinations here are separate from Yosemite National Park, with all trailheads lying within Inyo National Forest, Humboldt-Toiyabe National Forest, and Mono Lake Tufa State Natural Reserve, these spectacular locations remain intertwined with Yosemite's history. Hikes within this sprawling region include remote explorations into glacial lake basins, excursions through aspen groves that blaze with fiery color during fall, and short trips to several geologic oddities ranging from volcanic craters to the famous tufa on the shores of Mono Lake.

Numerous campgrounds and several lodges and motels provide lodging options for visitors to Lee Vining, the June Lake Loop, Lundy Canyon, and Virginia Canyon. Two wilderness areas—the Ansel Adams Wilderness and the Hoover Wilderness—lie south and north of State Route 120/Tioga Road, respectively. The Harvey Monroe Hall Research Natural Area encompasses a large swath of geography to the west of Saddlebag Lake Road, and it serves as a vast, living laboratory where scientists study characteristics of alpine and subalpine habitats. The research area is open to hikers, but only for day-use. Backpackers must confine camping to the Ansel Adams and Hoover Wilderness

Low effort, high scenery at the Nunatak Nature Trail

areas. The Mono Basin Scenic Area Visitor Center in Lee Vining provides information and interpretive programs, and Inyo National Forest's Lee Vining Ranger Station is a source of info for forest service trails and permits.

79 Nunatak Nature Trail

RATING/ DIFFICULTY	ROUNDTRIP	ELEV GAIN/ HIGH POINT	SEASON
**/1	0.5 mile	Negligible/ 9657 feet	July–Oct

Map: USGS 7.5-min Tioga Pass; **Contact:** Inyo National Forest, Mono Lake Ranger District; **Notes:** Day-use only. No restroom at trailhead. No food storage at trailhead; **GPS:** 37.9313, –119.2502

 This tiny gem of a hike offers a big lesson on *geologic processes. A nunatak is a ridge or mountaintop protruding from an icefield. Also referred to as glacial islands for their ability to preserve seed banks and species that then help to replenish the vegetation when glaciers retreat, nunataks appear on the Sierra Crest in the Tioga Pass area in several spots, most notably at Mount Dana, which towers above the three small, tranquil lakes along this easy, family-friendly route.*

GETTING THERE
From US Highway 395 in Lee Vining, drive west on State Route 120/Tioga Road for 9.9 miles to the Nunatak Nature Trail Trailhead on the right side of the road. Park along the road near the trailhead sign.

ON THE TRAIL
From the trailhead sign, head due west on a short connector path that leads directly to

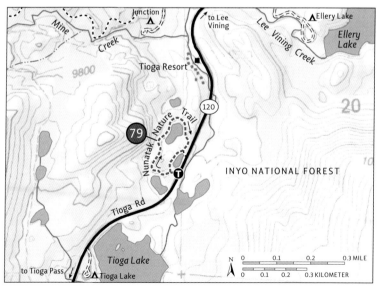

the looping nature trail. Turn left to make a clockwise loop, and begin a leisurely stroll pausing periodically to read the interpretive plaques that explain the geology of nunataks and the long history of glaciation in the Tioga Pass region. The three small lakes reflect the towering heights of Mount Dana as well as landmarks such as Gaylor Peak, the Dana Plateau, and Tioga Peak.

The loop returns to SR 120/Tioga Road at 0.4 mile; keep right to remain on the nature trail while skirting the western edge of the third and smallest lake. At 0.5 mile, turn left to return to the parking area. Although you can finish the hike in minutes, it's better to take your time absorbing geologic lessons and enjoying the tranquil habitats on display.

80 Bennettville and Fantail Lake

RATING/ DIFFICULTY	ROUNDTRIP	ELEV GAIN/ HIGH POINT	SEASON
***/2	3.4 miles	400 feet/ 9908 feet	July–Oct

Map: USGS 7.5-min Tioga Pass; **Contact:** Inyo National Forest, Mono Lake Ranger District; **Notes:** Day-use only. Vault toilet located within Junction Campground near trailhead. No food storage at trailhead; **GPS:** 37.9383, –119.2511

This unassuming and unexpected little trail delivers big on historic interest and scenic beauty. After a stop at the site of Bennettville, a mining colony that built the forerunner of today's Tioga Road, this mellow journey leads to a trio of beautiful alpine lakes basking in High Sierra sunshine at the base of the Sierra Crest.

GETTING THERE
From US Highway 395 in Lee Vining, drive west on State Route 120/Tioga Road for 9.3 miles to the junction of Saddlebag Lake Road and SR 120/Tioga Road. Turn right onto Saddlebag Lake Road, then in a few hundred feet turn left into Junction Campground. Park at one of the handful of spots immediately on the left before the bridge crossing Lee Vining Creek. Walk over the bridge and into the campground to find the signed Bennettville Trail adjacent to the camp host site.

Whether you catch anything or not, Fantail Lake is a fine place to spend an afternoon.

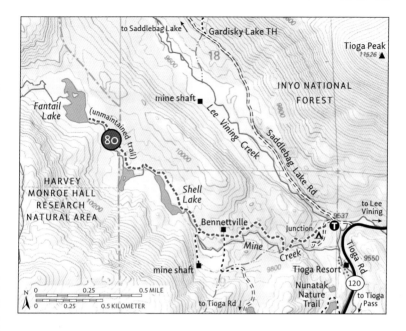

ON THE TRAIL

The Bennettville Trail leads away from the campground as it bobs and weaves in a generally westward direction along the banks of Mine Creek, which rumbles along through a willow-lined ravine on your left. After completing the bulk of the climbing over the first 0.7 mile, the trail tops out at a rocky ledge where two structures from the Bennettville mining colony remain standing thanks to forest service preservation. These fascinating old structures look a bit drafty today, but during Bennettville's heyday, the buildings served to house miners and to test the purity of the extracted minerals.

After contemplating a dusty, hard-knock silver-mining past, continue west past the remnants of an old road leading back to Tioga Road. Look to the left to see a segment of old mining road leading to the primary mine shaft on the opposite side of Mine Creek. One last bit of climbing brings you to the outlet of Shell Lake at 0.9 mile, a long, narrow lake boasting stellar views looking northwest toward North Peak.

As you work your way around Shell Lake's outlet and along its eastern shore, look out for a false trail at 1 mile. Keep right at this easy-to-miss junction to continue traveling northwest toward the second lake, which has no name. Another 0.5 mile of peaceful, nearly flat walking through subalpine forest leads to the boundary of the Harvey Monroe Hall Research Natural Area. Shortly beyond the boundary of the research area, the trail reaches Fantail Lake. This is the largest and prettiest of the lakes along the route, and it seems too good to be true that you can enjoy a scene this beautiful for such a modest amount of effort. There are several places to rest, relax, or fish along the eastern shore of the lake before it's time to return the way you came to the trailhead.

81 Gardisky Lake

RATING/ DIFFICULTY	ROUNDTRIP	ELEV GAIN/ HIGH POINT	SEASON
**/3	2.4 miles	800 feet/ 10,522 feet	July–Oct

Map: USGS 7.5-min Tioga Pass; **Contact:** Inyo National Forest, Mono Lake Ranger District; **Notes:** Suitable for backpacking (Gardisky Lake Trail). No restroom at trailhead. No food storage at trailhead; **GPS:** 37.9505, –119.2612

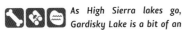 *As High Sierra lakes go, Gardisky Lake is a bit of an* anomaly. *For starters, it drains into two separate canyons from its perch atop the Tioga Crest. Additionally, instead of occupying a rocky glacial basin, Gardisky Lake is surrounded by a spacious meadow. And finally, the lake offers some gobsmacking views looking both west to the Sierra Crest and east to the Mono Basin. This unusual but eminently pleasant experience can be yours by following the short but very steep trail from Saddlebag Lake Road.*

GETTING THERE

From US Highway 395 in Lee Vining, drive west on State Route 120/Tioga Road for 9.3 miles to the junction of Saddlebag Lake Road and SR 120/Tioga Road. Turn right onto Saddlebag Lake Road and continue along the unpaved road for 1.2 miles to a small parking area on the left (west) side of the road. The Gardisky Lake Trailhead is just ahead on the right (east) side of the road.

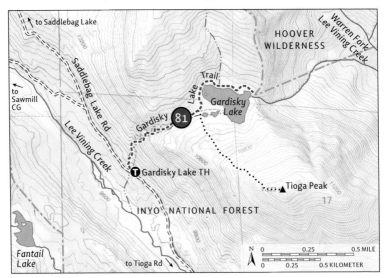

Sunrise over Gardisky Lake

ON THE TRAIL

Cross Saddlebag Lake Road and find the unmarked Gardisky Lake Trail on the east side of the road. The trail begins a steep ascent almost immediately, and you will soon be huffing and puffing your way through a dense forest of lodgepole pines. After 0.3 mile, the forest opens to views west toward the Sierra Crest, adding some scenic spice to the uphill grind. After another 0.1 mile, the trail reaches a series of tight, rocky switchbacks along the bank of Gardisky Lake's outlet creek before the grade finally eases at the mouth of a grassy meadow.

The grassy meadow heralds a transition into a different world. Gone is the dense pine forest. In its place lies an expansive meadow surrounding Gardisky Lake. Hike due east past a handful of small ponds on nearly flat terrain. At 0.7 mile, keep to the left to follow a faint fisherman's trail along the northern shore of the lake. This path will lead you to the lake's eastern outlet, from which point you can stand upon a precipice peering into the depths of Lee Vining Canyon and beyond toward Mono Basin. This is your turnaround point; return to the trailhead the way you came.

EXTENDING YOUR TRIP

If you've got the time and stamina, you can bag Tioga Peak by ascending the steep, scree-encrusted slope on the south side of the lake. Your mileage will vary depending on the route you take, but you can count on adding another 1050 feet of elevation over less than 1 mile.

82 Greenstone Lake

RATING/ DIFFICULTY	ROUNDTRIP	ELEV GAIN/ HIGH POINT	SEASON
**/2	4.1 miles	350 feet/ 10,179 feet	July–Oct

Map: USGS 7.5-min Tioga Pass; **Contact:** Inyo National Forest, Mono Lake Ranger District; **Notes:** Day-use only. Restroom adjacent to trailhead; **GPS:** 37.9657, –119.2704

Saddlebag Lake is both the largest lake in the area and a focal point for recreation in the upper Lee Vining Canyon area. This moderate loop stitched together from two trails that encircle Saddlebag Lake leads to beautiful Greenstone Lake for a taste of High Sierra splendor without a significant amount of energy expenditure.

GETTING THERE

From US Highway 395 in Lee Vining, drive west on State Route 120/Tioga Road for 9.3 miles to the junction of Saddlebag Lake Road and SR 120/Tioga Road. Turn right onto Saddlebag Lake Road and follow the unpaved road for 2.4 miles to the signed Saddlebag Trailhead parking on the right. After parking, follow the service road toward a second parking area above the Saddlebag Lake Resort. The trail begins at the east end of this second parking area.

ON THE TRAIL

From the trailhead, commence your wanderings with a short passage through a rocky garden of spring-fed willows that turn gold during the fall. After navigating the willow garden, the trail turns north to parallel the eastern shore of Saddlebag Lake about 50 to 75 feet above the surface of the lake. As you progress north, the distinctive shape of North Peak draws your eye, followed soon by Mount Conness as you near the lake's northern shore.

At 1.3 miles, the trail arcs to the west after entering a dense forest. Look to the left for an old ranger station at 2.1 miles, followed by a four-way junction. An informal path on the left leads downhill to the lakeshore if you desire a short diversion. Otherwise, continue straight and pass through a second junction at 2.2 miles before finally turning right on a spur trail that runs west along the outlet creek draining Greenstone Lake.

Opposite: *North Peak from the grassy banks of Greenstone Lake*

Head west along the creek to the shoreline of Greenstone Lake at 2.3 miles. This is the prettier of the two lakes, and this spot is a perfect place to stop and take an extended snack break.

Backtrack to the main trail to begin the return journey to the trailhead. Although the western leg of the loop around Saddlebag Lake is shorter, the jagged scree composing the trail's surface makes it seem more difficult and more tedious than the eastern leg of the loop. This long, uncomfortable section of hiking comes to an end at 3.9 miles near the dam impounding

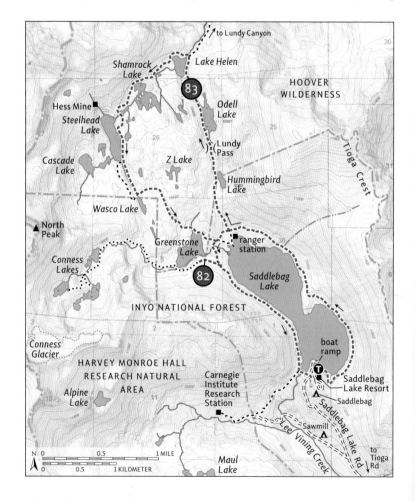

Saddlebag Lake. Cross over the dam and follow a path back to the road to return to your car at 4.1 miles.

83 Twenty Lakes Basin

RATING/ DIFFICULTY	ROUNDTRIP	ELEV GAIN/ HIGH POINT	SEASON
****/3	8.4 miles	1100 feet/ 10,361 feet	July–Oct

Maps: USGS 7.5-min Tioga Pass, Dunderberg Peak; **Contact:** Inyo National Forest, Mono Lake Ranger District; **Notes:** Suitable for backpacking (Saddlebag Lake Trail). Food storage lockers at trailhead. Restroom adjacent to trailhead; **GPS:** 37.9657, –119.2704

  This classic High Sierra adventure follows a beautiful, moderate trail through the Hoover Wilderness for a quintessential mountain experience with bountiful lakes and alpine views. The lakes along the way take on every shape and size, and the backdrop of the Sierra Crest culminating in North Peak and Mount Conness paints a perfect image of alpine splendor.

GETTING THERE
From US Highway 395 in Lee Vining, drive west on State Route 120/Tioga Road for 9.3 miles to the junction of Saddlebag Lake Road and SR 120/Tioga Road. Turn right onto Saddlebag Lake Road, then continue along the unpaved road for 2.4 miles to the signed Saddlebag Trailhead parking on the right. After parking, follow a service road toward a second parking area above the Saddlebag Lake Resort. The trail begins at the east end of this second parking area.

ON THE TRAIL
Begin from the trailhead on the eastern end of the Saddlebag Lake Resort parking area. Set out from the trailhead through a garden of willow trees that flash gold during fall. The trail bends to the north as it parallels the eastern shore of Saddlebag Lake about 50 to 75 feet above the waterline. The first views of North Peak and Mount Conness emerge at just over the half-mile mark—these two peaks will be constant scenic companions throughout the hike, although a grove of lodgepole and whitebark pines temporarily obscures the views at 1.3 miles.

At 2.1 miles, look for an old ranger station on your left just before a four-way junction. Turn right at this junction to hike north into the Hoover Wilderness toward Lundy Pass on a gentle ascent through open meadows dotted with whitebark pines. Shortly before you reach Lundy Pass, look to your right for an informal spur trail and follow it to Hummingbird Lake. Walk a short distance around the lake's grassy shores to get another look west toward North Peak—your faithful hiking partner for the day.

Beyond Hummingbird Lake, the trail crests Lundy Pass and then descends toward Lake Helen. Along the way, the trail traverses a rocky ledge above Odell Lake which lies tucked into a rugged basin on your right. Just past Odell Lake's outlet, the trail descends a narrow ravine where the trail surface devolves into jagged scree. This uncomfortable stretch of downhill hiking comes to a merciful end at the shores of lovely Lake Helen at 3.7 miles.

Lake Helen is a fine place to stop and take a break to enjoy cross-lake views of North Peak. For a quick diversion, you can wander a short distance down the Lundy Canyon Trail to peer into the depths of Lundy Canyon to

the north (Hike 89) from a rocky promontory. After returning to Lake Helen, cross the outlet creek and begin a staircase-like ascent over a series of broad, meadow-blanketed ledges to reach the next major lake on the route: Shamrock Lake. Shamrock Lake lies at the precise halfway point (4.2 miles), and it differs from previous lakes thanks to its numerous rocky bays and islands.

After completing the traverse of Shamrock Lake's northern shore, the trail passes a small, unnamed lake before arriving at a junction with an old mining road accessing the Hess Mine at 4.6 miles. Turn right onto the mining road and pass through a thicket of willows for about 40 yards to reach the shore of Steelhead Lake. This short diversion provides the best full views of Steelhead Lake framed by the Sierra Crest crowned by North Peak. You can also scramble up to the remains of the Hess Mine by following the degenerating mining road, but this diversion does not improve significantly on the scenery.

Complete your lakeside reconnaissance and backtrack to the main trail. Turn right and follow the trail south over a rocky knoll before settling into a groove along Steelhead Lake's east bank. Keep straight at a junction with a spur loop at 5.4 miles that leads to some possible campsites. At 5.6 miles, the trail turns away from Wasco Lake to descend through sparse lodgepole pine forest to grassy Greenstone Lake. After passing Greenstone Lake's northern shore and outlet creek, look for an unmarked informal path that leads through a grassy, wildflower-flecked meadow toward the lake's eastern shore and more views of North Peak.

After enjoying Greenstone Lake, conclude the hike by retracing your steps to the main trail. Turn right to follow the trail south along the western shore of Saddlebag Lake. Although the western segment of the loop trail around Saddlebag Lake is shorter than the eastern segment, the tread is rockier and less pleasant to walk on. The discomfort ends when you reach the dam across Saddlebag Lake's outlet. Cross the dam and follow a path upslope to the main road and the Saddlebag Lake parking area.

84 Conness Lakes

RATING/ DIFFICULTY	ROUNDTRIP	ELEV GAIN/ HIGH POINT	SEASON
***/3	6.2 miles	800 feet/ 10,784 feet	July–Oct

Map: USGS 7.5-min Tioga Pass; **Contact:** Inyo National Forest, Mono Lake Ranger District; **Notes:** Day-use only. Cross-country navigation required. Difficult terrain. Restroom adjacent to trailhead; **GPS:** 37.9650, –119.2721

This cross-country route follows informal trails into a glacial basin at the foot of Mount Conness. A quintet of lakes colored turquoise by glacial sediment awaits hikers comfortable with a bit of route-finding and rough terrain. Solitude and alpine beauty reward those who attempt the route, and rumor has it that the fishing isn't half bad either.

GETTING THERE
From US Highway 395 in Lee Vining, drive west on State Route 120/Tioga Road for

Opposite: Steelhead Lake and omnipresent North Peak

9.3 miles to the junction of Saddlebag Lake Road and SR 120/Tioga Road. Turn right onto Saddlebag Lake Road, then continue along the unpaved road for 2.4 miles to the signed Saddlebag Trailhead parking on the right. From the parking area, follow the service road toward a second parking area above the Saddlebag Lake Resort.

ON THE TRAIL

From the parking area, follow an unmarked path down to the dam impounding

Alpine splendor at the lowest Conness Lake

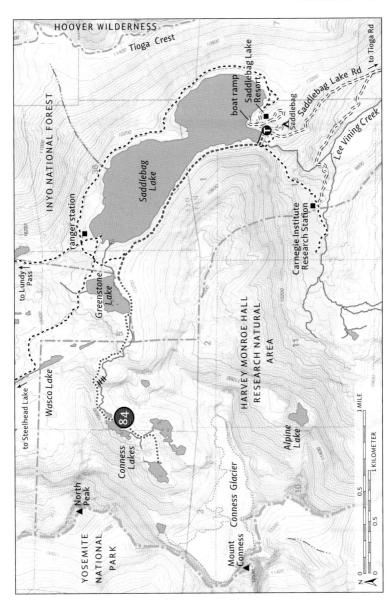

HOOVER WILDERNESS

Tioga Crest

Saddlebag Lake

to Tioga Rd

boat ramp

Saddlebag Lake Resort

Saddlebag

Saddlebag Lake Rd

Lee Vining Creek

INYO NATIONAL FOREST

Saddlebag Lake

ranger station

Carnegie Institute Research Station

to Lundy Pass

Greenstone Lake

to Steelhead Lake

Wasco Lake

HARVEY MONROE HALL RESEARCH NATURAL AREA

Alpine Lake

84

Conness Lakes

North Peak

Conness Glacier

YOSEMITE NATIONAL PARK

Mount Conness

N

1 MILE

1 KILOMETER

0.5

0.5

Saddlebag Lake. Cross the dam, and turn right to follow a jagged scree trail along the western shore of Saddlebag Lake. As you near the northern end of Saddlebag Lake, look for an unmarked informal path leading away on the left at 1.3 miles. Turn left here and follow the informal path as it arcs along the grassy southern shore of Greenstone Lake. North Peak rises over Greenstone Lake to the northwest, hinting at the alpine splendor that lies ahead. Once you reach the western end of Greenstone Lake, look for a continuation of the unmaintained path on the north side of the lake's inlet creek.

After rock-hopping the creek, follow the trail as it darts into a forest of lodgepole and whitebark pines before crossing into the Harvey Monroe Hall Research Natural Area. The increasingly rough trail climbs to a meadow through which the creek meanders lazily. The toughest stretch of climbing lies ahead with a cross-country scramble up granite slabs. Although it is possible to stick to the increasingly vague trail on the way up the slabs, it may be easier to climb straight up toward a notch to the right of a cascading waterfall.

Once at the notch, find the path that follows the north bank of the creek toward the first of the Conness Lakes. After following the shore of the first lake to its inlet, turn left to walk across a narrow, rocky isthmus that separates the smaller first lake from the second, larger lake. This rather stunning second lake sparkles with a turquoise sheen created by powdery granite sediment (a.k.a. "glacial milk") carried by runoff from the Conness Glacier nestled beneath the shadow of Mount Conness. Mount Conness itself punctuates the Sierra Crest directly ahead of you, daring alpine peak-baggers to have a go.

If you have had enough of scrambling and routefinding, you could stop at the second lake and call it a successful hike. However, three more lakes lie ahead, each requiring more scrambling than the last. The third and fourth lakes lie directly south from the second lake, and you can reach both by turning south and scrambling up and over a series of rocky ledges. To reach the fifth lake, follow the southern shore of the second lake toward the rocky slope of the final lake's moraine.

The easiest path toward the final lake follows the base of a rocky knoll on the east end of the fifth lake. However, since this is cross-country hiking, use your map and your best judgment to find a suitable route. After heading south and then west, this will bring you to a gap that leads to the lake's southeastern shore. Glacial runoff carrying more granite powder clouds the water and creates a striking turquoise color even more pronounced than the turquoise color at the second lake. This is your turnaround spot, from which you will retrace your steps back to the Saddlebag Lake parking area.

85 Parker Lake

RATING/ DIFFICULTY	ROUNDTRIP	ELEV GAIN/ HIGH POINT	SEASON
*****/2	3.6 miles	600 feet/ 8339 feet	June–Oct

Map: USGS 7.5-min Koip Peak; **Contact:** Inyo National Forest, Mono Lake Ranger Station; **Notes:** Suitable for backpacking

Opposite: Parker Lake is one of the loveliest spots on the east side of the Sierra.

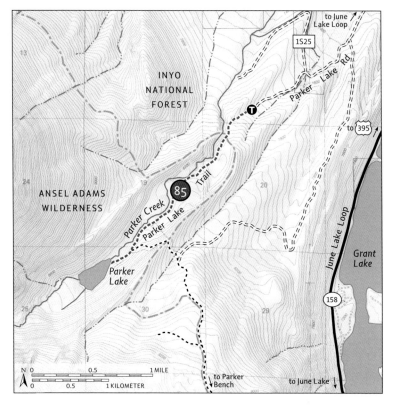

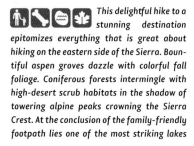

(Parker Lake Trail). No food storage at trailhead; **GPS:** 37.8530, −119.1345

This delightful hike to a stunning destination epitomizes everything that is great about hiking on the eastern side of the Sierra. Bountiful aspen groves dazzle with colorful fall foliage. Coniferous forests intermingle with high-desert scrub habitats in the shadow of towering alpine peaks crowning the Sierra Crest. At the conclusion of the family-friendly footpath lies one of the most striking lakes not only in the Yosemite region, but in the entire range: Parker Lake. Be sure to time this hike for early October when fall color is at its peak for a superlative hiking experience.

GETTING THERE

From the intersection of US Highway 395 and State Route 120/Tioga Road, drive south on US 395 for 3.6 miles to a junction with State Route 158 South (June Lake Loop), and turn right. Follow SR 158 South for 1.4 miles and veer right onto Parker Lake Road. Follow unpaved Parker Lake Road, which is usually passable for low-clearance, two-wheel-drive vehicles, for another 1.9 miles until a junction with Forest Route 1S25. Turn left here, continuing on Parker Lake Road for another 0.6 mile on dirt road; parking and the Parker Lake Trailhead are at the end of the road.

ON THE TRAIL

Locate the trailhead adjacent to an Inyo National Forest information kiosk. Follow the trail through a fragrant mixture of sagebrush and rabbitbrush on a steady incline. After 0.3 mile, the trail crosses into the Ansel Adams Wilderness. If you haven't stopped to catch your breath by now, make a point of stopping before the boundary sign and then turn around to enjoy the view across the Mono Basin toward Mono Lake. One last burst of climbing over the next 0.1 mile rounds out the bulk of the uphill work.

After the climb eases, the trail enters the first of a handful of sheltered valleys as it continues along the southern banks of Parker Creek. Aspen groves crowd along the creek in several sprawling groves, and the rust-colored ramparts of the Sierra Crest, crowned by Mount Wood, Parker Peak, Koip Peak, and Mount Lewis, add grandeur to the scene. The surrounding scenery graced by quaking aspen groves adds a sense of wonder to every step, particularly in the fall when the leaves transition into hues of lime-green, yellow, gold, orange, and red.

At 1.1 miles, the trail approaches Parker Creek, and consistent tree cover replaces the semi-open scrub habitats that defined the initial mile of the hike. There are several picturesque spots to pause along the creek as you continue a mellow incline heading southwest. This pleasant passage through pine and aspen forest continues for the next 0.7 mile. Continue straight through the junction with a trail leading south to Parker Bench at 1.6 miles, and in another 0.1 mile, reach the abrupt end of the forest at the shore of Parker Lake..

Even if you've seen the pictures and know what to expect, Parker Lake is still a revelation. With the rust-colored canyon walls rising more than 4000 feet above the lake, and bands of aspens streaking the canyon walls, the setting could hardly be more spectacular. This is a destination that merits an extended break to soak in every detail of the scene. Photographers who have the fortune to visit on a calm, partly cloudy day may walk away with world-class photos of a beautiful Sierra lake holding a perfect mirror image of montane splendor.

86 South Tufa

RATING/ DIFFICULTY	ROUNDTRIP	ELEV GAIN/ HIGH POINT	SEASON
****/1	0.9 mile	50 feet/ 6417 feet	Year-round

Map: USGS 7.5-min Lee Vining; **Contact:** Mono Basin Scenic Area National Forest Visitor Center; **Notes:** Day-use only. Day-use fee required. Interpretive trail. Pit toilet at trailhead; **GPS:** 37.9388, –119.0270

This short, easy hike leads to one of the more otherworldly natural features in the State of California, the tufa of Mono Lake. Tufa are limestone formations produced here by the interaction of subterranean spring water and Mono Lake's high concentration of dissolved inorganic carbon. Over thousands of years, carbon accumulations formed thousands of limestone pillars around these submerged springs. As Mono Lake's water level dropped, the tufa became exposed, leaving surrealistic pillars and towers along the shore and creating an unforgettable scenic destination. This short trail wanders among the tufa while periodic interpretive panels give you a primer on the geology, hydrology, human history, and natural history associated with the area.

GETTING THERE

Starting from the junction of State Route 120/Tioga Road and US Highway 395 just south of Lee Vining, drive south on US 395 for 4.7 miles and turn left onto SR 120. Continue for another 4.7 miles and turn left onto Test Station Road. This unpaved but easily traveled road continues for 0.9 mile to the parking area for the South Tufa Trail. **From the south:** drive 5.6 miles from the junction of State Route 158 (June Lake Loop Road) and US 395 for 5.6 miles and turn right onto SR 120, then proceed as above.

ON THE TRAIL

Hikers visiting this trail will invariably get the most out of the experience if they visit around sunrise. The ethereal geology of the tufa, the lake's vast waters, and the towering Sierra Crest to the west combine with golden light from the rising sun to produce an experience that is surreal, beautiful, and unforgettable. Photographers will enjoy testing their skills to capture scenes of tufa lit by golden light, and even a novice with a smartphone will walk away with photos they can rightfully brag about.

Navigationally speaking, the route is simple. Head north on the signed South Tufa Trail and keep left at a Y junction 50 feet from the trailhead. After the left turn, the trail transitions to boardwalk as it progresses north toward the lakeshore. Numerous interpretive panels highlight features of Mono Lake which, despite the lake's highly saline chemical composition, supports a surprisingly rich ecology, including unique plant and animal life. Mono Lake is as salty as it is because it occupies what scientists call an endorheic basin, which means that water flows into, but not out of, the lake. As a result, salts and minerals have nowhere to go, so they collect within the lake. The lake's salt content is so high that its waters are more buoyant than those of the Dead Sea in Israel.

Over time, the lake's salinity has increased because of diversion of the lake's inflow streams, especially Rush Creek, Lee Vining Creek, and Mill Creek, from the lake to the city of Los Angeles. This diversion caused a slow and steady decline in the lake's water level, along with its habitats, as the lake became saltier and saltier. The Mono Lake Committee along with the Sierra Club fought a long and difficult legal battle against California water interests to achieve a compromise so that a certain amount of water would continue to flow into the lake, thus increasing its water level and decreasing its salinity. The lake still has not reached its target level, but the habitats have begun to recover thanks to the efforts to balance the needs of a thirsty metropolis with the needs of a unique environment.

Normally, highly alkaline environments are not conducive to life, but a copious number of alkali flies thrive along the lake's shore, providing sustenance for the countless shorebirds and migratory sea birds that nest on Negit and Paoha Islands. The Mono people who inhabited the area prior to

Opposite: *Tufa create an otherworldly scene on the banks of Mono Lake.*

European expansion made the larvae of the alkali flies one of their primary food staples.

After 0.4 mile of gentle downhill walking, the trail reaches the shore of the lake. The water level is variable and depends largely on the time of year and the extent of the Sierra snowpack. If you're visiting in early May of a heavy snow year, the trail along the shore may be submerged, requiring you to either backtrack or to follow a separate path that steers away from the lake. At most other times, you can reach the edge of the lake

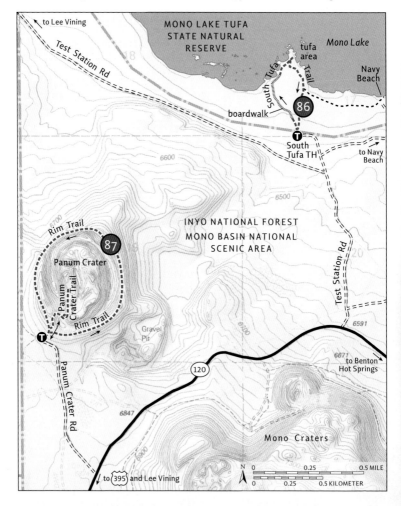

where the largest and most impressive tufa rise from the sandy shore. Informal trails allow you to wander through the tufa, but be sure not to touch and thus risk inadvertent damage to these rare and fascinating formations.

At 0.45 mile, the trail turns to the south, passing several additional tufa formations and a handful of beaches that are ideal for sunrise photography. Continue beyond these beaches and formations once you have taken enough pictures or soaked in enough scenery. On the return to the trailhead, look for a side trail leading east at 0.65 mile. This side trail will lead you toward Navy Beach, a popular swimming spot about 0.5 mile to the east; a visit adds a mile to the overall distance on this route. Continue past this side trail to reach the trailhead at 0.9 mile.

87 Panum Crater

RATING/ DIFFICULTY	ROUNDTRIP	ELEV GAIN/ HIGH POINT	SEASON
**/2	2.4 miles	600 feet/ 6957 feet	Year-round

Map: USGS 7.5-min Lee Vining; **Contact:** Inyo National Forest, Mono Lake Ranger District; **Notes:** Day-use only. No food storage

A lone Jeffrey pine grows in the volcanic soils of Panum Crater

at trailhead. No restroom at trailhead; **GPS:** 37.8530, −119.1345

 Stretching from Mammoth Peak to the north shore of Mono Lake, the Mono-Inyo Craters showcase an extended period of recent volcanic activity that has had a considerable impact on the landscape east of the Sierra Crest. For a dash of geological fascination, you can enjoy a short exploration through one of the youngest landscapes (a mere 600 to 700 years old) in California at Panum Crater for a scenic loop hike.

GETTING THERE

From the intersection of US Highway 395 and State Route 120/Tioga Road just south of Lee Vining, drive south on US 395 for 4.8 miles to a junction with SR 120. Turn left and continue east for another 3 miles to a junction with an unpaved road leading north to Panum Crater. Turn left toward the crater, then follow the bumpy, uneven dirt road for another 0.7 mile to the Panum Crater Trailhead and parking. This dirt road is rough and uncomfortable, but it is passable by low-clearance vehicles; be attentive and drive slowly.

ON THE TRAIL

The Panum Crater Trail leads east from the parking area on a moderate incline over sandy pumice toward the rim of the crater. After 0.1 mile, keep left and head north as the trail drops into a small declivity separating the rim of the crater from the obsidian plug dome residing within the middle of the crater. After a short dip into this declivity, the trail resumes a steep incline up to the top of the rugged, fractured plug dome. Rabbitbrush, which flowers yellow in fall, contrasts

against solitary Jeffrey pines and pillars of smooth, black obsidian as the trail weaves its way north toward a viewpoint at 0.5 mile with a partial view of Mono Lake to the north and impressive full views of the Sierra Nevada mountains to the west.

If the viewpoint and a 1-mile hike are all you have the inclination for, retrace your steps back to the first junction on the rim of the crater, and return to the parking area. If you wish to circumnavigate the crater and enjoy a full panorama of Mono Lake and its surrounding basin, turn left when you reach the rim of the crater instead of going right to the parking area, and follow the Rim Trail on a counter-clockwise loop around the rim. The trail rises and falls as you progress, with the route's highest point and best views coming at the 1.4-mile mark on the northeast point of the crater. From here, you can spot the South Tufa area, Paoha Island and Negit Island (both also volcanic craters related to Panum Crater), and the Bodie Hills to the north.

The toughest part of the hike comes after the northeast viewpoint, as the trail drops a quick 200 feet of elevation, only to regain it on an ascent along the western half of the crater. The rewards for this effort include more great views toward the Sierra Crest and south toward the Mono Craters and the June Lake area. At 2.3 miles, the loop closes at the trail leading back to the parking area. Turn right to conclude the hike.

88 Lundy Mine and Oneida Lake

RATING/ DIFFICULTY	ROUNDTRIP	ELEV GAIN/ HIGH POINT	SEASON
**/3	7.2 miles	1800 feet/ 9669 feet	July–Oct

A beautiful fall day on the banks of Oneida Lake

Map: USGS 7.5-min Dunderberg Peak;
Contact: Inyo National Forest, Mono Lake
Ranger District; **Notes:** Suitable for backpacking (Lundy Mine Trail). No toilet at
trailhead. No food storage at trailhead; **GPS:**
38.0313, –119.2194

A generous dose of scenery, fall color, and history combine with solitude and serenity on this off-the-beaten-path destination. Hike to the historic Lundy Mine that was part of the same era that produced Bennettville, Bodie, *and the Great Sierra Mines, and you'll find fascinating relics of mining history scattered about the site of the mine. Oneida Lake's spar-kling waters lie just a stone's throw away from these ruins, and its tranquil waters pro-vide an ideal lunch stop following a few pleas-ant hours of exploring the relics of a long-vanished era.*

GETTING THERE

From Lee Vining at the junction of State
Route 120/Tioga Road and US Highway 395,
drive north on US 395 for 6.7 miles to Lundy

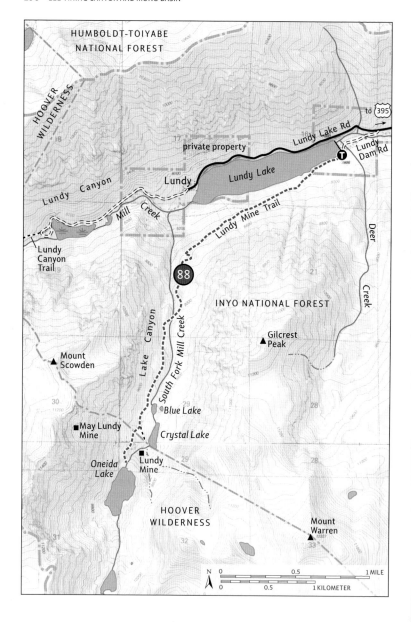

Lake Road and turn left. Continue west for 3.4 miles to Lundy Dam Road and veer left. After 0.2 mile, Lundy Dam Road terminates at a dirt parking lot for the Lundy Mine Trailhead.

ON THE TRAIL

The route begins from a signed trailhead kiosk just south of the Lundy Lake Dam. Find the remnants of an old mining road that have been converted to trail, then start by hiking west along the south banks of Lundy Lake through groves of quaking aspen. After 0.25 mile along the lake, the trail begins a long, oblique climb away from the lake on Lundy Canyon's southern slopes. Views of Lundy Lake as well as the red ramparts crowning Lundy Canyon's northern slopes emerge and improve as the climb progresses. Occasional spring-fed streams produce dense bursts of riparian vegetation to complement the common high-desert plant schemas consisting of sagebrush, mountain mahogany, manzanita, and some scattered, solitary Jeffrey pines.

At 1.6 miles, the trail takes a sharp switchback through dense vegetation nourished by more spring-fed streams, followed by a second switchback into Lake Canyon. Once the trail leaves the switchbacks and the dense vegetation behind, it's a fairly tedious slog along the rocky roadbed nearly all the way to the Lundy Mine. The trail crosses the creek at 2.3 miles, but this is the only eventful moment until the 3-mile mark when the trail emerges from lodgepole pine forest along a meadow overlooking marshy Blue Lake. This transition signals the final approach to the highlights of this hike: Lundy Mine and Oneida Lake.

The trail reaches an unmarked junction at 3.2 miles. The left fork of this junction leads to Lundy Mine. First prospected during the 1860s, the Lundy Mine and the May Lundy Mine, about 1600 feet upslope, first yielded ore in 1877, and the mining complex operated from 1879 into the early 1900s. The relics include an old stamp mill and some water tanks. Additional structures lie to the southeast near the shore of Crystal Lake, but reaching those ruins requires an uncomfortable bushwhack through willows. Also, bear in mind that the mining operation permanently poisoned the topsoil and water supplies below Oneida Lake with arsenic, which was used extensively in processing ore. If you need to refill water, or if you're camping, be sure to do so upstream at Oneida Lake.

The right fork from the junction at 3.2 miles climbs to the top of a massive pile of tailings left over when miners gouged out tunnels into the earth. Cables and railroad ties testify to the presence of a tram that once conveyed ore and people up and down between the upslope May Lundy Mine and the downslope processing facilities at the Lundy Mine. The tailings pile offers a nice view down-canyon and across Crystal Lake and Blue Lake. Beyond the tailings, the trail becomes vague as it follows the tram cables for a bit before passing through sparse lodgepole pine forest toward the banks of Oneida Lake. If camping, look for campsites scattered among the trees.

After reaching a dilapidated dam at 3.5 miles, the trail passes through a thicket of willows to arrive at the banks of Oneida Lake. The lake sits nestled into a glacial bowl bound by the Tioga Crest to the west and an unnamed ridge crowned by Mount Warren to the east. The lakeshore is a pleasant place to pass an hour or two, especially since few hikers ever seem to venture this way. When you've had your fill of solitude, head back down the trail the way you came to return to the trailhead.

89 Lundy Canyon

RATING/ DIFFICULTY	ROUNDTRIP	ELEV GAIN/ HIGH POINT	SEASON
***/2	3.8 miles	800 feet/ 8851 feet	July–Oct

Maps: USGS 7.5-min Lundy, Dunderberg Peak; **Contact:** Inyo National Forest, Mono Lake Ranger District; **Notes:** Suitable for backpacking (Lundy Canyon Trail). Restroom at trailhead; **GPS:** 38.0225, –119.2619

Rich in history and not lacking in scenic beauty, colorful Lundy Canyon provides one of the most memorable and most accessible day hikes in the Hoover Wilderness.

Once the site of several bustling and productive mines, today's Lundy Canyon now reverberates only with the sounds of rumbling waterfalls and the gentle rustle of quaking aspen leaves, which turn brilliant shades of orange, yellow, lime, and red during late September and early October.

GETTING THERE

From Lee Vining at the junction of State Route 120/Tioga Road and US Highway 395, drive north on US 395 for 6.7 miles to Lundy Lake Road and turn left. Continue north for another 6.6 miles, passing Lundy Canyon Campground, then Lundy Lake, and then Lundy Lake Campground, until the road terminates at a looping parking area. The trailhead is on the farthest western end of the loop.

Golden foliage and cascading waterfalls deep within Lundy Canyon

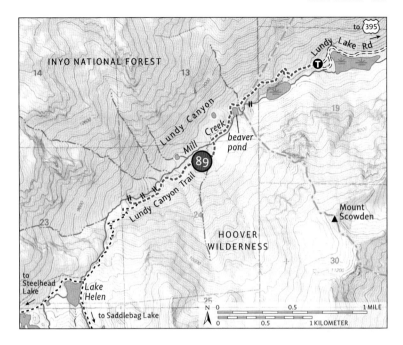

ON THE TRAIL

Set out from the parking area, traveling west along a moderately ascending trail that runs parallel to Mill Creek on your left. After 0.25 mile, keep right at a spur trail that drops down to the shore of a marshy lake, unless of course you want to fish or just enjoy a short lakeside diversion. The trail bends to the north, climbing away from the lake toward the first of several expansive groves of quaking aspens. At 0.6 mile, the trail climbs up and over a ridge, from which point you can peer west toward the hike's first waterfall, framed in colorful deciduous trees. Views up-canyon are outstanding from this spot, especially in fall when golden aspens appear to spill down the canyon bottom and walls like rivers of molten gold.

At 0.9 mile, the trail reaches another small pond that appears to be the work of beavers. The trail wraps around the western edge of the pond to resume a southwestward descent through a dense forest of quaking aspen sprinkled liberally with lodgepole pines. Cross Mill Creek at 1.25 miles and enjoy a prolonged stretch of barely perceptible climbing through the aspen and pine forest. Around the 1.5-mile mark, keep your eyes peeled for the remains of an old cabin testifying to activity in the canyon over a century ago.

At 1.8 miles, the trail reaches the first in a set of three cascading waterfalls. Willows and aspens frame each of these, which thunder in the late spring and early summer. By fall, the waterfalls become gentler, and the golden autumnal color of willows and aspens framing the falls combined with the deep-red metamorphic bedrock composes idyllic scenes underscored by a gentle aqueous soundtrack. Turn around at the third waterfall to retrace your steps back to the trailhead.

90 Virginia Lakes

RATING/ DIFFICULTY	ROUNDTRIP	ELEV GAIN/ HIGH POINT	SEASON
***/2	3 miles	600 feet/ 10,400 feet	June– Oct

Map: USGS 7.5-min Dunderberg Peak; **Contact:** Humboldt-Toiyabe National Forest, Bridgeport Ranger District; **Notes:** Suitable for backpacking (Virgina Lakes Trail). No food storage at trailhead. Vault toilets at trailhead; **GPS:** 38.0480, –119.2632

Technically, the Virginia Lakes lie outside of the Mono Basin Scenic Area in a different watershed governed by a different national forest by virtue of their location north of Conway Summit. However, by withholding a trail description to this beautiful lake basin, which lies only minutes from Lee Vining, this author feels he would be doing a disservice to anybody who is interested in visiting a gorgeous chain of lakes accessible with only a modest amount of effort. If you're one of those interested visitors, you can count on experiencing no fewer than six subalpine lakes for the low, low price of a moderate 3-mile hike.

GETTING THERE

From the intersection of US Highway 395 and State Route 120/Tioga Road, drive north on US 395 for 13.8 miles to Conway Summit

and a junction with Virginia Lakes Road. Turn left onto Virginia Lakes Road and follow it for 6.1 miles to its terminus at the Virginia Lakes Trailhead. The trailhead lies just to the north of the vault toilets.

ON THE TRAIL

This hike requires one caution: The trailhead sits at an elevation of 9850 feet. If you haven't acclimated to this altitude, there is a danger of developing altitude sickness. If you've spent a night or two at a high altitude, the elevation shouldn't be an issue except for particularly sensitive individuals.

After finding the trailhead, follow the Virginia Lakes Trail west through lodgepole forest along the shore of Big Valley Lake, the largest of the lakes along the route. Informal side paths allow you to reach the shore until the trail turns away from the lake after 0.1 mile. The trail winds through more lodgepole forest on an easy grade that picks up a modest amount of elevation as it passes a small lake that lies just below much larger Blue Lake at 0.4 mile. The trail skirts the north shore of Blue Lake and begins to make a more pronounced climb over rust-colored scree before entering another dense thicket of lodgepole trees. Just before you cross a tributary draining Moat Lake to the north, look for the ruins of an old prospector's cabin on the left at 0.7 mile. Look east from the ruins for a nice view across Blue Lake.

Beyond the cabin ruins, cross the Moat Lake tributary, and make a stiff climb over a heavily wooded moraine impounding the upper Virginia Lakes. At 1.1 miles, arrive at the first and largest of the upper lakes, sparkling Cooney Lake. Sculpted peaks and glaciated canyons serrate the sky in the landscape beyond Cooney Lake, and a brief flat stretch along the lake's north shore

A splendid alpine scene at the Frog Lakes

eases the climb long enough for you to thoroughly enjoy the scene.

One last final stretch of climbing awaits beyond Cooney Lake, and after crossing Virginia Creek at 1.3 miles, you reach the first of the three Frog Lakes. This marshy trio of lakes does not attain the same size and scale as Cooney, Blue, or Big Valleys Lakes, but the alpine setting creates a more scenic backdrop. The second Frog Lake is accessible by way of an informal trail that skirts the east bank of the first lake. This trail peters out at the second lake but not before splitting off toward some decent campsites. To reach the third lake, continue past the creek crossing to find a short spur trail leading to the third lake's northeastern shore. The third Frog Lake is your turnaround. Trace your steps back to the trailhead.

EXTENDING YOUR TRIP

If you're in the mood for a much longer affair, you can continue west along the Green Creek Trail, up and over a pass at 4.3 miles

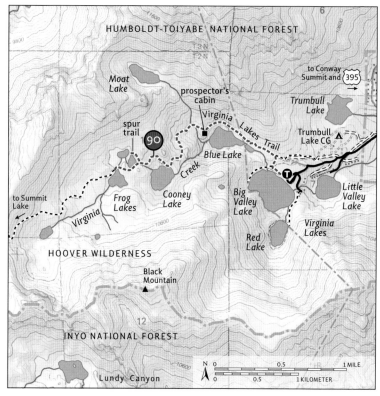

that divides Virginia Creek from Green Creek. From there, descend for another 1.6 miles to a junction. If you turn left at the junction, the trail leads west for another 0.4 mile to Summit Lake, which lies just east of the Yosemite National Park border. If you turn right at the junction, the Green Creek Trail leads northeast past a series of lakes, beginning with the Hoover Lakes (5.1 miles), Gilman Lake (6.1 miles), East Lake (6.5 miles), and Green Lake (8.3 miles). If you have two cars and two drivers, you could even leave a car parked at the Green Creek Trailhead for a one-way hike covering 12.2 miles with 1700 feet of elevation gain and 3600 feet of elevation loss.

Acknowledgments

The first and foremost acknowledgment for this guide belongs to Yosemite itself, a vast, complex, transcendent, and occasionally frustrating national park that I had the privilege of exploring for twenty-two months starting in the wildfire days of late 2018 and concluding in the depths of the COVID-19 pandemic in summer of 2020. Throughout the madness of those times, I returned to Yosemite sixteen times to complete this book, and every time Yosemite sent me away with an appreciation as durable as Sierra Nevada granite.

I also wish to thank the following individuals for their support: Kelly Turner for continuing to encourage me to go deep into the wilderness alone even though it means my absence for long stretches of time. Hank Turner for providing some of the silliest and sweetest distractions while I was trying to proofread this book. Don Endicott for sharing his resources, sharing his expertise, and spending a week in the high country with me while awakening me to the wonders of cross-country exploration in the Cathedral Range. Kate Rogers for encouraging me to do this even though I was originally on the fence because of so much adulting that needed to be adulted. Matthew Stasiak for giving a stranger a ride and helping me avoid a lot of redundant hiking. Scott Jirous and Cassidy Cortright for sharing the final moments of the field work with me atop Mount Dana. Antonia Reed-Felstead for camaraderie on Sentinel Dome. The Yosemite History Facebook Group for pointing me in the direction of some good historical resources. I appreciate the editorial work of Mary Metz at Mountaineers Books and freelancers Ginger Oppenheimer, Lynn Greisz, and Emily Barnes; I also thank Melissa McFeeters for doing such a fine job with the layout and Ben Pease for his diligence in creating maps. The Yosemite Park staff deserve my sincere appreciation as well. Finally, very special thanks to the person who found my driver's license at the Smith Meadow Trailhead.

Opposite: *Half Dome looms large from the north rim of Yosemite Valley (Hike 33).*

Appendix I
Bonus Hikes

My original plan for this guide was to include 100 hikes, with additional routes outside of Yosemite National Park in the adjacent national forests. However, I scouted the last 20 percent of the book at the start of the COVID-19 pandemic, and I had to sacrifice some hikes for the sake of expediency. However, that should not stop you from learning about some of the off-the-beaten-path gems in and around Yosemite.

In this appendix, I include basic information to aid your research if you are interested in exploring these routes. The National Geographic map covering the park is a good aid in charting these routes.

I also include basic information with reference to more thorough sources on a handful of famous backpacking routes that were too big to include in the book, but which are too well-known and important to ignore. Please note that there are also great backpacking routes referenced in the "Extending Your Trip" sections of more than a dozen day hikes described in this guide.

The routes are arranged according to region, matching the geographical order in this book. For the backpacking routes, the region name is given in parentheses after the route title.

WAWONA DAY HIKES

Nelder Grove
Trailhead coordinates: 37.5369, –119.6535
Distance: Up to 7.6 miles

Elevation gain: Up to 1200 feet
This small grove of sequoias inhabits a lush basin a mere 7 miles to the southeast of Mariposa Grove. Parts of the grove were badly damaged in the 2017 Railroad Fire, and at the time of writing, both the Graveyard of the Giants Loop and the Shadow of the Giants Recreational Trail were closed. However, the Chimney Trail Loop remains open—provided the road gets fixed.

Wawona Trail to Wawona Point
Trailhead coordinates: 37.5369, –119.6535
Distance: 14.6 miles
Elevation gain: 2750 feet
This historic and strenuous footpath connects Wawona to Mariposa Grove. Follow the trail east and southeast out of Wawona's valley up to the grove. Upon reaching the Perimeter Trail, turn left to follow it all the way to Wawona Point for stellar views of the Wawona area.

BIG OAK FLAT ROAD DAY HIKE

Hite Cove
Trailhead coordinates: 37.6545, –119.8873
Distance: 6.8 miles
Elevation gain: 1200 feet
The 2018 Ferguson Fire swept through this historic hiking path, obliterating sections of trail and destroying some of the structures from the historic Savage's Trading Post along the South Fork of the Merced River. The trail remained closed through

the scouting period for this guide, but when it opens up (call Sierra National Forest in advance to check status), hikers will again have a chance to enjoy the legendary springtime wildflower displays along the undulating riverside trail.

HETCH HETCHY DAY HIKES

Laurel Lake
Trailhead coordinates: 37.9464, –119.7876
Distance: 14.4 miles
Elevation gain: 3000 feet
This route to a tranquil subalpine lake follows segments of a historic roadbed connecting Hetch Hetchy Reservoir to Lake Eleanor. Follow the trail through the tunnel on the north side of the O'Shaughnessy Dam to a junction on the left signed for Laurel Lake. This trail leads north on a steady incline to Beehive Meadow, at which point you turn west to reach the lake. Laurel Lake can also be the first stop on a three-day backpacking adventure that also visits Lake Vernon, Tiltill Valley, and Rancheria Falls before returning via Wapama Falls.

Preston Falls
Trailhead coordinates: 37.8787, –119.9506
Distance: 8.2 miles
Elevation gain: 400 feet
Follow the Tuolumne River on a gentle incline to a thundering waterfall. This lower-elevation route on Stanislaus National Forest land is at its best during spring when the river is high and temperatures are low. The Kirkwood Powerhouse also offers a dash of historical interest since it sits on the site of an older powerhouse that was instrumental in the construction of Hetch Hetchy Reservoir.

Kibbie Lake
Trailhead coordinates: 37.9880, –119.8874
Distance: 12.2 miles
Elevation gain: 2400 feet
This secluded lake lies in the quiet northwest corner of Yosemite National Park. Accessible only through the Cherry Valley area of Stanislaus National Forest, Kibbie Lake receives little visitation. Suitable for backpacking and great for solitude.

WHITE WOLF TO TENAYA LAKE DAY HIKES

Eagle Peak via Yosemite Creek
Trailhead coordinates for Yosemite Creek Campground: 37.8263, –119.5965
Trailhead coordinates for Tioga Road Trailhead: 37.8521, –119.5779
Distance: 15 miles from Yosemite Creek Campground; 19.6 miles from Tioga Road TH
Elevation gain: 2000 feet from Yosemite Creek Campground; 2800 from Tioga Road TH
This alternate route to Eagle Peak eschews the tough climbing from the valley floor and substitutes it for longer distances. If the road to Yosemite Creek Campground is open, that trailhead is preferable since it shaves off 4.6 miles. The route from Tioga Road is more suitable for backpacking. The "reveal" from Eagle Peak is more exciting from this direction, but this route is also only accessible when Tioga Road is open, usually between June and October.

LEE VINING CANYON AND MONO BASIN DAY HIKES

Thousand Island Lake via Rush Creek Trail
Trailhead coordinates: 37.7831, –119.1279

Distance: 17.4 miles

Elevation gain: 3400 feet

One of the most beautiful places in the Sierra Nevada, this gorgeous alpine lake offers great backpacking and incredible vistas. There are a few ways to get there, including a southbound, overnight route from Tuolumne Meadows or north from Reds Meadow in Mammoth Lakes. However, the Rush Creek Trail, while steep and long, is the option listed here, as it also visits several other alpine jewels, including the appropriately named Gem Lake.

Bloody Canyon

Trailhead coordinates: 37.8725, –119.1588

Distance: 10 miles

Elevation gain: 3200 feet

This historic route once served as the primary footpath for the Mono people to travel from Mono Basin into the Yosemite high country. The rust-red rocks contrast beautifully against fall color from abundant aspen groves. A pair of lakes offers good camping options, and backpackers can extend their trip with day hiking forays into the Mono Pass/Spillway Lake areas of Yosemite National Park. High-clearance vehicle recommended for the drive to the trailhead.

Black Point Fissures

Trailhead coordinates: 38.0273, –119.0847

Distance: 2 miles

Elevation gain: 500 feet

This cross-country route climbs, due west, straight up to the top of Black Point, where you'll find a fascinating set of fissures that are the width of slot canyons. You can explore the fissures for an entire morning, and the views across Mono Lake are equally rewarding.

Glacier Canyon

Trailhead coordinates: 37.9213, –119.2546

Distance: 5 miles

Elevation gain: 1650 feet

Glacier Canyon lies below the soaring heights of Mount Dana, and within minutes you will experience a primeval landscape dotted with alpine tarns and Dana Lake. The route is cross-country, and the terrain is tough.

BACKPACKING ROUTES

The John Muir Trail (Access Points at Yosemite Valley and Tuolumne Meadows)

Trailhead coordinates for Happy Isles: 37.7324, –119.5579

Trailhead coordinates Whitney Portal: 36.5869, –118.2404

Distance: 211 miles

Elevation gain: 40,225 feet (35,800 feet of loss)

Beginning from Happy Isles, the legendary John Muir Trail (JMT) follows the spine of the Sierra southbound to the range's highest point, Mount Whitney. Along the way to Whitney, the JMT passes through the Ansel Adams Wilderness, the John Muir Wilderness, Kings Canyon National Park, and Sequoia National Park before exiting out of Whitney Portal. Although her book focuses primarily on the Pacific Crest Trail, which runs concurrent with the JMT from Tuolumne Meadows to Mount Whitney, Shawnté Salabert's guide, *Hiking the Pacific Crest Trail: Southern California*, provides a wealth of information to help you prepare. Permits for the JMT are always in high demand, and you can find details on obtaining permits at: www.nps.gov/yose /planyourvisit/jmtfaq.htm.

The High Sierra Camps
(Tuolumne Meadows)

Trailhead coordinates: 37.8777, –119.3386

Distance: 47 miles

Elevation gain: 7500 feet

For hikers interested in the backcountry experience without having to do the hard work of backpacking, this beautiful and historic route starting from Tuolumne Meadows connects Yosemite's six High Sierra Camps, where hikers can camp in relative luxury. The six camps contain tent cabins, linens, beds, meals, and vault toilets. This guide describes routes leading to four of the five camps (May Lake, Glen Aulin, Tuolumne Meadows, Vogelsang, and Sunrise), which will give you a good start on researching the route. Reservations for the ever-popular camps are available through Yosemite Hospitality, which awards reservations through an annual lottery. Visit the website, www .travelyosemite.com, to enter the lottery and (hopefully) secure your reservation. You can also follow this route as a backpacking trip with stops at backpacker camps adjacent to each of the High Sierra Camps.

The Pacific Crest Trail from
Tuolumne Meadows to Sonora Pass
(Tuolumne Meadows)

Trailhead coordinates for Tuolumne Meadows: 37.8767, –119.3458

Trailhead coordinates for Sonora Pass: 38.3281, –119.6373

Distance: 71 miles

Elevation gain: 12,750 feet (11,750 feet elevation loss)

Section hiking of the Pacific Crest Trail (PCT) has increased in popularity over the last decade, and this approach to hiking the PCT is a way for folks who can't take six months off to hike the entire trail. The section from Tuolumne Meadows to Sonora Pass features some of Yosemite's more remote wilderness areas along with access to stellar destinations like Virginia Canyon and Matterhorn Canyon. For more in-depth information on this route, check out Philip Kramer's *Hiking the Pacific Crest Trail: Northern California: Section Hiking from Tuolumne Meadows to Donomore Pass*.

The Clark Range Loop
(Glacier Point Road)

Trailhead coordinates: 37.6713, –119.5850

Distance: 50 miles

Elevation gain: 8000 feet

This multi-day route encircles the Clark Range by way of the Merced Pass Trail. Before Merced Pass, follow the Ottoway Lakes Trail up and over Red Peak Pass and through an alpine wonderland. The route then drops down to the Merced River near Washburn Lake before returning west to Mono Meadow past Merced Lake, Little Yosemite Valley, and Nevada Fall. The last segment follows the Panorama Trail to a connecting trail leading back to Mono Meadow.

Appendix II
Agency Contacts

VISITOR CENTERS

Mono Basin Scenic Area Visitor Center
1 Visitor Center Drive
Lee Vining, CA 93541
(760) 647-3044
http://monolake.org/visit/vc

Tuolumne Meadows Visitor Center
8.3 miles west of Tioga Pass
(209) 372-0200
www.nps.gov/yose/planyourvisit/tm.htm

Wawona Visitor Center
8308 Wawona Road
Wawona, CA 95389
(209) 372-0200
www.nps.gov/yose/planyourvisit/waw
   .htm

Yosemite Valley Visitor Center
9035 Village Drive
Yosemite Valley, CA 95389
(209) 372-0200
www.nps.gov/yose/planyourvisit/yv.htm

RANGER AND INFORMATION STATIONS (Includes Wilderness Permits)

Bass Lake Ranger District Office (Sierra National Forest)
57003 Road 225
North Fork, CA 93643
(559) 877-2218
http://usda.gov/recarea/sierra
   /recreation/camping-cabins
   /recarea/?recid=45422&actid=29

Big Oak Flat Information Station
6107 Big Oak Flat Road
Groveland, CA 95321
(209) 372-0200
www.nps.gov/yose/planyourvisit
   /permitstations.htm

Bridgeport Ranger District Office (Humboldt-Toiyabe National Forest)
75694 US Highway 395
Bridgeport, CA 93517
(760) 923-7070
www.fs.usda.gov/detail
   /htnf/about-forest
   /districts/?cid=fseprd754240

Hetch Hetchy Entrance and Information Station
Hetch Hetchy Road
Groveland, CA 95321
(209) 372-0200
www.nps.gov/yose/planyourvisit/hh.htm

Mono Lake Ranger District (Inyo National Forest)
1.4 miles west of intersection of US
   Highway 395 and Tioga Road/State
   Route 120
US 395, Lee Vining, CA 93541
(760) 647-3044
www.fs.usda.gov/recarea/inyo/recarea

Tuolumne Meadows Wilderness Center
6.6 miles west of Tioga Pass
(209) 372-0200
www.nps.gov/yose/planyourvisit
   /permitstations.htm

Wawona Visitor Center
8308 Wawona Road
Yosemite Valley, CA 95389
(209) 372-0200
www.nps.gov/yose/planyourvisit/waw
.htm

Yosemite Valley Wilderness Center
Yosemite National Park Road
Yosemite Valley, CA 95389
(209) 372-0200
www.nps.gov/yose/planyourvisit
/permitstations.htm

MUSEUMS AND HISTORICAL SITES

The Ahwahnee Hotel
1 Ahwahnee Drive
Yosemite Valley, CA 95389
(888) 413-8869
www.nationalparkreservations.com
/lodge/yosemite-ahwahnee-hotel

Ansel Adams Gallery
9031 Village Drive
Yosemite Valley, CA 95389
(209) 372-4413
www.anseladams.com

Happy Isles Art and Nature Center
Happy Isles Loop Road
Yosemite Valley, CA 95389
(209) 372-0631
www.yosemite.com/what-to-do/
yosemite-art-center

Pioneer Yosemite History Museum
4100 Forest Drive
Wawona, CA 95389
(209) 372-0200
www.yosemite.com/what-to-do
/pioneer-yosemite-history-museum

Yosemite Museum
9039 Village Drive
Yosemite Valley, CA 95389
(209) 372-0200
www.nps.gov/yose/learn/historyculture
/yosemite-museum.htm

HELPFUL WEBSITES

Yosemite Park
www.nps.gov/yose/index.htm

Yosemite Conservancy
https://yosemite.org

Travel Yosemite
www.travelyosemite.com

Inyo National Forest Wilderness Permits
www.recreation.gov/permits/233262

OTHER SERVICES

**Badger Pass Ski Area
(December through March)**
7082 Glacier Point Road
Yosemite National Park, CA 95389
(209) 372-1000

Curry Village Gift & Grocery
9020 Curry Village Drive
Yosemite Valley, CA 95389
(209) 372-8344
www.travelyosemite.com/things-to-do
/shopping-supplies-groceries

Mountain Shop at Curry Village
9020 Curry Village Drive
Yosemite Valley, CA 95389
(209) 372-8344
www.travelyosemite.com/things-to-do
/shopping-supplies-groceries

US Post Office
9017 Village Drive
Yosemite Valley, CA 95389
(800) 275-8777
www.travelyosemite.com/things-to-do
  /shopping-supplies-groceries

Village Store
9011 Village Drive
Yosemite Valley, CA 95389
(209) 372-1253
www.travelyosemite.com/things-to-do
  /shopping-supplies-groceries

Yosemite Medical Clinic
9000 Ahwahnee Drive
Yosemite Valley, CA 95389
(209) 372-4637

Yosemite Mountaineering
School & Guide Service
9020 Curry Village Drive
Yosemite Valley, CA 95389
(209) 372-8344
www.yosemite.com/what-to-do
  /yosemite-mountaineering
  -school-guide-service

TRANSPORTATION

Glacier Point Tour Bus
 (888) 413-8869
www.travelyosemite.com/things-to-do
  /guided-bus-tours/

Yosemite Area Rapid Transit System
(YARTS)
369 W. 18th Street
Merced, CA 95340
(877) 989-2787
https://yarts.com

Yosemite Shuttle, Mariposa Grove
Shuttle, and Tuolumne Meadows Shuttle
www.nps.gov/yose/planyourvisit
  /publictransportation.htm

Yosemite Valley to Tuolumne
Meadows Hiker Bus
 (888) 413-8869
www.travelyosemite.com/things-to-do
  /guided-bus-tours

PARK PARTNERS

Friends of the Inyo
621 W Line St, Suite 201
Bishop, CA 93514
(760) 873-6500
https://friendsoftheinyo.org

Friends of Sierra National Forest
P.O. Box 25306
Fresno, CA 93729
www.friendsofsierranationalforest.org/

NatureBridge
9040 Village Drive
Yosemite National Park, CA 95389
https://naturebridge.org/locations
  /yosemite

Yosemite Conservancy
101 Montgomery Street, Suite 1700
San Francisco, CA 94104
https://yosemite.org
(415) 434-1782

Yosemite Hospitality
(Park concessionaire)
 (888) 413-8869
www.travelyosemite.com

Appendix III
Recommended Reading

NATURAL HISTORY

Laws, John Muir. *The Laws Field Guide to the Sierra Nevada.* Berkeley: Heyday Books, 2007.

———. *Sierra Birds: A Hiker's Guide.* Berkeley: Heyday Books, 2019.

Schoenherr, Allan A. *A Natural History of California,* 2nd ed. Berkeley: University of California Press, 2017.

Spencer, Shirley. *Living Among Giants.* San Francisco: Yosemite Conservancy, 2017.

HUMAN HISTORY

Clark, Galen. *Indians of the Yosemite Valley and Vicinity.* CreateSpace, 2015.

Giacomazzi, Sharon. *Trails & Tales of Yosemite & The Central Sierra.* Fort Bragg, CA: Bored Feet Press, 2001.

Johnston, Hank. *The Yosemite Grant 1864–1906: A Pictorial History.* San Francisco: Yosemite Association, 1995.

LeConte, Joseph. *A Journal of Ramblings through the High Sierra of California.* San Francisco: Sierra Club, 2012.

O'Neill, Elizabeth Stone. *Meadow in the Sky: A History of Yosemite's Tuolumne Meadows Region.* Fresno, CA: Panorama West Books, 1984.

Salcedo, Tracy. *Historic Yosemite National Park.* Guilford, CT: Lyons Press, 2016.

Simpson, John W. *Dam! Water, Power, Politics, and Preservation in Hetch Hetchy and Yosemite National Park.* New York: Pantheon Books, 2005.

Walklet, Keith S. *The Ahwahnee: Yosemite's Grand Hotel.* San Francisco, CA: Yosemite Conservancy, 2004.

MUIR

Muir, John. *The Mountains of California.* San Francisco: Sierra Club, 1989.

———. *My First Summer in the Sierra.* Boston: Houghton Mifflin, 2011.

———. *The Yosemite.* New York: Century Company, 2007.

Stetson, Lee. *The Wild Muir: Twenty-Two of John Muir's Greatest Adventures.* San Francisco: Yosemite Conservancy, 2013.

Wurtz, Mike. *John Muir's Grand Yosemite: Musings and Sketches.* San Francisco: Yosemite Conservancy, 2020.

GEOLOGY

Glazner, Allen and Greg Stock. *Geology Underfoot in Yosemite National Park.* Missoula: Mountain Press Publishing Company, 2010.

Huber, N. King. *Geological Ramblings in Yosemite.* San Francisco: Yosemite Conservancy, 2007.

Tierney, Timothy. *Geology of the Mono Basin.* Lee Vining, CA: Mono Lake Committee, 1995.

Wise, James M. *Mount Whitney to Yosemite: the Geology of the John Muir Trail.* Createspace, 2009.

RECREATION GUIDES

Barbier, John. *Angler's Guide to the Eastern Sierra: (Bridgeport to Bishop).* Berkeley: PGW Publishing, 1995.

Kramer, Philip. *Hiking the Pacific Crest Trail: Northern California: Section Hiking from Tuolumne Meadows to Donomore Pass.* Seattle: Mountaineers Books, 2017.

McAllister, Harley and Abby McAllister. *Yosemite National Park: Adventuring With Kids*. Seattle: Mountaineers Books, 2019.

Salabert, Shawnté. *Hiking the Pacific Crest Trail: Southern California: Section Hiking from Campo to Tuolumne Meadows*. Seattle: Mountaineers Books, 2017

Schifrin, Ben. *Emigrant Wilderness and Northwestern Yosemite*. Birmingham, AL: Wilderness Press, 1990.

Turner, Scott. *Hike the Parks: Sequoia and Kings Canyon National Parks*. Seattle: Mountaineers Books, 2020.

ART & PHOTOGRAPHY

Adams, Ansel. *Ansel Adams' Yosemite.* Boston: Little, Brown, & Company, 2019.

Adams, Ansel and Andrea G. Stillman. *Ansel Adams in the National Parks: Photographs from America's Wild Places*. Boston: Little, Brown, & Company, 2010.

Frye, Michael. *The Photographer's Guide to Yosemite*. San Francisco: Yosemite Conservancy, 2012.

Obata, Chiura, Janice T. Driesbach, and Susan Landauer. *Obata's Yosemite: Art and Letters of Obata from His Trip to the High Sierra in 1927.* San Francisco: Yosemite Conservancy, 1993.

Osborne, Michael. *Granite, Water and Light: The Waterfalls of Yosemite Valley*. San Francisco: Yosemite Conservancy, 2009.

MAPS

Harrison, Tom. *Half Dome Trail Map*. San Rafael, CA: Tom Harrison Maps, 2012.

———. *Hetch Hetchy Trail Map*. San Rafael, CA: Tom Harrison Maps, 2006.

———. *Tuolumne Meadows*. San Rafael, CA: Tom Harrison Maps, 2015.

———. *Yosemite High Country*. San Rafael, CA: Tom Harrison Maps, 2014.

National Geographic Maps, *Yosemite National Park Map & Day Hikes Map Pack*. Evergreen, CO: National Geographic Maps, 2020.

Index

1% for Trails

Where would we be without trails? Not very far into the wilderness. That's why Mountaineers Books designates 1 percent of sales of select guidebooks in our Day Hiking series toward trail maintenance. Since launching this program, we've contributed more than $22,000 toward improving trails.

For this book, our 1 percent of sales is going to Yosemite Conservancy (yosemite.org), the primary nonprofit partner to Yosemite National Park.

Yosemite Conservancy inspires people to support projects and programs that preserve Yosemite National Park and enrich the visitor experience. Thanks to generous donors, the Conservancy has provided more than $130 million in grants to the park in recent years to restore trails and habitat, protect wildlife, provide educational programs, and more. The Conservancy's guided adventures, volunteer opportunities, wilderness services, and bookstores help visitors of all ages connect with Yosemite. Please visit yosemite.org to learn more and get involved.

Mountaineers Books donates many books to nonprofit recreation and conservation organizations. Our 1% for Trails campaign is one more way we help fellow nonprofit organizations as we work together to get people outside, to both enjoy and protect our wild public lands.

If you'd like to support Mountaineers Books and our nonprofit partnership programs, please visit our website to learn more or contact mbooks@mountaineersbooks.org.

About the Author

Scott Turner has hiked a thousand miles each year for the last decade. He has contributed more than three hundred trail descriptions to Modern Hiker, the West's most widely read hiking website. Scott has written three other books for Mountaineer Books, all in the Hike the Parks series, about Joshua Tree, Zion and Bryce Canyon, and Sequoia and Kings Canyon National Parks. He also updated the fifth edition of Jerry Schad's longstanding *Afoot and Afield: San Diego County*, published by Wilderness Press.

When Scott isn't hiking and writing about trails, he works as a marriage and family therapist providing mental health treatment for teenagers and adults. Scott lives in northern San Diego County with his wife, Kelly, his son, Hank, and his cat, Dingleberry.

MOUNTAINEERS BOOKS

SKIPSTONE   BRAIDED RIVER

recreation · lifestyle · conservation

MOUNTAINEERS BOOKS, including its two imprints, Skipstone and Braided River, is a leading publisher of quality outdoor recreation, sustainability, and conservation titles. As a 501(c)(3) nonprofit, we are committed to supporting the environmental and educational goals of our organization by providing expert information on human-powered adventure, sustainable practices at home and on the trail, and preservation of wilderness.

Our publications are made possible through the generosity of donors, and through sales of more than 700 titles on outdoor recreation, sustainable lifestyle, and conservation. To donate, purchase books, or learn more, visit us online:

MOUNTAINEERS BOOKS

1001 SW Klickitat Way, Suite 201 • Seattle, WA 98134
800-553-4453 • mbooks@mountaineersbooks.org • www.mountaineersbooks.org

An independent nonprofit publisher since 1960

Mountaineers Books is proud to support the Leave No Trace Center for Outdoor Ethics, whose mission is to promote and inspire responsible outdoor recreation through education, research, and partnerships. The Leave No Trace program is focused specifically on human-powered (nonmotorized) recreation. For more information, visit www.lnt.org.

YOU MAY ALSO LIKE:

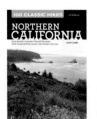
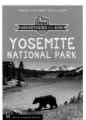